The Down Easters

American Deep-water Sailing Ships

1869–1929

BASIL LUBBOCK

Dover Publications, Inc., New York

Dedicated to

All those Merchant Adventurers and Master Mariners,
Shipwrights and Sawyers and Shellbacks
and other Seafaring Folk who
built up America's Mighty
Sailing Marine

This Dover edition, first published in 1987, is a slightly altered republication of the second edition, 1930, of the work originally published by Brown, Son & Ferguson, Ltd., Nautical Publishers, Glasgow, in 1929. The sequence of plates has been altered and six immaterial pages (blanks and part-titles) have been omitted from this edition.

Manufactured in the United States of America
Dover Publications, Inc., 31 East 2nd Street, Mineola, N.Y. 11501

Library of Congress Cataloging-in-Publication Data

Lubbock, Basil.
  The down easters.

  Reprint. Originally published: 1st ed. Glasgow : Brown, Son & Ferguson, 1929.
  Includes index.
  1. Sailing ships—United States—History—19th century. 2. Sailing ships—United States—History—20th century. 3. Navigation—United States—History—19th century. 4. Navigation—United States—History—20th century. I. Title.
VK23.L79 1987   387.2′2′0973   86-24340
ISBN 0-486-25338-4

PREFACE

WHEN I first began hunting up sailing ship records some years before the War I was early struck by the romance of the Cape Horn passage round the Americas, and I at once started to collect logs and journals of the famous American clippers which raced round the Horn to California and China in the fifties.

I should probably have published my efforts but for the fact that the late Captain Arthur H. Clark forestalled me, and treated the subject in a far superior manner to anything I could have done, in his *Clipper Ship Era*. I noticed with regret, however, that he had confined his records to the out-and-out clippers, and that numbers of what were then called half or medium clippers were not mentioned, nor was the work carried on into the period which followed the North and South War.

In this book I have endeavoured to complete the history of the American square-rigged sailing ship which has been so ably begun, not only by Captain Clark but by such gifted writers as Samuel Eliot Morison, R. D. Paine, J. R. Spears, Winthrop L. Marvin, and others. *The Down Easters* makes no pretence to be a literary effort; my main—my only—concern in compiling it is to preserve the memory of a number of beautiful ships sailing under the Stars and Stripes, and to give pleasure to the few remaining old shellbacks who sailed them.

I have done my best to get at the truth—no easy matter in dealing either with the present or the past—but mistakes are sure to occur, though I hope there will not be many. We are all fallible,

iii

and our memories are far from perfect. This must be my excuse, to be coupled with my apology, for any mis-statements. I have tried to deal fairly with every sailorman mentioned in the book, and have done my best to avoid hurting the feelings of anyone.

I have to thank a great number of old sailors and shipping people for information, which could have been obtained in no other way, and also for a great many of the illustrations, which I hope will give the layman some idea of the beauty and majesty of the old Down Easter, with her gleaming cotton canvas and shining masts and spars.

CONTENTS

v

CONTENTS

CHAPTER VI.—THE DOWN EASTERS OF THE NINETIES.

CHAPTER VII.—THE LAST OF AMERICA'S SQUARE-RIGGERS.

APPENDIX.

INDEX.

ALASKA

Delineated to the pr̄
by Gerhard Kremer
more commonly kno

Bristol Bay

Gulf of
Alaska

Skaguay
Juneau

Sitka

Pt. Rupert
Essington

DOMINION

Here a
Salmon
Packers
Barque

Aleutian Is.

Here a school of
porpoise disport

Vancouver
Victoria

Vancouver
Seattle
Tacoma

Astoria

Portland

UNITE
9

Here a schooner
carrying lumber

San Francisco

Here
Glory of the Seas
breaks the
Pacific Record

Los Angeles
S. Diego
Ensanada

PACIFIC OCEAN

Here flying fish

Tropic of Cancer

Hawaian Is.

Honolulu

Hawaii

Here a hungry
Albecore

CHART of NORTH AMERICA
to illustrate the positions of ships & ports
in "DOWN-EASTERS" by Basil Lubbock.

Three-masted Ship.

Two-masted Schooner.

Ketch

Four-masted Barque

Three-masted
Schooner

Full-rigged
Brig

ILLUSTRATIONS

ILLUSTRATIONS

LIST OF PLANS

THE DOWN EASTERS

CHAPTER I.

THE SAN FRANCISCO GRAIN TRADE.

A Yankee ship came down the river,
Blow, boys, blow !
Her masts and spars they shine like silver,
Blow, my bully boys, blow!

The Cape Horners.

THE Down Easter was built to fight Cape Horn and carry the Californian grain. Although she was well known throughout the twenty-five to thirty years of her existence in every sailing ship port of any size, from Calcutta and Cape Town to Hongkong and Honolulu, it is as a Cape Horner that she will take her place in history.

It was the hurry and scurry to gather the grains of gold dust which produced the Yankee clipper and drove her round the Horn to the port of El Dorado. It was the more satisfying grain of wheat which drew the Down Easter to the Pacific Coast for cargoes of the golden corn, which was distributed by their means not only through the Eastern States but in the British Isles and on the Continent of Europe.

A variety of untoward and unexpected circumstances combined to shorten the clipper ship era and bring on that of the grain carrier. First came the great financial depression of 1857, then the devastating North and South War, and, right on top of this, the advent of iron into shipbuilding, which gave Great Britain an immense advantage in the world trade, helped, as she undoubtedly was, by unwise American navigation and tariff laws.

Iron-built clippers from the Clyde and other British yards were soon covering the seas, whilst the Stars and Stripes at the monkey-gaff of a soft-wood three-skysail-yarder became something of a rarity in any but American ports, and there is little doubt that but for the rapid growth of the Californian grain trade in the sixties the American Mercantile Marine would have had to fall back on its own coastal trade. During the War nearly all the world-famous Yankee clippers were either sold abroad or destroyed by the *Alabama* and other Confederate cruisers, and scarcely a couple of dozen were left to take advantage of the growing trade between San Francisco and the European ports.

Grain is an awkward cargo and requires a well-built and well-found ship, and clippers which had been hastily put together in the boom days of the Californian gold rush, and afterwards driven hard on the severe Cape Horn passage, soon became too expensive in upkeep and repairs to pay well in the freight-cutting grain trade. Nevertheless, as we shall see, two of the most renowned of the early American clippers were most successful as grain carriers around Cape Horn, and stayed with the trade through thick and thin until the middle of the eighties.

The Down East builders were, however, quick to realise that the out-and-out clipper, requiring a big crew and lacking carrying capacity, was no longer a necessity in the Californian trade, and they began to build a medium clipper of greater power, yet with a good turn of speed, very strongly put together and economical to work, yet requiring only half the men needed by an out-and-out flyer. These medium-built Cape Horners came to be known as Down Easters because they were all built in the Down East ports—of Maine, such as Bath and Thomaston; of Massachusetts, such as East Boston and Newburyport; of New Hampshire, such as Portsmouth; and of Connecticut, such as Mystic and Stonington.

The designers and builders of these ports managed to evolve a magnificent type of a wooden full-rig ship, which soon became known the world over for her smart, spick and span appearance, and fierce discipline. But it was to San Francisco and her grain that these fine ships mostly owed their dividends, and it will thus be of interest to examine into the growth of this trade.

Some Statistics of the 'Frisco Grain Trade.

The following table, taken from Bates' *American Marine*, gives one a good idea of the extent of the trade between 1872 and 1892:

SAN FRANCISCO GRAIN TRADE.

Year	Number of American Ships Employed	Number of Ships of Other Nationalities Employed	Total Number of Ships Employed
1872-3	136	203	339
1873-4	91	156	247
1874-5	62	203	265
1875-6	82	92	174
1876-7	94	213	307
1877-8	50	59	109
1878-9	83	186	269
1879-80	113	160	273
1880-1	132	224	356
1881-2	154	405	559
1882-3	169	202	371
1883-4	81	210	291
1884-5	116	255	371
1885-6	88	161	249
1886-7	55	227	282
1887-8	33	165	198
1888-9	60	229	289
1889-90	55	229	284
1890-1	52	213	265
1891-2	39	234	273

In examining this table one should keep in mind the fact that the tonnage per ship greatly increased during the twenty years, thus the amount of grain carried by the 273 ships in 1891-2 was very much greater than that in the holds of the 339 ships in 1872-3.

According to the *Maritime History of Massachusetts*, the first consignment of grain from San Francisco was carried by the clipper barque *Greenfield* in 1855, and she was followed by the Boston clipper ship *Charmer*, which took a full cargo of wheat at 28 dollars a ton to New York. In 1860, 1088 tons of wheat and 58,926 barrels of flour were exported from San Francisco. Ten years later, 1870, the figures had risen to 243,199 tons of grain and 352,969 barrels of flour. In the bumper harvest year of 1882 the 559 ships carried 1,128,031 tons of wheat and barley, and 919,898 barrels of flour.

Amongst the grain carriers that year there were no less than twelve magnificent Down Easters registering over 2000 tons apiece.

BATES' TABLE FOR THE BOOM YEARS OF THE GRAIN TRADE.

Nationality	No. of Ships	Average Tonnage	Average Cargo in Centals	Freight Rate in Sterling	Average of Passages in Days	Best Passage	Worst Passage	No. of Ships Wrecked	No. of Ships Missing	No. of Ships Abandoned	No. of Ships Lost Spars and Sails
AMERICAN											
Wood ..	418	1634	52400	47/5⅔	125	105	179	1	–	1	12
Iron ..	5	1201	40799	58/3¾	124	118	140	–	–	–	–
BRITISH											
Wood ..	198	1272	42394	51/9¼	131	96	150	2	1	1	4
Iron ..	761	1356	44618	51/5 1/16	130	91	181	2	3	1	28
GERMAN											
Wood ..	39	1196	37697	49/0⅞	135	118	157	–	–	–	2
Iron ..	41	1007	31999	48/3½	136	112	168	–	–	–	–
NORWEGIAN ..											
Wood ..	20	929	29346	54/9¼	127	114	151	–	–	–	1
Iron ..	2	1111	37711	50/-	137	136	138	–	–	–	–
FRENCH											
Wood ..	16	628	20680	58/9¾	139	125	165	–	1	–	1
Iron ..	7	806	27541	50/8½	151	138	169	–	–	–	–
ITALIAN											
Wood ..	12	881	28527	46/2	141	128	158	1	–	–	–
BRITISH											
Steamers	11	1761	61330	59/8¾	84	66	91	–	–	1	1

Let us now look into the building statistics of the American Merchant Marine as regards square-riggers. As usual, there was a boom after the War, and from 1865 to 1870 an average of 90 ships were built per annum. This dropped to 28 ships per annum for the years 1871-1873. Captain Bates accounts for this by the increase of insurance rates made by Lloyd's on American wood ships. This may have had some slight effect, but one must always expect a slump, or, at any rate, a steadying down, after a boom. From 1873 the building of Down Easters kept at a steady level until 1886, when the real slump set in. Captain Bates has collected some very interesting data for the four years preceding 1886 when the grain trade was booming. First of all he states that,

STOWING TOPSAILS.

SHIPPING IN 'FRISCO BAY, "HEREWARD" IN FOREGROUND.

Lent by Capt. L. R. W. Beavis.

between July, 1881, and July, 1885, 128 American deep-watermen were launched—an average of 32 per annum. The number dropped to 11 in 1886, 7 in 1887, 4 in 1888, and 1 in 1889, in which year there were 30 Down Easters employed in the 'Frisco trade to United Kingdom and Continent as against 167 British, 11 German, and perhaps a dozen of other nationalities.

In the foregoing table the best passages were made by the following:

American wood barque, *Cassandra Adams*, 1127 tons, built at Seabeck, Washington, in 1876—105 days.

American iron barque, *Annie Johnson*, 997 tons (formerly British ship, *Ada Iredale*)—118 days.

British composite ship, *City of Hankow*, 1195 tons, built by Stephen of Glasgow in 1869—96 days.

British iron four-mast barque, *Loch Moidart*, 2000 tons, built by Barclay, Curle of Glasgow in 1881—91 days.

Bates in his *American Marine* cries out for protection against the economical Clyde-built iron ship, but he never succeeded in effecting his object. Congress would not listen, and in the end the Down Easter was driven out of the foreign trade and compelled to rest content with the American inter-coastal trade round the Horn.

Running Expenses and Profits.

The Cape Horn voyage was without doubt the most wearing voyage that a sailing ship could undertake, and this was well realised by the owners of the wooden Down Easters.   Both for their rigging outfits and their food scales these fine ships bore a splendid reputation.   There was no such thing as pound and pint aboard a Yankee Cape Horner, any more than there was a rotten gasket or a cut ratline.   The biscuit—or bread, as the sailor always called it— was excellent, Californian hard-tack being celebrated the world over ; then a variety of preserves was served out to the fo'c'sle, "air-tights," as they were called, being used quite as much as the salted meat of the harness cask.

As regards rigging, sails, rope and spars were of the best, the gear being at once replaced directly it showed the least sign of wear.   Thus the running of a 2000-ton Down Easter averaged close on 25,000 dollars per annum ; yet, during the twenty to thirty years when the trade was at its best, these ships almost invariably paid good dividends, from 15 to 20 per cent. being by no means unusual. Just at the last, when owners were struggling vainly against the cheaply-run, cheaply-built steam tramp, food and upkeep as well as dividends dropped below their usual high standard, but this was only to be expected.

The Construction of a Down Easter.

The builders of the American square-rigger rarely imported foreign materials, being quite satisfied with their native woods. The frame of a Down Easter, with stem, stern-post, breast-hooks and other principal parts, was of white oak. The outside planking and inside lining were of pitch-pine; and this useful wood was also selected for deck beams. The bigger Down Easters were three-deckers, though the lower deck was only partly laid, a few planks in the wings and a platform forward and another aft. The keel and keelsons were also massive logs of pitch-pine. The knees were all cut with the natural growth from the native Maine hackmatack, and were fastened with locust wood tree-nails. Some ships had yellow metal or copper bolts throughout, but others used iron bolts above the ballast loadlines.

The bottom planking was, of course, felted and coppered up to the normal salt water draught. Deckhouses were usually painted, being framed with oak and planked with white pine. In the cabin, the ornamental work was either of mahogany or bird's-eye maple, but simplicity and neatness were aimed at rather than expensive wood carving, and the lining, which was only picked out with polished hardwoods, was generally white-painted pitch-pine.

In many ways these medium-built Cape Horners resembled the earlier clippers in appearance, especially by the way in which their bowsprits were run into the sheer, instead of on top of it, as in British and most foreign ships. But their lines were neither so sharp nor so hollow, and they were, of course, full-bottomed for cargo carrying, without any dead rise to speak of.

The Yankee clipper was proud of her gingerbread work, her figure-head, scrollboards and stern frame being most elaborately and beautifully carved; but the Down Easter was often content with a neat fiddle-head.

Rigging and Deck Plans.

In their rigging plans, three skysails were very popular; it was rare for a Down Easter to cross double topgallant yards, and the three upper yards squared to a hair at equally spaced distances gave a very smart look to an American vessel in port and gained for her a great deal of well-deserved admiration.

In comparison with British ships, the American carried short lower masts and very long topmasts, it being no unusual thing for their upper topsails to have two rows of reef-points. The masts, like the hulls, were of wood; the lower masts were usually built up of three pitch-pine logs bolted together, rounded off and then banded by 6-inch iron hoops. Most American skippers kept their masts scraped bright and varnished, whilst the hoops were painted either with white or red lead, but sometimes black.

The *Joseph B. Thomas* had her masts panelled with long white strips between the hoops, which, with the brilliant red lead of the hoops themselves, satisfied the most hard-to-please of nautical critics. Bowsprits and jibbooms were generally of pitch-pine, the former black painted and the latter scraped bright and varnished. Martingales were of oak with chain backropes and bowsprit shrouds.

Stunsails went out with the clippers, though one or two captains tried to keep in touch with old times by setting a fore topmast stunsail. Only three ships still carried stunsail booms in the nineties; these were the *Paul Revere, Jabez Howes,* and *Indiana.* The two latter contented themselves with fore topmast and lower stunsails, but *Paul Revere* had a full suit, which, it was said, added 1000 square yards to the ship's canvas and put 2 knots on to her speed.

Very few Down Easters carried a standing spanker gaff, this sail being always furled on the boom instead of being brailed into the mast as was the custom in British ships. A small monkey-gaff was carried at the mizen topmast head for the signal halliards.

The Cape Horners invariably bent a main spencer as soon as they reached 50° S. This sail was made of No. 0 duck, and had a standing gaff about 20 feet long, the luff of the sail reaching to within 3 or 4 feet of the maintop. The spencer was a steadying sail, very useful when head-reaching or hove-to in a gale of wind, and American masters trusted a great deal to this sail in the stormy weather down South.

Some of the ships carried such light weather kites as a main royal staysail, a jib topsail, and a Jimmy Green.

The chief points to notice in the deck plans of Down Easters were their carvel-built boats, big wheelhouses and monkey-poops. The long-boats on the skids of the midshiphouse were often kept upside down, and were awkward to handle quickly in time of need, but beautiful whale-boats swung from davits on either quarter. The wheelhouse, a great institution on American ships, was divided into forward and after portions; the wheel, compasses, bell, and log line were in the forward portion of the house, also that most necessary article, the helmsman's spittoon, into which went the juice of several sticks of chewing tobacco every week.

In the after part of the house was the rudder head and tiller, both of massive oak, the wheel ropes and their polished lignum vitae blocks, the pigeon-hole case for signal flags, life-buoys, and fog horn.

The accommodation aft on a Down Easter was excellent, being generally divided into a dining saloon forward and captain's cabin aft, with a number of staterooms on either side, besides the captain's bathroom, the steward's pantry, a store-room, and a chart-room. Besides two exits on to the maindeck forward, there was an exit on to the poop aft, which faced the wheelhouse; this was for the captain's use only. The lazarette could also be gained by a companionway from the poop, and this was also useful as an emergency entrance to the hold in bad weather.

The pumps were a very important part of a Down Easter's specification. Besides the main pumps just abaft the mainmast there were two wing bilge pumps in the waist of most ships. These were found very handy by the mate who wished to shine up old irons in a sleepy middle watch, when the ship was laying over on a wind.

Donkeys or winches were almost unknown on a Down Easter; but besides a powerful maindeck capstan, and the windlass capstan

SOUTH STREET, NEW YORK, IN THE DAYS OF SAIL

BENDING A LOWER TOPSAIL.

on the fo'c'sle-head, there were usually a couple of small handy wing capstans on most ships.

Spit and Polish.

The Down East mate was without a rival in his love of spit and polish. He was the only human being I can think of who would have dared to paint the lily and gild the rose. No sergeant-major of the Guards was ever more particular about his accoutrements, no Horse Artillery Number One more pernicketty about his breech-block and harness than the mate of a Down Easter was about his decks and rigging.

In all that pertained to a smart, shipshape appearance aloft and alow, the officer from Maine or Massachusetts always showed himself a super-seaman; and if he was called a "bucko" and a slave-driver he never spared himself, and his efforts were all for the honour of his ship. No newly-fledged middy or just-joined subaltern ever had more *esprit de corps* than the mate of a Cape Horner. His pride in his ship was his ruling passion, and he often went to unheard of lengths in his efforts to uphold her reputation for smartness.

One enthusiastic bucko made a habit of sending both watches aloft on quiet moonlight nights in order to scrub the yards with sand and canvas. Another expended much time and energy on his 'tween decks ; these were holystoned and oiled, and the stringers painted in alternate stripes of white and light blue, over which was hung a lining of canvas. When the ship was unloaded this canvas was taken up, scrubbed and put away to await the advent of the next cargo.

Decks were always a great source of anxiety and trouble, and woe betide the man who was caught expectorating tobacco juice or dropping spots of paint on a Down Easter's maindeck. Few Yankee chief officers were satisfied with the appearance of their decks until they had been carefully holystoned, oiled, then coated all over with coal tar, and finally scrubbed until they came up as white as snow.

It was always easy to tell an old Cape Horner—that is to say, a seaman who had sailed for any length of time in American ships—

by his wonderful aptitude in ship cleaning, in the use of sand and canvas, holystones, bibles and prayerbooks, and other back-breaking instruments of toil such as the deck-bear, though he was often a very indifferent marlinspike seaman.

Here is a good picture of a Down Easter in a foreign port, written by a British master mariner for a shipping magazine :

> I remember a case in Port Chalmers, New Zealand, in 1875 or 1876. There was lying at the wharf an American ship, the *General Maclellan*, discharging timber from Puget Sound. She carried three skysail-yards, and all her spars, masts, etc., from truck to deck were scraped and oiled. Her sails were all white cotton canvas and stowed with a lovely harbour stow.
>
> All her running gear was stowed up and down the shrouds and fastened with narrow strips of canvas. The jibboom was rigged in and all the head-stays set up taut to the bowsprit. The yards were squared as though with a tape line, and there was not a slack rope or anything untidy or out of place from stem to stern.

No yacht was ever more neat and shipshape aloft, or more spick and span on deck than the typical Down Easter; though the latter certainly lacked the elaborate finish of the British tea and wool clippers, whose decks were one mass of carved teak and inlaid brass, his spotless white paint and shining bright work were the admiration of all sailormen.

The Builders.

In the days of the Californian gold rush, when ships were actually built in the woods and hauled to the waterside by teams of oxen, every farmer learnt to use the adze and the caulking mallet. No doubt much of the boom shipbuilding of that time was very rough, hurried work, for we are told that many a brand-new ship, on her arrival inside the Golden Gate, sailed straight away on to the mud flats in order to spell her crew at the pumps and keep from sinking. But twenty years later the sons of those shipbuilding farmers had become skilled shipwrights, and we owe the splendid Down Easters of the seventies and eighties to their fine workmanship.

Though the big yards of New York and Boston had by this time almost ceased to turn out wooden sailing ships, the Northern ports of the New England coast amply made up for their defection. In his splendid *Maritime History of Massachusetts*, Samuel Eliot

Morison very truly observes : "But it was Maine rather than Massachusetts that kept the flag afloat at the spanker gaff of sailing ships." Maine, indeed, abounded in old-fashioned yet very efficient shipyards, where the slowly dying art of the wood sawyer was preserved and the steel riveter kept at a distance.

Every year gangs of lumbermen were employed cutting timber in the forests of Maine, and even as far south as Virginia, for the busy shipyards of Bath, Thomaston, Richmond, Damariscotta, Frankfort, Yarmouth, Phippsburg, Camden, Waldoboro, Newcastle, Searsport, and Kennebunk.

At Bath there were the yards of Flint and Chapman ; Goss, Sawyer and Packard ; of the Sewalls and the Houghtons. At Thomaston old Sam Watts built in rivalry with Ed. O'Brien. Mills and Creighton also turned out some notable ships from that port. At Kennebunk N. L. Thompson was responsible for the good looking *Vigilant*; and the *L. Schepp*, generally known as the "Hell of a Ship," was built by Titcomb & Thompson at Kennebunkport. J. Pascal built the *Wandering Jew*, with her novel double deck, at Camden. At Yarmouth there were the yards of Blanchard Bros. and C. F. Sargent ; whilst at Richmond the big *Eureka* and *Commodore T. H. Allen* were built by T. J. Southard, and the *Hagarstown* by J. M. Hagar. Phippsburg was represented by C. V. Minott, and A. R. Reed had a yard at Waldoboro. Soule's rather box-shaped vessels were built at Freeport, and Carleton, Norwood & Co., whose captains were considered the hardest nuts in the Cape Horn fleet, had a shipyard at Rockport. Searsport, though it boasted no less than twelve building yards along its 6 miles of water frontage, of which the chief were Pendleton's, Carver's, McGilvery's, Packard's and Merrithew's, was more noted for its skippers than its ships, which were mostly under 1500 tons.

In Massachusetts George Thomas at Quincy built three very beautiful ships—the *Northern Light*, once the command of that wonderful single-hander, Joshua Slocum; the *America*, remembered until quite recently as a Pacific Coast timber droghuer; and the main skysail-yarder, *Red Cloud*, which ended her days under the German flag.

At Newburyport on the Merrimac John Currier also turned out an occasional square-rigger, but at such ports as Medford, Massachusetts, and Mystic, Connecticut, from which so many packet ships, and clippers had been sent afloat, an all wood square-rigged Down Easter soon became quite a rarity on the stocks and an object of curiosity.

The old-time method whereby the building of a deep-water sailing ship was financed still continued in the New England ports. Though the ships were generally managed by brokers in New York or Boston, the shares were mostly owned by their builders, captains, sailmakers, ship chandlers, opticians, and a few old retired skippers ; and many a fine ship was built by some such casual proposition as the following, "Let's build a ship for Captain Smith," which was voiced, perhaps, in the captains' room at some ship chandler's, or in a builder's drawing-loft, where the chief shipping men of the port were accustomed to collect together and yarn. And at such seamen's gatherings the lines of the future Down Easter were not only discussed in detail from every point of view, but debated with much heated argument by these same old sea dogs, before the plans could be finally settled upon.

The Naming of the Down Easters.

Donald MacKay, who had a strong romantic strain in his nature, started the craze for calling clipper ships by high-flown names, such as *Flying Cloud* and *Sovereign of the Seas*. Then the Californian gold rush sent a dozen or more "Golden" thises or thats afloat.

But when we come to the naming of the Down Easter we find that the romantic outlook of the gold seeking argonauts has given way to the more individualistic outlook of the shrewd New England business man. Thus the later American ship, whether square-rigger or fore-and-after, was generally named for or called after—the expression differs by the width of the Atlantic Ocean—her largest shareholder. As a rule this was her builder or her broker, but occasionally someone who was quite unknown beyond the limits of his own town was advertised all over the world by means of the name boards and stern of a beautiful three-skysail-yard full-rigger.

There was one ship whose name had to be changed. She was named for a well-known financier. Two or three years after she had been launched this money magnate so over-reached himself that he was obliged to make a bolt of it across the Canadian border in order to escape the clutches of the law.

Only two firms that I know of ever departed from this custom of ship nomenclature. They were the Sewalls of Bath, who preferred such beautiful old Indian names as *Shenandoah* and *Susquehanna*, *Roanoke* and *Rappahannock*, and the Houghtons, who went in for the names of countries which ended in "ia," such as *Columbia*, *Arabia*, and *Servia*.

There has come one advantage from the personal method of ship nomenclature, and that is that it gives one an historical list of all the chief men connected with American shipping between 1870 and 1890, whether builders or brokers, captains or clerks.

CHAPTER II.

BULLY CAPTAINS, BUCKO MATES AND
CAPE HORN SHELLBACKS.

And if you go further and pause to admire
A ship that's as neat as your heart could desire,
As smart as a frigate aloft and alow
Her brasswork like gold and her planking like snow . . . .
Look round for a mate by whose twang it is plain
That his home port is somewhere 'round Boston or Maine.
(C. Fox-Smith.)

Yard-oh ! Yard-oh ! Then we'll wring the yard, oh !

Character Making.

IF we are to believe American nautical writers on their own ships and seamen, their captains were all bullies, and their mates buckos, whilst the seamen were a mixture of all the most degraded, down-trodden and undesirable aliens that ever trod a deck.

Here is a typical statement, taken from the latest of American seamen authors :

And the figure of the bucko mate, belaying-pins in his short boots and knuckle-dusters on his fists, comes back out of the past, not as an adjunct to morbid romance but as a cruel fact. He broke men and killed them on the cruel blue sea without the aid of fire.

This sounds a bit highly coloured, yet Captain Felix Riesenberg knows from personal experience what he is writing about.

There was far more, however, to the make-up of the American deep-water mate than the picturesque belaying-pin and cruel knuckle-duster. He was a distinct American type, a virile type, in the same category and with much the same outlook on life as those frontiersmen, the cowboy and the miner and the lumberman. He was also a product of the times, obeying that law called "the survival of the fittest," for one must remember that he invariably began life as a ship's boy, a "red-neck" or a "greenhorn," a lamb for slaughter ; surviving which he became an able seaman ; then, through a show of initiative or powers of leading in times of stress, was promoted petty officer, and finally by sheer character and driving force fought his way to the quarterdeck.

There are two distinct grades of humans, positive and negative : the bucko mate was aggressively positive, and he was often a cruel, hard taskmaster, because his own struggle to rise out of the ruck had been so cruel hard that it had toughened the fibre of his nature and steeled his heart to an almost incredible degree.

The sea undoubtedly makes character with a heavier tool than does the land. Old Ocean uses the adzc or the axe where Mother Earth uses the smoothing plane. But the man who backs the blizzard or the sea in its fury has often found that his greatest testing has come from his own species. It takes character to blaze a difficult trail successfully, just as it takes character to handle a ship in a hurricane, or steer one through a Cape Horn snorter; but, more than these, it takes character to hold one's own in the wilds where no law runs but the law of the six-shooter, or on the deck of a windjammer, where a knife thrown in the dark, or a block dropped from aloft, may mean a sudden exit from this world.

The one quality that has been the making of the great American nation is that of nerve force, known under various slang terms such as "grit" and "sand."

It is curious that, when a man holds an excess of nervous energy in his composition, he is in more danger of becoming an oppressor than a supporter of his weaker neighbours. More often than not it is just this excess of nervous energy—perhaps one should call it vital force—which has produced the bad men and the outlaws of the wild and woolly West, and the bullies and the buckos of the blood-boat.

The Curse of Drink.

There was just one other cause—or curse, shall I call it?—which turned the strong man into a brutal tyrant, and that was the curse of drink.

New Orleans cotton ships were noted in the old days for the lively time put up both by their fore and after guards whilst towing to sea. This was almost entirely due to a powerful drink called "Old Levee Tanglefoot," which put a reckless Dutch courage into the weak and an insane fury into the strong, ingredients which produced the most spectacular of handspike and belaying-pin battles.

Here is a description of a typical "rough house" aboard a Mississippi outward bounder:

"Was it the first mate who struck me ? " (This question is asked by a shellback who has just come to in the fo'c'sle, after being knocked senseless.) His friend replies:

"You were too reckless, old man, ye oughter ha' watched for the mate. He's a holy terror; he half killed all hands yesterday ; that's why we couldn't stand by ye better. He jumped off the fo'c'sle on to Dennis, an' the two o' them kicked him all round the fore hatch. David was knocked endwise with a heaver for going to windward o' the skipper, an' his teeth are all gone. Lars got soaked at the wheel—that's agin the law ; an' ye see him get it again to-night. Dutch Ned let go the to'gallant sheet, an' the second mate sent him 20 feet. I got it in the nose just 'fore goin' below at 8 bells, for no reason on earth but 'cause I was the only man left who hadn't got soaked."

This towing down battle with all hands full of tanglefoot was a recognised custom of the Mississippi. There is the well-known story of a New Orleans packet-rat exclaiming during an unusually quiet towing to sea: " Hell ! Four bells and nobody hurted yet ! What de matter, I guess ? "

An anecdote of the same description is told of the notorious Captain Shotgun Murphy, of the four-master, *Shenandoah.*

When coming out of 'Frisco, bound for Liverpool one voyage, finding everything unusually quiet and peaceful at the start, he called his mates aft and addressed them as follows :

"What's the matter aboard this here ship ? Have I got a couple of old women for mates ? Here, we've been out of 'Frisco more'n a week and I ain't seen any blood running in the scuppers yet."

There was another potent drink down South in the old days, and this was called "Tarantula juice." It consisted of about two quarts of alcohol, a few burnt peaches, and a plug of black tobacco put into a keg with five gallons of water. This was no "knock-out drop" but an everyday tipple for strong men. Then

FOC'S'LE-HEAD AWASH.

CATCHING BONITO.

there was the milk whisky sold along the West Coast, which not only drove men mad but killed them.

Up in the Klondyke, away back in the gold rush days, I once shared blankets in a bunk-house with a man who had six notches on his revolver and a devastating reputation. Yet he was a most mild and inoffensive citizen except when he had had a drop, but when this was the case I got out of bed and slept on the sanded floor.

Another time I remember the landlord of the Pack Train Inn at Bennett going crazy from drink on the Queen's birthday. At midnight he went round the bunks slashing the canvas to pieces with a carving knife. Luckily all hands were out celebrating, except a sick man who was so thin that the knife missed him. That landlord was dead before daybreak. His own liquor had killed him.

It was not even the worst liquor that could kill a real Down East American mate, but it very often gave him a jaundiced view of life, in which foremast hands took on the aspect of rats, only fit to be clubbed and broken.

"The Red Record."

When a nation is in the making men of great force of character are required, men ready to fight Nature and drive their own kind to the limits of human endurance.

On land such men were the pioneers of civilisation, the trail breakers, the cattle foreman, the lumber boss, and the master of the railway gang; at sea they were the skippers and the mates of deep-water ships.

Ashore when such men broke the law they became desperadoes, such as Slade of the Pony Express and Soapy Smith of the Skagway Trail. At sea a ship's officers had almost unlimited power in the old days over their men, and it required very little skill to sail a 2000-ton ship through not only the laws and regulations of the United States, but the sixth commandment itself. And this freedom from restraint, allied to a superabundance of vital force, and a soured or savage temper, produced by over-indulgence in bad drink, turned many a decent sailorman into a bully skipper or a bucko mate.

As a proof of the above statement, there is a curious human document called the *Red Record*, which was published at San Francisco in the nineties as a supplement to the *Coast Seamen's Journal*, the official organ of the National Seamen's Union of America. This record covers seven years only, from September, 1888, to November, 1895, and details 64 cases of cruelty and murder on the high seas in the American Cape Horn fleet.

These cases make lurid reading, and many of them will find a mention when I come to describe the ships on which they occurred. But the really astonishing thing about this document is the way in which the bucko law breakers invariably escaped punishment according to the law of the land.

Here are a few typical entries :

> The mates deserted the ship while towing up the Delaware ; the captain also disappeared for a time. (Ship *Solitaire*, April, 1889.)
>
> Warrant sworn out for mate's arrest; mate disappeared and could not be found. (Ship *Standard* at San Francisco October, 1889.)
>
> The latter officer (second mate) skipped as the *Reuce* was towing through the Golden Gate. (Ship *Reuce* at San Francisco, November, 1889.)
>
> On the arrival of the *Belknap* in New York the second mate disappeared. (Ship *Robert C. Belknap*, December, 1889.)
>
> McNichols (first mate) disappeared upon arrival of the *Eureka*. (At San Francisco, November, 1891.)

And so the record goes on ; when the case was considered serious enough, the officer likely to get into trouble invariably left the ship before she came to an anchor. But where bucko officers were daring enough to stand trial it was usually a matter of " Case dismissed for ' lack of evidence '," or else on the ground of " justifiable discipline."

It came to be the accepted dictum, at last, amongst Consuls and magistrates, that an officer of an American deep-water ship had to be rough and able to fight his weight in wild cats in order to maintain discipline and carry on the ship's work.

And so it came about that Americans began to take a queer pride in this buckoism, as they called it, just as they revelled in the gory doings of their Western desperados.

As a type the bucko officer was certainly a most interesting study, and sea writers have given him certain recognised characteristics, which undoubtedly have been taken from real men.

The Bucko in Print.

Here is a quotation from Morgan Robertson :

Captain William Belchior was more than a martinet : he was known as " Bucko Belchior " in every port where the English language is spoken, having earned this prefix by the earnest readiness with which, in his days as second or chief mate, he would whirl belaying-pins, heavers and handspikes about the decks, and by his success in knocking down, tricing up, and working up sailors who displeased him.

With a blow of his fist he had broken the jaw of a man helplessly ironed in the 'tween deck, and on the same voyage, armed with a simple belaying-pin, he had sprung alone into a circle of brandishing sheath-knives and quelled a mutiny.

He was short, broad, beetle-browed and grey-eyed, of undoubted courage, with the quality of sympathy left out of his nature.   During the ten years in which he had been in command he was relieved of much of the executive work that had made him famous when he stood watch, but was always ready to justify his reputation as a bucko should friction with the crew occur past the power of his officers to cope with.

His ship, the *Wilmington*, a skysail yard clipper, was rated by sailormen as the "hottest " craft under the American flag, and Captain Belchior himself was spoken of by Consuls and Commissioners, far and near, as a man peculiarly unfortunate in his selection of men ; for never a passage ended but he was complainant against one or more heavily ironed and badly used up members of his crew.   His officers were, in the language of one of these defendants, " o' the same breed o' dorg."   No others could or would sign with him.   His crew were invariably put aboard in the stream or at anchorage, never at the dock.

Here is a note on the appearance of bucko officers by the same writer :

He was a giant with a giant's fist and foot, red-haired and bearded, of sinister countenance.   But he was no more formidable in appearance than his captain, who was equally big, but smooth-shaven, and showing the square jaw and beetling brows of a born fighter.

The bully captains and bucko mates of fiction generally ran to size, strength and fighting fitness, but the second mates were invariably gnarled old men of an incredible toughness, as was often the case in fact.

No doubt the clear-cut portrait of the second mate, Garnett, in Jenkins Hains' *Windjammers* was taken from real life.

Here is the quotation :

Captain Enoch Moss was said to be a hard man among hard men.   His second mate was a man named Garnett, a fellow who had been so smashed, shot and stove up, in the innumerable fracases in which he had taken part, that to an un-nautical eye he appeared an almost helpless old man. His twisted bow-legs, set wide apart, gave him a peculiar lurching motion when he walked, and suggested the idea that he was continually trying to right himself into equilibrium upon the moving world beneath his feet.

Here is another type of second mate, described from life by an American foremast hand :

Our second mate was what is commonly known among English-speaking sailors as a "white-washed Yank." He was a long, lean, leathery-faced, piratical-looking brute who prided himself upon a record of crime and bloodshed, who swore by Yankee institutions "because on American ships, by God, a man was a man, by God, and there wasn't no damned laws, by God, that prevented you from gouging a dam' Dutchman's eyes out if he shipped as an able seaman, by God, and didn't know his business."

Here is still another second mate, also taken from fact, not fiction :

The second mate was a long, bony Nova Scotiaman, by name McDonald. The second mate of a packet is supposed to be a "horse," and Mr. McDonald filled the bill to perfection. The man who would give him a fight was the man he loved.

The best description, however, that I have come across of a Cape Horner's second officer is that given by Paul Eve Stevenson in the first of his sailing ship classics, which runs as follows :

A word or two here about the second mate would not be amiss, I believe, as he is a genuine character. His name is Kelly, and his hailing port Thomaston, Maine, the home of so many of our deep-water sailors. His age, I should think, is in the neighbourhood of fifty years, and his face sufficient proof of the assertion that he had, until this voyage, averaged one round trip a year between New York and San Francisco for thirty-two years, making sixty-four times that he has doubled the Horn. His countenance, seared by the sun of the Equator and hardened into leather by Cape Horn gales, would have long ago won him a fortune as an artist's model. He has no eyelids, and it is impossible to tell the colour of his deep-set eyes (little holes in his face they look like), continually blood-shot from staring into sou-west gales in the Southern Ocean, ably seconded by bad rum. His face is further adorned with an enormous red moustache, extending down each side of his mouth, with large, bushy ends. It is known ashore sometimes as the "car-driver's moustache."

But most curious of all is the shape of his legs. He is the most bow-legged man it is possible to conceive of ; in fact, from his waist down he is the shape of an egg, and a stout, healthy pig could jump through his legs without touching either knee. I have often seen the men put their hands before their mouths to smother a grin when old Kelly rolls forward on the maindeck. His deformity has its advantage, though, as during the severest rolling he stands seemingly fixed to the deck, and maintains his equilibrium with no apparent effort; for, by placing his feet a few inches from each other, his knees will be more than a foot apart, and he sways from side to side so comfortably that I often envy him the perfection of his art.

The cold, steely nerve of the Western gun-man was equally a necessary attribute of the bucko officer. Down East mates for the most part believed that it was necessary to instil terror into all foremast hands, and they usually succeeded in doing this without straining themselves.

The Mutiny of the "Neptune's Car."

The best story I know of to illustrate this power of instilling fear is one told by Admiral Fitzgerald in his *Memories of the Sea*. It is worth while quoting his words in full :

While we were lying at Singapore we witnessed a mutiny on board an American merchant ship. She was lying close to us, and was one of those splendid well-kept clippers that were seen in all parts of the world prior to the American Civil War. About five o'clock one afternoon we heard a great row going on on board the *Neptune's Car*. The crew all came aft on the quarterdeck and apparently began arguing with the three mates, who were standing at the poop-rails. The altercation was obviously a very angry one, and then suddenly some of the crew rushed to the fife-rails, pulled out the iron belaying-pins, and let fly at the three officers on the poop, who dodged as best they could ; but while this was going on something was happening which no one on board the *Neptune's Car* could see, though we could.

A boat rowed off from the shore, came under the stern of the ship, and a little man swarmed up the rope ladder which was hanging over the stern, and suddenly appeared at the break of the poop with something in his hand. He was a very small boyish-looking little fellow, but the effect of his appearance was magical. The whole crew turned and fled like a flock of sheep before a dog. They fled on to the forecastle and the little man after them. They swarmed out on the bowsprit, out on to the jibboom, out on to the flying jibboom, and then they began dropping off the end of the flying jibboom into the water like dead flies.

One of our cutters happened to be manned alongside, and she was immediately sent away and picked up some of them and brought them on board the *Retribution*, where they were lent clothes while their own were drying, and then sent on shore and handed over to the United States Consul.

All the Yankee swank was taken out of them, and they were as tame as kitchen cats ; and when we asked them what on earth induced them to go overboard in a sharky place like Singapore, all we could get out of them was, "That captain of ours is a snotty little cuss."

The Skipper's Speech.

One expects wit in an after-dinner speech, learning with a scattering of Greek or Latin tags in a University professor's speech, and a quibbling and distortion of facts in a politician's speech, but for sheer, forceful, direct-to-the-point eloquence nothing could beat the customary speech made by the captain of an American sailing ship at the start of a voyage.

Here is a typical piece of sea captain's eloquence, taken from a little book called *Among our Sailors*, written by a United States Consul and published by Harpers in 1874 :

Men ! My name's Captain Halyard. I'm master of this ship and I want to start square with you. We've got a long voyage before us and there's plenty of work to be done. I want you to understand I'm great on discipline, and you can have hell or heaven on board, just as you please. All you've got to attend to is to do your duty and obey orders : that's what you shipped for, and that's what you're paid for. If you do your duty, it will be all right: and if you don't, it will be all wrong.

The first man that disobeys my orders I'll put daylight through him—quick, and here's the little joker I'll do it with (exhibits a revolver). If any of you men try to make trouble aboard of this ship I'll make it—hot for you. I'll make mince-meat of some of you quicker'n hell's scorch a feather !

I hear that some of you are from the *White Swallow*—(the crew of the *White Swallow* mutinied in the China Sea because of harsh treatment)—where you gave much trouble. Well, this is not the *White Swallow*, and you've got bloody Jock Halyard to deal with. Now you know who I am, and what you've got to expect. Go forward !

Here is Morgan Robertson's description of a Yankee skipper's speech :

. . . . the crew mustered aft and listened to a forceful speech by Captain Bacon, delivered in quick, incisive epigrams, to the effect that if any man aboard his ship—whether he believed himself shipped or shanghaied, a sailor, a priest, a policeman, or a dry-nurse—showed the slightest hesitation at obeying orders, or the slightest resentment at what was said to him, he would be punished with fists, brass-knuckles, belaying-pins or handspikes—the officers were there for that purpose—and if he persisted, he would be shot like a mad dog. They could go forward.

The captain of a Down Easter was of no use unless he had supreme self-confidence, and was ready to take his ship to sea without a real sailor in his fo'c'sle.

Captain David Bone, in *The Brassbounder*, by no means exaggerated when he put the following words into the mouth of Bully Nathan, captain of the American ship, *J. B. Flint* :

Give me grave-diggers or organ-grinders, boys, if ye kyant get sailormen. Anything with two hands an' feet. I guess I'm Jan K. Nathan, and they'll be sailormen or " stiffs " before we reach aout!

No wonder the Cape Horn shellback declared wearily : "What with hard-case mates here and Hiram K. Satan down below, it seems to me that a poor sailorman is in for a very thin time."

Bully Captains.

When I headed this chapter " Bully Captains, etc. . . " I had in mind the American adjective " bully " rather than the English noun, which my dictionary translates as " a quarrelsome fellow." When one leaves highly coloured fiction for honest fact, one invariably finds that there is not so much " blood and thunder " in this world as the word-artist would have one imagine. Thus the American Merchant Marine was not entirely composed of bullies and buckoes, and the American master mariner was more often a bully specimen of manhood rather than a bully of those under him.

He was no " Nancy," it is true, and was far from suffering fools gladly, neither would he put up with the incompetent nor the slacker, but he was a prime sailorman whose equal it would be hard to find nowadays amongst those who "go deep-water."

Of Puritan Stock.

And if he was a strict disciplinarian, this is not surprising when one remembers that he almost invariably came from the old Puritan stock and inherited much of that stern stoicism and iron sense of duty, which together made up the corner-stone of the great American nation.

It is not necessary to go to Salem or Nantucket to find the old English names; right up through Maine they run from port to port along the wild ragged Down East coast. And almost without exception the Anglo-Saxon surnames have Biblical Christian names in front of them.

Nowhere else in the world do you find such names as the following, taken at random from an old list of Maine shipmasters :—

Osias Blake
Phineas Pendleton
Nathan P. Carver
Caleb F. Carver
Jesse T. Carver
Lebbeus Curtis
Eben Curtis
Amos A. Dow
Levry Dow
Josiah L. Emery

Amasa D. Field
Jasper N. Nichols
Peleg B. Nichols
Cyrus G. Nichols
Jeremiah H. Park
Ephraim Pendleton
Timothy C. Pendleton
Simon Ross
Asa A. Waterhouse

These mariners all came from Searsport, Maine, and commanded some of the finest of the Down Easters.

Searsport Shipmasters.

Less than fifty years ago the little New England town of Searsport supplied more than 10 per cent. of America's sea captains. According to local statistics, in 1889 Searsport had 2000 inhabitants, 77 of whom were in command of American sailing ships, and 33 of whom were the proud masters of full-rigged Cape Horners.

Ever since those hardy pioneers from the Old Country cleared their holdings along that thickly wooded New England seaboard, salt water has run in the blood of their descendants. The State of Maine has always wrested a living from the forests and the sea.

The first ship commanded by a Searsport captain is said to have been the *Henry Leeds*, of 379 tons, built in Prospect Marsh in 1834 for Captain Jeremiah Sweetser of Prospect, which was, of course, the old name for Searsport. Since that date there have been three Sweetsers in command of American ships : Jeremiah Sweetser (senior), ship *Henry Leeds*; Jeremiah Sweetser (junior), ship *Mary Goodell*; Joseph P. Sweetser, ship *Zephyr*.

But there were many other families living at Searsport who could beat this record. Out of seven Blanchards commanding ships during the latter half of the nineteenth century five brothers were all lost at sea at different times.

The churchyard at Searsport is said to contain many more tombstones than coffins; and the record " lost at sea " is carved over many a non-existing grave. Here is a typical inscription :

In memory of Captain John G. Pendleton, son of Captain Phineas, Jr., and Wealthy

SEARSPORT CAPTAINS.

Standing :—Wm. Parse, Ned Meyers, Amos Nichols, Wm. Goodell, B. F. Colcord and Wm. R. Gilkey.
Sitting :—Nathan Gilkey, Daniel Nichols, Henry Curtis, Charles Nichols, Joseph Sweetser and AndrewRoss.

CAPT. ANDREW M. ROSS.

CAPT. ANDREW J. ROSS.

Photo 1871.

C. Pendleton, born April 23, 1836, master of the ship *Solferino*, which was lost at sea with all on board, bound from Rangoon to London, last spoken off Cape of Good Hope, December 21, 1863.

An earlier John G. Pendleton was lost at sea on December 2, 1847. There were no less than fourteen Pendletons amongst Searsport shipmasters, namely :

Phineas Pendleton (second)	ship	*Vistula.*
Phineas Pendleton (third)	,,	*Henry B. Hyde.*
Benjamin F. Pendleton	,,	*Nancy Pendleton.*
John G. Pendleton (senior)	,,	*Solferino.*
John G. Pendleton (junior)	,,	*William H. Connor*
James G. Pendleton	,,	*Bell Rock.*
Nathan Pendleton	,,	*Dumbarton.*
Ephraim Pendleton	,,	*Statesman.*
George W. Pendleton	,,	*Henry S. Sanford.*
Timothy C. Pendleton	,,	*Louis Walsh.*
Frank I. Pendleton	,,	*W. H. Connor.*
James H. Pendleton	,,	*Mary L. Cushing.*
Charles Pendleton	,,	*Golden Rocket.*
Andrew S. Pendleton	,,	*Aryan.*

John G. Pendleton Carries Sail.

One cannot give the history of each one of these Pendleton skippers, though it would be intensely interesting, but there is only space for a few scattered anecdotes. Here is a yarn of the sail-carrying John G. Pendleton, who had the *William H. Connor.*

He married Sara Gilkey, belonging to another of Searsport's great seafaring families, and took her to sea with him. One day, when outward bound, Mrs. Pendleton crept up on deck and said to her husband : " It's getting awfully trembly in the cabin. Wouldn't it be as well to shorten sail ? " The captain, who was a very big man, looked down at her with lifted eyebrows. No other person aboard would have dared to suggest touching a sheet or halliard. But hardly had she finished speaking before the main topgallant sail blew out of the bolt-ropes and vanished down wind, whereupon Captain Pendleton said calmly in what he thought was a soothing tone of voice, "Well, my dear, there's the main topgallant sail gone anyway." At which Mrs. Pendleton went below somewhat, if not altogether, relieved of her anxiety. And here comes the point of the story—before the watch was out another main topgallant sail had been bent and set ! !

The *William H. Connor* was the last square-rigger built at Searsport. She is said to have cost young John Pendleton 110,000 dollars, but within three years of her launch he had received back her cost in freights. This was no unusual profit for, according to a Searsport tradition, one of his ships paid 1600 per cent. to her lucky shareholders.

The second Phineas Pendleton was the captain who brought the first Hereford cattle from England in the ship *Astoria*.

The *Henry B. Hyde*, generally considered to be the finest Down Easter ever built, was commanded by Phineas Pendleton the third, her chief shareholders being Pendleton, Carver, and Nichols, all Searsport men.

In the Appendix will be found a list of these famous Searsport captains, and the ships they commanded. I have only given the most notable command of each skipper, as it would have needed a list of a hundred ships to give all their commands. For instance, Captain Benjamin F. Colcord, besides commanding the *Centennial*, was master of the *James G. Pendleton, Henry S. Sanford, Governor Robie, Abner Coburn*, and *William H. Connor*.

Captain Daniel C. Nichols had the *Commandor Du Pont* and the *Robert Porter* before commanding the *Wandering Jew*, and after that ship was burnt in Hongkong harbour he took over the *Emily Reed*. This ship was sold at Tacoma in March, 1900, and the old captain, for the next five years, sailed the *Manuel Llaguno*. When she was sold at New York in September, 1905, Captain Nichols retired, after 45 years in deep-water sailing ships.

Another Searsport captain of long experience in sail was Captain Henry G. Curtis, who commanded the ships *Hope, John C. Potter, State of Maine*, and *Belle of Bath*.

Captain Charles M. Nichols, whose commands consisted of the barque *Patmos* and ships *Henrietta, S. F. Hersey, Lucy A. Nickels*, and *A. J. Fuller*, was one of the few Searsport captains who ended up in steam.

There are still nearly a couple of dozen of these Searsport shipmasters alive and hearty, and during the summer of 1927 a dinner was given to sixteen of these survivors of a bygone shipping era by Mr. Wingate F. Cram, President of the Bangor-Aroostook Railroad, when the group opposite page 24 was taken.

The Town of a Hundred Captains.

This was the proud title which Thomaston gave to itself. Amongst these hundred captains were numbered no less than 25 members of the Watts family, one of the best known of whom was Captain Edwin Watts, who was lost off the Horn in the barque *Minnie M. Watts* in 1883. This Thomaston shipmaster had previously commanded the *James Nesmith* and *L. B. Gilchrist.*

The *James Nesmith,* which he commanded as far back as 1860, had the unhappy distinction of being cut down to the water's edge by the *Great Eastern* when that unlucky leviathan was acting as a cable steamer.

Young Captains.

Many of these Down East master mariners commanded their own ships at a very early age. The latest example of a young American captain that I know of was I. N. Hibberd, who took over the command of the big skysail-yarder *Cyrus Wakefield* in the early nineties at the age of 25, and proceeded to make a record Cape Horn voyage in her. This youthful " old man " has been immortalised in *Cappy Ricks.*

But there have been younger captains of Down Easters than Hibberd. Captain Bert Williams, son of old Bully Williams, was only 21 when he was given the command of the *St. Paul.* Captain John Wallace was actually under 20 years of age when he assumed command of the *J. B. Walker,* whilst Captain Jim Walls was in his twentieth year when he took the *John T. Berry* round the Horn.

Another well-known skipper who obtained command at a very early age was Captain Jim Murphy, who was given the command of the *David Brown* in 1872, when he was only 22 years of age.

These young captains were, however, the exception in the Down Easters, and mere ability without good fortune and family interests did not prevent a long hard service through every grade of a sailor's calling before the coveted promotion was obtained. A good ship deserves a good captain, for a captain can either make or mar his ship's name.

Captain David Sherman Babcock of the "Young America."

The *Young America* was lucky in coming out under the skilful guidance of Captain David S. Babcock, one of those old-time aristocrats of the sea, who was born of a distinguished family and went afloat more for the love of the life than for any need of money.

A fine photograph of this famous American master mariner forms one of the illustratiõns of Clark's *Clipper Ship Era*.

Captain John A. Burgess of the "David Crockett."

Another of the same type as Babcock was Burgess of the *David Crockett*. Captain Burgess was educated at the Brown University, and, like many another, was sent to sea in order to conquer a delicacy of health, and, as so often happened in these cases, Old Ocean turned the delicate boy into a 200-lb., 6-ft., broad-shouldered man, who stood square on his feet to the four winds, a master of his craft.

Burgess was not only a navigator of national reputation, but one of those seamen who delighted in the art of driving a ship under sail. Though a strict disciplinarian, he would allow no bucko methods, and was one of those rare self-controlled master-men who were never known to swear or use bad language. His mates, Griffiths and Conrad, were men of the same type, who could get work out of an indifferent or vicious crew without using belaying-pins or knuckle-dusters.

Burgess was washed overboard off the Horn in attempting to cut some wreckage away forward, a dangerous job which he preferred to do himself rather than risk another man's life.

Captain Joseph Limeburner of the "Great Republic."

Another very superior type of captain, and an artist in the craft of handling a square-rigged ship, was Limeburner of *Great*

Republic. He also was a man who would allow no rough handling of his crew, yet managed to manoeuvre his ship in masterly fashion and to keep her in apple-pie order.

Captain George Cummings of "Young America" and "Three Brothers."

Captain George Cummings was also considered at the top of his profession, but he was cast in a rougher mould than Babcock, Burgess or Limeburner, and he was not above having a rough and tumble with one of his own officers. There was a noted second mate of the *Three Brothers* called Welsh Lewis, who claimed that he had thrown Captain Cummings through the glass door of the ship's after cabin. Though Cummings vehemently denied this, Welsh was a noted wrestler and a typical bucko who was quite capable of giving his own captain a severe drubbing.

Captain Cummings, it is said, would never dip his flag to a British ship, because the *Alabama* flew British colours when she captured and destroyed his beautiful clipper ship, the *Winged Racer*, in November, 1863.

Gates of the "S. P. Hitchcock" and Banfield of the "St. James."

In the last days of the Down Easter there were two captains who were noted in every sailors' boarding-house in every sailor-town the wide world over for their good treatment of the men under them. These were Captain E. V. Gates and Captain Banfield. There was no scrimmaging on the maindeck aboard their ships, no belaying-pin soup on dark nights, no booting off the yards, no lurid curses or savage blasphemies, yet both the *S. P. Hitchcock* and the *St. James* not only made fine passages but earned good dividends, whilst boarding-house runners had to use the strongest dope to entice their men away.

Captain William J. Lermond.

Captain William J. Lermond, of the *Samuel Watts* and *Joseph B. Thomas*, was another much respected American ship-master, and no bucko methods or hazing were allowed aboard his ships.

Captain Lermond had a strong vein of humour, and he was wont to declare laughingly that his make-up formed the ideal mixture. His great-grandfather came to Maine from County Antrim, Ireland, ran wild in the woods and married an Indian girl, a Maine Pocahontas, without the aid of a parson.   All the rest of his forebears, Captain Lermond averred, were real white ; it was clearly evident from his appearance that he had quite a dash of Indian blood in his veins.

Captain Lermond was a superb seaman, and his spyglass bore testimony to his skill, for it was presented to him by the underwriters, when he saved the dismasted *Samuel Watts* in mid-Atlantic and brought her into New York under jury rig.

He was commander and part-owner of the *Joseph B. Thomas* from 1881 to 1908, and sailed her with great success.

The Tragedy of the " Washington B. Thomas."

At the beginning of the twentieth century the American coasting trade was carried on chiefly by fast, shapely, three and four-mast schooners.   The late William F. Palmer, a New Englander of the old school and one of those shipping men who not only had a keen eye for a ship but a very keen business sense, is said to have been the first man to make a success of the four-masted fore-and-aft coaster.   But when he followed up his nicely designed four-masters with clumsy, huge, box-shaped five-masters, the lack of sail area soon brought many of his vessels to grief.   To show the tragic ends of these big unwieldy schooners I give a list of the Palmer fleet on page 31.

When the *Joseph B. Thomas* was sold to the Californian Shipping Co., Sam Watts built a four masted schooner for Captain Lermond. The old square-rig skipper made such a financial success of this fore-and-after, taking deals from St. John, N.B., to Bristol, and then coal up the Mediterranean, that it was decided to build him a bigger vessel, a five-master of great carrying capacity.   This schooner was called the *Washington B. Thomas* in honour of the junior partner of the Boston firm.

Captain Lermond handed over the four-master to his chief officer, Ed. E. Drisko, took the new ship from the ways and superintended her fit-out. Then he set off in ballast to the Virginia coal ports, where he loaded for Portland, Maine.

Winter had set in when Captain Lermond took his new schooner to sea with her first cargo, 4000 tons of coal. After leaving Newport News very heavy weather was experienced. At last it became so bad that Captain Lermond decided to take shelter under Stratton's Island, four miles off the Old Orchard.

THE PALMER FLEET.

Date Built	Name	Rig	Tons	Remarks
1900	*Maude Palmer* .	4-mstr.	1745	Foundered at sea with all hands.
1900	*Marie Palmer* ..	,,	1904	Wrecked on Frying Pan Shoals, 1909.
1901	*Baker Palmer* ..	5-mstr.	2792	Foundered.
1901	*Rebecca Palmer* ..	,,	2556	Sold to Greeks, who scrapped her.
1902	*Prescott Palmer* ..	,,	2811	Foundered 1914.
1902	*Paul Palmer* ..	,,	2193	Burnt at Provincetown.
1903	*Dorothy Palmer* ..	,,	2872	Wrecked on Massachusetts coast ; last survivor of fleet, had crew of only 9 men.
1903	*Elizabeth Palmer*	,,	3065	Sunk in collision with *Washingtonian* off Delaware coast.
1904	*Harwood Palmer*	,,	2885	Torpedoed off French coast, 1917.
1904	*Jane Palmer* ..	,,	3138	Abandoned off Bermuda, 1920.
1904	*Singleton Palmer*	,,	2859	Run down and sunk by steamer off the Delaware coast, 1921.
1905	*Davis Palmer* ..	,,	2965	Foundered off Boston harbour, 1909, crew of 9 drowned.
1907	*Fannie Palmer* ..	,,	2233	Foundered Christmas Eve, 1916.
1908	*Fuller Palmer* ..	,,	3060	Foundered, 1914.

At about 10.30 p.m. that night, when the easterly gale was at its height, the unwieldy schooner dragged on to the rocks and began to break up. The only chance for her crew was that the masts would stand, for all hands were obliged to take refuge in the rigging from the huge seas which were already washing the coal out of the vessel.

Captain Lermond was taking his young second wife to sea for the first time, and this terrible shipwreck was too much for her nerves ; indeed, she was so terrified that he could not get her to leave the deck-house. Whilst he was begging the half-demented woman to get into the rigging, a big sea swept over the vessel, smashed the deck-house to smithereens, and took the captain and his wife

overboard. Both were washed ashore on Old Orchard beach;
the captain was pulled out of the breakers when at his last gasp,
but his wife was quite dead, her skull having been fractured when
the deck-house was broken in.

The following morning the crew, some of whom were in a bad
way, were rescued by the coastguard and life-saving apparatus.

Misfortune now piled its full weight upon the poor old captain ;
whilst he was slowly recovering from the terrible battering he had
received in the surf, the news was broken to him that, by some over-
sight, his share in the schooner, which was practically every dollar
he possessed, had not been covered by the insurance, and thus,
at the age of 70, he was a ruined man.   For a time his many friends
tried to help him to eke out an existence by means of a few brokerage
commissions and the like, but he was glad at last to find a refuge in
the Sailors' Snug Harbour, that magnificent home for American
seamen on the shores of New York harbour.

Here, in 1918, the grand old skipper breathed his last.

The Sail Carriers.

Amongst the most noted sail carriers amongst the Down
East skippers were Dave Rivers of the *A. G. Ropes*, Phineas
Pendleton of the *Henry B. Hyde*, Eben. Curtis of the *Tillie E.
Starbuck*, Jim Murphy of the *Shenandoah*, R. J. Graham of the
Erskine M. Phelps, J. Allen of the *Benjamin F. Packard*, and
Dan Nichols of the *Wandering Jew*.

The sailing ship skipper would rather have a reputation for
sail carrying than for any other seamanlike attribute, and I fear
there may still be retired American shipmasters alive who will
take me to task for omitting their names from this list.   However,
there were captains on the American Register who were notorious
for other reasons than that of hanging on to their canvas.

Ed. Masters and His Tar Pot.

There was a Thomaston shipmaster named Ed. Masters, who
was so great a believer in tar as a wood preservative that he
spoilt the appearance of every ship he commanded.   When he took
over the handsome *Baring Brothers* from Captain Dick Thorndike

CAPT. WM. J. LERMOND AND HIS SON,
Master and Chief Officer of *Joseph B. Thomas.*

Lent by J. Randall, Esq.

CAPT. JAMES F. MURPHY.

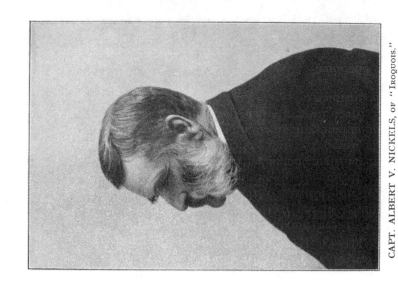

CAPT. ALBERT V. NICKELS, OF "IROQUOIS."

CAPT. JASPER NICHOLS.

he not only tarred her topsides from waterline to rail, but had the white paint scraped off her deck-houses so that they also could be anointed with prime Stockholm.

Dave Libby of the "General Knox."

Captain Dave Libby deserves a mention because of his goodness to all who were under him. He had one of those kindly natures which made him beloved by his crews to whom he acted in every way like a father, and the boys who started sea life under his benevolent and helpful rule were lucky.

Shotgun Murphy and His Irish Flag.

Captain Murphy of *Babcock* and *Shenandoah* fame was an enthusiastic Irish-American, and it was his custom on making port to fly the Harp without a crown on a green burgee beneath the Stars and Stripes at his monkey gaff. This habit was the chief theme of a "Come-all-ye" composed by a sailor called Johnny Clark, and sung to the tune of " The Banks of Newfoundland." The verses will be found in *Roll and Go*, by Joanna C. Colcord; he changes the well-known chorus to the following :

We'll wash her and we'll scrub her down, and we'll work without a frown,
For on board of the saucy *Shenandoah* flies the Harp without a crown.

Some Famous Down East Mates.

In that splendid sailor's book of reminiscences, *Fair Winds and Foul*, the old Down East mate, Fred Perry, gives brilliant thumb-nail sketches of his own contemporaries in the Cape Horn fleet, the mates who used to gather together on South Street, New York City, either at Fred Colcord's, near Peck Slip, or at Orrin Nickerson's, opposite Pier 19, or at Sam Dale's, a block or so east of South Ferry.

In this way he immortalises " Long-hen Toque " of the *Cutwater*, the yarn spinner, who so mixed his threads that he often found himself in Portland (Maine) and Portland (Oregon) on the very same evening ; and Glass-eye Mitchell, with his " long, drooping red moustache, tousled mop of red hair, and bushy eyebrows, topped off with a broad-brimmed black felt hat of the California

Forty-niner type, which was set at a slouchy angle on the back of his head."

Another man who remembered Glass-eye Mitchell declares that he was one of the smartest mates " in or out of Liverpool." He had a hard reputation in the Cape Horn trade, but Perry says he was not really so tough as he was painted. Ashore he was undoubtedly fond of his whisky and not averse to a rough house; and he had a very disconcerting habit, when out of tobacco, of taking his glass eye out of the socket and putting it in his mouth. Mitchell was for a long time mate of the third *Sovereign of the Seas.* His last ship, I believe, was the *Alfred Watts.*

Others of Perry's contemporaries were " Bull-dog " Penfield of the *George Peabody,* so-called because of his facial resemblance to a terra-cotta bull-dog. " Hell-roaring " Taylor, " who had a voice like a bass viol, which increased in volume when he was angry and made a combination of sounds half-way between a Chinese orchestra and a South Sea Island bull fiddle." (Captain Henry Merritt gave him this soubriquet when Taylor was mate under him in the *Charger.* Merritt used to declare that he could get no sleep at night owing to the roaring voice of Taylor shouting at and cursing his watch.) Charley Butcher, who was knifed whilst his ship was towing up the Hooghly and dumped over the side without ceremony. Dinky Bunker, of the *C. F. Sargent,* champion lightweight of Maine, who weighed only 135 lbs. but could knock a 6-ft. 200-lb. sailor clean across the main hatch.

Another boxer amongst the mates was Big Parker of the *North American.*

Then Perry goes on to mention Big Lou Holmes of the *Lucile,* who " with several of his mates fought and put to flight some 30 Greek and Italian sailors in Joe, the Greek's Coffee-house, just off Williamson Square, Liverpool, one Christmas Eve, for making disparaging remarks about the American flag."

Other mates in Perry's gallery were Big Rube Lawrence, nicknamed " Cut-throat Lawrence " owing to a scar from ear to ear, the mark of a murderer's knife. This happened whilst he was mate of the New Orleans cotton packet, *Richard Harvey.* Lawrence had beaten up his captain, Bully Brown, one of the most notorious buckos in the American Merchant Marine, and the captain hired one of his packet-rats to do Lawrence in on the first suitable dark night.

Previous to this Perry states that Brown, in a fit of fury, had marooned his own son, who was then his mate, on a barren island in the Pacific.

It was Brown's vainglorious boast that no mate dared sail a second voyage with him; but Lawrence, in spite of his cut-throat and other attempts at murder, refused to back-water, and in the end that terrible old man Brown had to confess that he was beaten.

Lawrence was afterwards mate of the three skysail-yarder *Triumphant* before gaining command.

Then we must mention One-eye Wilson, mate of the *Levi C. Wade,* a large husky man, a driver and a hard drinker who lost his eye through the snapping of a hawser. Jerry Donovan, a big-fisted Irishman, who was lost in the *St. John Smith*; and Fatty Storms of the *Pactolus,* who was short and fat, a hard drinker much given to lurid language and no mean artist with his dukes.

Perry does not mention Slippery Dick Martin, the mate of the *Glory of the Seas,* in his book. Martin was a first-class officer, a wonderful navigator and a linguist of some ability; he was also a swell dresser, with all the outward appearances of a gentleman. But after he had sold a hawser, a new mainsail, and several coils of manila rope to a junk-man at San Francisco, the "old man" of the *Glory of the Seas* declared that, though Martin was beyond reproach as an officer, he was a bit too slippery for him, and he went on to remark that if he had not returned from his ranch when he did he would have found that Martin had sold the " whole blooming ship."

Red Rogers of the *Columbia* was considered the most proficient swearer in the Cape Horn fleet. It is stated that he burst a blood vessel whilst cursing a deaf boilermaker—who had been shanghaied aboard his ship—and died of haemorrhage.

Perhaps the best known deep-water mate since Perry's time was Donald Nicholson of the *Tillie E. Starbuck,* described as a " big, rangy fellow, a typical bucko, hard of jaw and hard of fist, who feared neither God, man nor devil." He afterwards commanded in steam on the Honolulu and inter-island run, and only died a few years ago.

Amongst the really purple-dyed buckos were Black Watts of the " bloody " *Gatherer*, Harris of the infamous *Sunrise*, and Dick Hoffmann of the *Richard Robinson*.

Perry quotes a verse which refers to Charley Watts' extradition from Queenstown :

> Mr. Watts of *Gatherer* fame returns to clear his clouded name,
> Not because he thought it best, but because of the law's behest,
> Reinforced by bands of steel round his hands and round his heel,
> Made it rather awkward for Mr. Watts to snub the law.

Watts was found guilty of cruelty on the high seas and spent a long term in Folsom Prison.

" Sunrise Harris " was also condemned at San Francisco, though Perry considered it a miscarriage of justice in his case.

Dick Hoffman, however, made a get-away to South America and settled down at Valparaiso.

Old Mose Doyle, who was second mate with the terrible Captain Bob Merriman for many years, was another really tough specimen of the genus bucko.   Fred Perry thought very badly of his manners when he sneaked aboard Perry's ship in Valparaiso Bay and walked off with her largest and best snatch-block, which he sold ashore for the price of enough aqua-vitae to make himself and Dick Hoffman very drunk.   Hoffman, after the *Richard Robinson* mutiny, had escaped from jail and made his way to Valparaiso, where he was on the beach.   The two reprobates were safely locked up in the calaboose before morning, but Perry never recovered his snatch-block.

None of the above find a mention in the *Red Record*, which only starts in 1888.   The blackest character amongst the mates indicted by the *Red Record* appears to have been R. Crocker, who was accused of cruelty when second mate of the *Commodore T. H. Allen* in 1892 ; again when second mate of the *Tam o' Shanter* in 1893, and lastly as mate of the *Francis* a few months later.   Crocker stood 6 ft. 3 ins. in his socks and weighed 260 lbs.   He knocked seamen about from pure devilment, and even chased them from aloft in order to hammer them.   Such a man could rarely show himself in port, and usually spent that period of a voyage in hiding.

The Humour of the Down East Mate.

It must not be supposed that the American officer could only get work done or maintain discipline by violent methods. He was the master of a curious kind of sardonic humour, which was most effective with the men. Indeed, the tongues of some Down East mates were more dreaded than their fists. Sarcasm and ridicule were the two points of the attack, and past masters of both were often found amongst the after-guard of an American ship.

"Hop On, Hop Ever."

The nineteenth century will always be noted for its piety— or perhaps I should say its outward show of religion. Tracts were handed about all over the world, and texts pasted up in the most unlikely places. Thus at one time it was not uncommon for pious owners or captains to emblazon the break of the poop, the boat skids, or even the spare spars with mottoes and texts.

It happened that during this craze a ship lying in Calcutta had to find a new chief officer. This vessel had the words, "Hope on, Hope ever!" painted in large letters across her boat skids. The new mate, to the general alarm of the ship's company—she was a British ship—turned out to be a perfect specimen of the Down East type, a steely-eyed, close-lipped, lean, sinewy New Englander. After one contemptuous glance at the text on the boat skids, he sent for a pot of white paint and proceeded, slowly, neatly, and deliberately, to paint out the last letter of "hope," thus making the sentence read, "Hop on, Hop ever!"

He then called all hands and addressed them as follows: "That thar motto, I guess, war a sur' enough good 'un, but yew kin neow blink yew'r gol-darned eyes on a better—" He halted impressively, then went on in a tone to strike terror, "An' remember, when I say 'Hop!' hop lively!"

"Sunday."

Here is another yarn of the same description. This time the ship was a "Blue-nose," bound across to St. John, N.B., from Liverpool. At 8 bells on the first Sunday morning at sea, after the decks had been washed down, the mate, who hailed from the State of Maine, turned to one of the ship's boys and said: "Jump an' get that board out o' my locker." The boy fetched the board and was then told to hold it up so that all hands—both watches being still on deck—could read the word "Sunday " painted across it in large letters. " Neow," said Mister Mate in a slow, clear drawl, "all o' you take a good look at that board, for that's all the Sunday you'll see aboard this ship." Then, in a lighter tone, "All right, sonny, put it away, and you men, come along for'ard and we'll get ahead with that chafing gear." And that was all the Sunday that crew did see on a long, hard passage across the Atlantic.

" Crow ! And Crow Lively or I'll Let Fly at Ye ! "

Perhaps the best example of the power of ridicule was witnessed by the late Captain W. B. Whall, when a " mid " in the Blackwall frigate *Hotspur*. Let me give the yarn in his own words:

On one occasion a fine Boston packet lay outside us, the mate of which was a genius ; this fellow took most refined methods to drive his crew away. (Here I must explain that " running a crew out of a ship," when she was expected to make a long stay in port, was considered the duty of both American and British mates in those bad old days, in order to save the owners an unnecessary wages bill.) They were Scandinavians, who are naturally a meek and mild race. He hazed these poor devils around until they were almost crazy, but they hung on well. At last he hit on a grotesque refinement of cruelty, which had the effect he wanted.

One morning, at sunrise, whilst we were washing decks, we heard this character howl out, " Naoe ! Yup thar ! Crow ! And crow lively or I'll let fly at ye ! " There stood Mister Mate on the roof of the deck-house, revolver in hand, looking aloft. Following his gaze we beheld, perched on the main royal yard, six of these unhappy beings; and, as we looked, there came down to us the faint strains of "Cock-a-doodle."

He had actually made them climb aloft and crow like roosters when they saw the sun rise. This sufficed. The next day they were missing and safe ashore in the hands of the crimps.

A Formula for Bracing Yards.

It was rare to find an open humorist amongst New England mates, but on the rare occasions when an American mate did make a joke you may be sure that the watch brought down the skies with the heartiness of their laughter. Whereupon, as likely as not, they would be turned upon and withered into an uneasy silence by some such hissed-out sentence as the following : " Don't you kid y'selves you understand humour, yew scum. Cut that cackle an' git on with y'r work."

I can only recall one instance of a Yankee mate who prided himself on a sort of droll badinage. He was a man named Gibson, and he had a regular formula for bracing yards, which he would bawl out in a voice of thunder : " A small pull on the weather main brace ; topsail brace the same ; topgallant brace likewise ; royal brace also ; skysail brace ditto."

The Cape Horn Shellbacks.

The men who shipped before the mast in American Cape Horners—the despised shellbacks—have been lauded in print by Paul Eve Stevenson as the bravest of the brave.

As a matter of fact, you were liable to find any nationality, any profession, and any kind of a human being in the fo'c'sle of a Yankee Cape Horner, from a stiff-bristled pug-ugly to a spineless cur, from a prime true-blue to a useless hobo ; for the crimps, Shanghai Brown, Red Jackson, and the like, with their jackals of the type of Larry Marr and Three-finger Daily, were not particular as to the status or the fitness of the unfortunates whom they tossed aboard a Cape Horner in a doped condition the night before sailing.

One or two American sea writers have declared that their captains picked a mixed crowd of mongrels on purpose. Let me quote :

No skipper'll ship an American sailor whilst there's a Dutchman left in the shipping office. He wouldn't think it safe to go to sea with too many American sailors forward to call him down and make him treat 'em decent. He picks a Dago here and a Dutchman there, and all the Souwegians he sees, and fills in with the rakins and scrapins o' hell, Bedlam and Newgate, knowing they'll hate one another worse than they hate him, and never stand together.

I have met some of these Souwegians, with their " heavy foreign faces, greasy canvas jackets and blanket trousers." They were mostly fine seamen, superb ship cleaners, a bit clumsy aloft, perhaps, and slow, but lacking that trouble-making devilry and strain of fighting blood, so common in the Anglo-Saxon race ; which blood-strain, by the by, forms the backbone not only of John Bull but Brother Jonathan

It must not be imagined for one moment that a foremast crowd had to be easy and docile in order to please a Down East skipper and his mates. That was very far from being the case. American officers prided themselves on being able to handle a hard crowd and revelled in a " rough house."

" You know a man has to be rough going deep-water. When you get a tough or weak or know-nothing crowd for'ard, as sometimes happens, you have to handle them rough or you'd never get the ship's work done," was the general opinion from the mates' side of the deck.

And they even studied the various methods of taming a man without rendering him unfit for duty. Said an old Cape Horn skipper to his young officer: "Never strike a man near the temple, especially with an iron belaying-pin or a hand-spike; and when you have him down, kick him on the legs or above the short ribs. It's altogether unnecessary to disable a man, and unwise with a short crew."

And here is the rooted opinion of the Cape Horn shellback: " I'd rather be in hell without claws than aboard of a Yankee ship with the mates down on me."

CHAPTER III.

THE CLIPPERS IN THE CAPE HORN TRADE.

Jump away, Jonathan, jig along, Jemima,
California's made of gold ; we'll get as rich as Lima ;
Come, lads, leave your dads, to search for gold be brisk, oh ?
Cut stick, right slick, and sail for San Francisco.

(Californian Gold Rush Song.)

OF the famous American clippers which were launched in the early fifties only a few survived the North and South War and took their place in the grain trade from San Francisco round the Horn to the Eastern States and Europe, but the two rivals, *Young America* and *David Crockett*, not only made by far the best records in the Cape Horn trade, but survived over thirty years of hard buffeting, a longer period than many a heavier built, more powerful Down Easter could lay claim to. The late Captain Arthur H. Clark, in his *Clipper Ship Era*, credits the *David Crockett* with an average of $109\frac{7}{12}$ days for her best dozen outward passages between New York and San Francisco, and the *Young America* with an average of $110\frac{7}{12}$ days. It is evident, therefore, that there was not much to choose between them in the matter of speed.

In the Appendix I give a complete list of the *Young America's* voyages until she was sold abroad, and also a list of *David Crockett's* outward and homeward passages round the Horn.

Though many a clipper and many a carrier was built in Down East yards with whose model and construction it would be hard to find a fault, no more perfect wooden sailing ships were ever built than that famous pair of valiant Cape Horners, *Young America* and *David Crockett*. Both were launched in 1853, which might well be called the zenith year of American shipbuilding, for in that year close on 100 out-and-out clippers were sent afloat from Down East

41

yards, besides an equal number of medium and full-built ships. The list of clippers included such world-famed vessels as the *Dreadnought, Red Jacket, Great Republic, Romance of the Seas, Chariot of Fame, Neptune's Car, Eagle Wing, Reporter, Ocean Herald, David Brown, Dashing Wave, White Swallow, Empress of the Seas, Pampero, Panama, Sweepstakes, Herald of the Morning,* and two *Morning Lights.* During this *annus mirabilis* of American shipbuilding, the East Boston shore from Jeffries Point to Chelsea Bridge was one continuous line of sailing ships under construction, and amongst the vessels on the stocks no less than eleven owed their form to the genius of Donald McKay.

The same shipbuilding boom was raging in the New York yards, and William H. Webb, who built the *Young America,* was then at the height of his production, which not only included clippers but packet ships, mail steamers and even foreign men-of-war.

A great deal has been printed of late years about Donald McKay and his Boston-built marvels, but in the fifties William H. Webb was considered the leading shipbuilder and designer in the United States of America. In 1851, besides building the notorious *Challenge* and other clippers, such as the *Comet, Swordfish, Invincible* and *Gazelle,* he launched the Pacific Mail steamer, *Golden Gate,* and the Havre packet ship, *Isaac Bell.* The next year his best known ships were the extreme clipper, *Flying Dutchman,* and the Black Star packets, *America* and *Australia*; then on April 30, 1853, he launched the *Young America* from the stocks. Out of not less than 150 ships for which the great shipbuilder was responsible the *Young America* was his favourite and the nearest approach to his conception of a well-built clipper ship.

The " Young America."

This famous ship cost $140,000 to build, and her construction was carefully superintended by her future commander, Captain David S. Babcock, who gave up the *Swordfish* to take Webb's new masterpiece. The *Young America* was a big ship for her day, her tonnage being 1961 tons old measurement and 1439 tons new. Length of her keel was 239 ft. 6 ins., and on deck 243 ft. Extreme beam was 43 ft. 2 ins. ; depth of hold 26 ft. 9 ins.; mean draft 22 ft.; and dead rise at half floor 20 ins., with long lean bow lines, a clean run, and very graceful sheer. She had no figure-head, but her elaborately carved trail boards terminated in what Americans called a billet-head. Her stern was elliptical and with slightly more overhang and counter than many of the American clippers, and this, with her long bow, gave her a very racy appearance.

She was built as strongly as it was possible to build a ship, with iron frames, diagonally braced and only 4 ft. apart. There were three decks, and under a poop deck 42 feet long a number of cabins were handsomely furnished for passengers of whom she generally carried a few during the first half of her life.

Like most of the American clippers, *Young America* crossed three skysail yards and she was both lofty and square, for it is said that her mainyard was 104 feet long before she was cut down and given double topsails. With such a big sail plan she required a large crew, and on her maiden voyage she sailed from New York with a complement of 75 all told, including 4 mates and 60 able seamen. Her freight list on this occasion came to 86,400 dollars. Twelve years later she was considered to be very favoured by the shippers, when she sailed for San Francisco with a freight amounting to 50,442 dollars, as against the brand-new *Seminole's* 45,369 dollars.

From the first the *Young America* proved herself a good money maker, and considering the severe knocking about sustained in the Cape Horn trade she was singularly free from dismastings and other mishaps. Only once did Cape Stiff succeed in doing more than smash in bulwarks, stove boats, and break down deck-house doors, and this was on her third voyage during the night of May 18, 1856. When hove-to off the Horn the *Young America* took a heavy sea over, which broke her jibboom into three pieces and did sundry other damage.

On October 30, 1862, when bound to Antwerp from the Antipodes, she put into Plymouth for repairs, having lost her fore topmast, main topgallant mast, and had her main topsail yard sprung during a tornado squall in 9° S., 32° W.

Her worst experience was on December 3, 1868, when she was caught aback in a pampero and went over on her beam ends.

Captain Cummings had just given the order for axes to the weather lanyards, when the mizen topmast broke off at the lower cap and took with it the main topgallant and fore royal masts. The ship was 41 days out, the port of Monte Video was handy, and Cummings had to decide whether he would refit at sea with the Cape Horn passage ahead, or put up with a long delay and costly repairs in the South American port. He decided to carry on at sea, and this decision, which was rewarded at San Francisco by a 1000-dollar gift from the underwriters, shows the stiff-lipped nerve of the " old man," for the ship was half full of water, had a cargo of railway iron which, it was supposed at the time, was all adrift and shifted to leeward; also her crew were worn out and on the verge of refusing duty, and her passengers, who included the captain's wife and son, were scared stiff as they floundered about amidst broken crockery in the flooded cabin. But "old man" Cummings kept cool where all was panic and hysteria.

For 24 hours, though the pampero had passed, a nasty cross sea swept the maindeck whilst all hands spelled each other at the pump brakes. Then as soon as the pumps sucked every tackle in the ship was clapped on to the wreckage of spars alongside.

It took a week of superb seamanship and severe man-driving to get the *Young America* jury-rigged on the mizen. Then, on December 11, a heavy sou-wester with high sea threatened to undo the work, and induced Captain Cummings to cut down his new mizen topsail to a three-reef instead of a four-reef sail. On December 15 the main topgallant mast was fidded, and the sail bent and set. On the 20th one of the worst Cape Horn snorters in the captain's memory attacked the ship, and the following day he had to threaten his hard-worked crew with the bilboes to keep them going ; Christmas brought better weather, and on December 25 the *Young America* was abreast of the Horn in fine, clear weather.

Captain Cummings brought his ship into San Francisco on February 17, looking like a yacht, and received great praise from the whole shipping community. The subsequent repairs cost 18,000 dollars.

The *Young America* seems to have been very tight for a wooden ship. In 1862 she got aground on the New Zealand coast, but came to no harm; but in 1865, when bound to San Francisco, she sprang a bad leak in the South Pacific, and the pumps had to be kept going until she arrived, which was only a matter of 17 days, a quick run, from the Equator. In 1870 she ran on a reef off Cape San Roque, but, after jettisoning cargo, came off after hours without leaking.

Young America's two record passages are worthy of being given in detail. On October 12, 1872, she left Liverpool for San Francisco, and, after discharging her pilot off the Tuskar on October 16, made the splendid run to the Equator of 15 days 6 hours, and was abreast of Pernambuco 17 days 13 hours after dropping the pilot.

Her first 11 days totalled the following 24-hour runs : 340, 268, 230, 300, 207, 212, 255, 260, 227, 225, and 223. She was off Cape Horn in 43 days 12 hours, and crossed 50° S. in the Pacific 51 days out.

The passage would have beaten every record if she had not had very poor winds in the South Pacific, so that between 30° and 20° S. she only covered 727 miles. The Pacific Equator was crossed on January 3, 1873, and *Young America* was 100 miles S.W. of the Golden Gate on January 18, 94 days out ; she was then, however, obliged to tack offshore and did not make the anchorage until January 20.

On her record run to New York the *Young America* left San Francisco on March 15, 1870, crossed the Equator in the Pacific 16 days out, rounded Cape Horn 42 days out, and crossed the Equator in the Atlantic 64 days out. At 8 a.m. on June 4, when only 81 days out and 10 miles from Sandy Hook lightship, the ship was shrouded in fog and unable to find a pilot. On June 5, when 20 miles east of Sandy Hook, she received her pilot, and anchored in New York harbour on June 6. This is called the record passage for a loaded ship.

It will be noticed that her best run from San Francisco to Liverpool was no better than 103 days. The record for this passage was made by the American clipper, *Panama*, namely 86 days 17 hours ; she left San Francisco on October 27, 1860, and anchored in the Mersey on January 21, 1861.

The *Young America's* best piece of sailing to be recorded was a 4-day run of 1423 miles, when homeward bound in 1876. On this occasion she made four consecutive 24-hour runs of 365, 358, 360, and 340 miles respectively.

Another remarkable record by the *Young America* was made between July 17 and 23, 1876, when she sailed round the Horn from 50° S. Atlantic to 50° S. Pacific in six days. This is undoubtedly the most difficult traverse for a sailing ship in the whole world. Many and many a fast, well-found ship has spent one and even two months over it; and there are many instances of vessels putting their helm up in despair and going east about the whole way round the world rather than face another bout with the merciless Cape Horn snorter.

George Daniels was the *Young America's* first owner, but it is more than probable that her builder and her captain, David Babcock, each held a considerable number of 64th shares. At the beginning of the sixties she was registered as owned by Abram Bell's sons, then Robert L. Taylor had her for a few years until about 1870, when she came into the hands of George Howes & Co. along with her old rival, *David Crockett*. When the business of the Howes brothers was wound up John Rosenfeld of San Francisco acquired the fleet.

In October, 1883, after a leaky passage from San Francisco, the old ship was sold in New York for 13,500 dollars. She then came under the Austrian flag and was renamed *Miroslav*. After staggering to and fro across the stormy North Atlantic for a couple of years the gallant vessel succumbed to the westerly gales; she left Delaware breakwater on February 17, 1886, for Fiume, and was posted as missing.

The " David Crockett."

The *David Crockett*, *Young America's* great rival in the Cape Horn trade, was built to run as a packet ship between New York and Liverpool. Her builders, Greenman & Co., of Stonington, Connecticut, were not known as clipper ship builders, but the *David Crockett* turned out a masterpiece, and could hardly have been improved upon as a Cape Horner, being possessed not only of unusual speed and strength but of good carrying capacity.

"YOUNG AMERICA."

FIGURE-HEAD OF "DAVID CROCKETT."

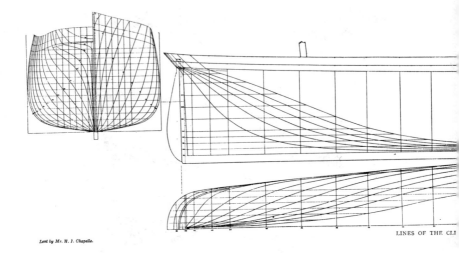

LINES OF THE CLI

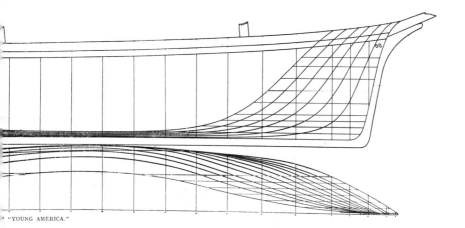

"YOUNG AMERICA."

ORIGINAL SAIL PLAN

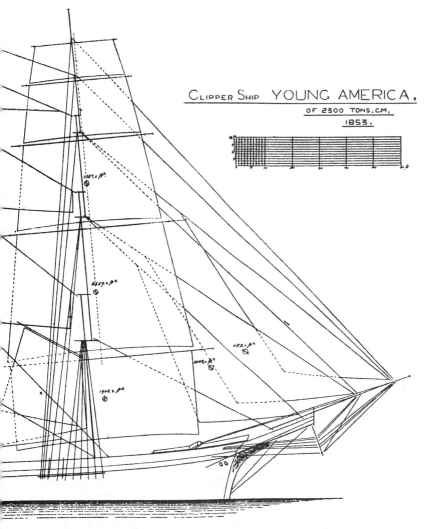

CLIPPER SHIP YOUNG AMERICA,
OF 2300 TONS. C.M,
1853.

OUNG AMERICA."

"GREAT REPUBLIC" IN 1860.

Lent by Francis B. C. Bradlee.

She was not so heavily rigged as the *Young America,* but she crossed three skysail yards, and when her single topsails were replaced by the double the single mizen topsail was retained Perhaps a comparison of measurements with regard to the two famous Cape Horners will be of interest :—

	Tons old	Tons new	Length	Breadth	Depth
Young America ..	1961	1439	243	43·2	26·9
David Crockett ..	1679	1547	218·8	41	27

As regards her carrying capacity, *David Crockett* loaded a grain cargo of 2200 short tons.

Throughout her career she was a great money maker, and it is stated that her net earnings up to 1876 were half a million dollars ; considering that her total cost was 93,000 dollars this is good work.

The *David Crockett* had a famous figure-head, which may now be seen at the San Francisco Chamber of Commerce. This figure-head was apparently kept for harbour use, being carefully unscrewed and stowed away whilst at sea.

With the exception of an East India voyage in 1855, when she went out to Aden from Liverpool in 85 days and came home from Bombay in 104, the *David Crockett* was serving as a packet ship in Handy & Everett's Line from 1853 to 1857, and she evidently did nothing outstanding in the way of quick passages, or the fact would have been noted in the New York or Liverpool papers.

Her first experience of Cape Horn came in 1857, and the passage of the dreaded Cape was by no means pleasant. *David Crockett* was fighting hard westerly gales for a fortnight off the pitch of the Horn, during which time her maindeck was swept bare.

Her worst experience off Cape Stiff was probably in 1879, when she arrived within sight of the Horn on May 28, 63 days out from New York. For the next eleven days she battled unavailingly with a succession of Cape Horn snorters, with terrific hail and snow squalls, until at last she was driven back as far as Cape St. John. The chief damage sustained during this time of stress was the carrying away of two chain plates in the main rigging, and the gammoning of the bowsprit, whilst that dreadnought of a sail, the main spencer, was split from top to bottom. Captain Anderson always declared that this was his worst experience of Horn weather.

On June 11, the *David Crockett* was once more abreast of Cape Stiff ; this time she got a slant, and in two days had crossed 50° S. in the Pacific.

Though she was often severely knocked about by the elements, the *David Crockett* was so well handled by her different captains, notably by Captains Burgess and Anderson, that she was never dismasted.

On September 11, 1882, when eight days out from the Golden Gate, in 16° N., 117° W., the *David Crockett* ran into a cyclone, which played havoc with her for 20 hours. This time her hard weather sails, such as the lower topsails, were blown clean out of the bolt-rope. The masts held, however, though the ship herself did not escape damage. As she was being run off before it she was pooped by a sea, which started the stern frame, broke in portholes and skylights, and flooded the cabin, washed away the binnacle, and set the spare spars on the maindeck adrift.

The following was her fastest run out to San Francisco :

Nov.	6,	1871	Left New York		
„	26	1871	Crossed Equator 20 days out		
Dec.	26	1871	Crossed 50° S. in Atlantic	50 days out	
Jan.	7	1872	Crossed 50° S. in Pacific	62	„
Jan.	27	1872	Crossed Equator in Pacific	82	„
Feb.	17	1872	Arrived San Francisco	103	„

I do not believe that the *David Crockett* was capable of the big runs made by *Young America*, and probably her best speed per hour was not much over 15 knots ; but she was one of those all-round vessels, which were hard to keep up with, and still harder to get away from in any type of weather or condition of wind.

Lawrence Giles & Co., of New York, were her first owners in the Cape Horn trade, then about 1870 she came under the celebrated Howes flag along with *Young America*, and was also taken over by John Rosenfeld along with the rest of Howes' fleet, in 1880. In 1883, when the fleet was again dispersed, she went to Thomas Dunham's Nephew & Co. In 1889 we find her still ship-rigged and owned by Thos. Daggett of New York.

Finally, like so many splendid American sailing ships, she

was converted into a coal barge, being bought by Messrs. Peter Wright & Son of Philadelphia in May, 1890, for this purpose.

The end came in February, 1899, when the wood three-mast schooner barge, *David Crockett*, Captain B. G. Pendleton, owner F. L. Neall of Philadelphia, was wrecked.

The "Great Republic."

No description of the American Cape Horners would be complete without some mention of the *Great Republic*. This famous vessel was designed and built by Donald McKay at East Boston in 1853. He intended her to be not only the largest but the finest and fastest sailing ship in the world, and there is no doubt whatever that at the date of her launch, October 4, 1853, this was the case.

Donald McKay built her entirely at his own expense on spec, and when the shipping experts, on seeing the newly laid keel of the huge ship, declared that she was too large to pay, and that she would go bankrupt, the great shipbuilder replied : "Let friends and foes talk, I'll work."

The launch of the *Great Republic* was a public holiday in Boston, and 60,000 people gathered to see the vessel take the water. Longfellow has immortalised the occasion in his poem, " The Building of the Ship."

> Then the Master
> With a gesture of command
> Waved his hand :
> And at the word,
> Loud and sudden there was heard,
> All around them and below,
> The sound of hammers, blow on blow,
> Knocking away the shores and spurs.
> And see ! She stirs !
> She starts—she moves—she seems to feel
> The thrill of life along her keel,
> And, spurning with her foot the ground,
> With one exalting, joyous bound,
> She leaps into the ocean's arms !
> And lo ! from the assembled crowd
> There rose a shout, prolonged and loud,

That to the Ocean seemed to say—
"Take her, O bridegroom, old and grey,
Take her to thy protecting arms,
With all her youth and all her charms ! "

The launch was in every way successful, except that a few old croakers and gay topers prophesied evil when they saw that Captain Alden Gifford christened her with Cochituate water instead of champagne, in order as some declared, to please the temperance advocates of Boston.

In a number of other ways the *Great Republic* was a record breaker. To begin with she was a four-master, of the rig called shipentine in America and four-mast barque in Great Britain, and she was the first four-masted sailing ship since the advent of the Canadian log ships. Then her masts and yards were longer and heavier than any that had been stepped or crossed before. Her mainmast, from deck to truck, was 228 feet long, and the lower mast was 44 inches in diameter. Her mainyard was 120 feet long and 28 inches in diameter, and all other masts and yards were in proportion, so that she was able to spread no less than 15,653 yards of canvas. She had four laid decks, with 8 feet of head-room between each deck, and her registered tonnage under the American rule was 4555 tons. A magnificent golden eagle decorated her stem, and across the stern-board was another beautiful carving of an eagle with wings outstretched.

The complement of McKay's " great ship " consisted of 100 men and 30 boys ; and the builder's brother, Lauchlan McKay, who had superintended the building, took command.

Before sending her round to New York in order to load for Liverpool, Donald McKay made 1000 dollars for the Seamen's Aid Society by charging the public a dime or so to see over his masterpiece. After this the *Great Republic* was towed round to New York. Then came the tragedy of Donald McKay's life—his masterpiece, when loaded and ready for sea with sails bent, was burnt to the water's edge on Boxing Day, 1853, through her tarred rigging becoming ignited by sparks blowing across her from the fire in Front Street at the premises of the Novelty Baking Company.

The history of this disastrous fire, which also destroyed the ships, *White Squall* and *Joseph Walker*, and of the *Great Republic's* rebuilding under the direction of Captain Nat Palmer, has been recounted in print often enough. But there are one or two points which need to be emphasised.

First of all, the crew of the *Great Republic* fought heriocally to save their ship ; whips were rove and water hauled up to men stationed in the tops, and when, in spite of drenchings, the foresail burst into flames, followed by topsails and topgallant sails, these men made a great effort to cut the burning canvas from the yards, until they were driven to the deck, scorched and exhausted.

Then Captain McKay and Captain Ellis, who had hurried to the scene to act for the underwriters, decided to cut away the masts. This was probably a mistake, for the flaming masts and yards not only fell on deck, smashed up fire engine, boats and deck-houses, and drove the firemen away, but pierced their way through the decks to the hold and set fire to the cargo. After this, the last remedy of scuttling was taken, but this, though it put out the fire below decks, caused the grain in her cargo to swell and strain the hull in every direction. Also the ship was only submerged aft, and the greater part of her superstructure was destroyed by the fire, which continued to burn for two days.

After the reconstruction by Captain Nat Palmer, her new owners, A. A. Low & Brother, put her on the berth at New York for a trans-Atlantic cargo, but she was a very different ship to that which had astonished the world in October, 1853. She had lost a deck, and her huge spars had been greatly reduced, as much as 17 feet being cut off the lower masts and 20 feet off the lower yards. The beautiful eagle which decorated the bow was gone, and a plain billet-head did not help the appearance of the rather straight stem, which was a characteristic of McKay models.

Captain Joseph Limeburner now took over the command, and he remained in the ship until 1864.

Leaving New York on February 24, 1855, *Great Republic* made the land in 12 days, and arrived in the Mersey 13 days out. Here she was unable to dock owing to her great draft, and when she sailed round to the Thames there was not a dock in London deep enough to take her, and Captain Limeburner was compelled to discharge his cargo into lighters.

With transports badly needed to convey troops and stores to Crimea, *Great Republic* was speedily chartered by the French along with a number of other American clippers, such as *Ocean Herald, Queen of Clippers, Titan, Monarch of the Sea,* and *White Falcon.* But first of all the *Great Republic* went round to Liverpool, where she took on board 1600 British troops, which she landed at Marseilles. It was here that her portrait was painted by the French marine artist, Francois Roux, who was photographic in his rendering of the smallest detail of the great ship's appearance under sail.

It was not until the end of the year 1856 that the *Great Republic* returned to New York from her war service in the Mediterranean. And now at last she was loaded in the Cape Horn trade, taking on 5000 tons of general cargo for San Francisco. Before joining the Cape Horn fleet her jigger mast was removed and she was converted into a typical American three skysail-yarder.

Sailing from New York in December, 1856, Captain Limeburner dropped his pilot outside Sandy Hook lightship at 3 p.m. on December 7, and then proceeded to make the record run of 15 days 18 hours from Sandy Hook to the Line. On the fifth day of the passage the *Great Republic* made the best 24-hour run of her career— this was 413 miles, 360 of which were covered at the rate of 19 knots. Captain Luther, who was before the mast in McKay's wonderful ship in 1863, declared that, when bound from Callao to London, she logged $19\frac{3}{4}$ knots for several hours in the North Atlantic with the wind abaft the beam and topmast stunsails set.

On her first trip to California *Great Republic* passed the dreaded Cape San Roque in 19 days 14 hours ; she was off the pitch of the Horn in 45 days 7 hours, and sailed round the stormy Cape with skysails set. A week later she had crossed 50° S. in the Pacific. The Equator was crossed in 118° W. on February 17, 1857, and the clipper was within 500 miles of the Golden Gate on the 87th day out from Sandy Hook. But calms and fogs spoilt Captain Limeburner's chance of beating *Flying Cloud's* record, and *Great Republic* took another 5 days to get in, thus making the passage in the splendid time of 92 days.

There was no chance of a return cargo from San Francisco for such a monster as the *Great Republic* at that date, and Captain Limeburner was forced to go to Callao for Chincha Island guano. The run down the Pacific was made in 52 days. The *Great Republic's* first experience of a guano cargo was by no means pleasant; she loaded 4500 tons for London. All went well until she was to the southward of the Horn, but there she shipped a sea which fell with such force amidships that it stove in the planking and broke four deck beams. This allowed sea water to reach the guano in the hold, and the resulting chemical action on the cargo so tainted the ship's provisions that Captain Limeburner was obliged to put in to Port Stanley, Falkland Islands, for food. Arriving in this harbour of refuge on September 8, 1857, Captain Limeburner hired the sealing schooner, *Nancy*, and sent her to Monte Video for provisions. As soon as these were received the ship, which in the meantime had been repaired, was able to proceed, and arrived in the Thames on January 11, 1858.

On her second passage to San Francisco, in 1858, *Great Republic* was 41 days to the Equator instead of 15, the weather in the North Atlantic being very unfavourable. Her time from the Line to port was the same as on previous passage, 79 days, which was very good work. Leaving 'Frisco in ballast she raced the clipper *Talisman* to New York, and was beaten by four days, their times being :

Talisman left 'Frisco February 10, 1859   Arrived New York May 18— 96 days
Great Republic left 'Frisco February 10, 1859   Arrived New York May 22—100 days

Leaving New York again on November 23, 1859, *Great Republic* raced the *Ocean Telegraph* out to California, both ships arriving in San Francisco Bay on the same day, but owing to very light winds in the South Atlantic their times were spoilt, *Ocean Telegraph* taking 109 days and *Great Republic* 110 days. Again the latter was obliged to make the long homeward passage in ballast and was 96 days to New York.

In 1860 the *Great Republic* left New York on October 24 ; crossed the Equator on November 17, 24 days out; rounded Cape Horn on December 18, 55 days out ; took 11 days between the " fifties " : crossed the Line in Pacific on January 16, 1861, 84 days out ; and arrived San Francisco February 5, 1861, 104 days out.

This year she managed to load a grain cargo for Liverpool, and made the passage in 96 days. At Liverpool, with all the upset occasioned by the North and South War, *Great Republic* was unable to get any freight for New York, so crossed the Atlantic in ballast, taking 32 days. She had no sooner arrived than she was seized by the U.S. Government, owing to the fact that ten-sixteenths of her shares were owned by Southerners in Virginia and South Carolina. A. A. Low & Brother circumnavigated this difficulty by buying out the Southerners, and chartering the ship to the Government as a transport.

Her first trip was to Port Royal and back. Then in February, 1862, she formed one of the transports in the Butler Expedition to Ship Island. On this service Captain Limeburner had all the trouble he wanted. During a south-east gale the *Great Republic* dragged across the transport *Idaho*, and both ships went ashore. The great clipper came off without damage, but a fortnight later she was again ashore, in the Mississippi, after which Captain Limeburner was glad to give up transport work and return to the Cape Horn trade. Sailing from New York at the end of November, *Great Republic* had a very nasty night of it in a wild winter gale off Cape Hatteras, in which her mainsail and topsails were torn from the jackstays, and both fore and main upper topsail yards carried away. This occasioned some strenuous work, but the mate, Wall, was a hustler, who would have dealt generously in belaying-pin soup if the "old man" had allowed it, and he had new yards aloft and new sails bent within the space of a watch.

That very night the *Alabama*, which was on the lookout for the McKay clipper, was reported to have burnt a ship 60 miles to eastward of Captain Limeburner's position. But the *Great Republic* was not an easy vessel to catch, and she made a splendid passage to San Francisco, the epitome of which was as follows :

Left New York	November 24 1862		
Crossed the Equator	December 17 1862	.. 23 days out	
Crossed 50° S. Atlantic	January 13 1863	.. 50	,,
Crossed 50° S. Pacific	January 25 1863	.. 62	,,
Crossed the Equator	February 16 1863	.. 84	,,
Arrived San Francisco	March 6 1863	.. 102	,,

This year Captain Limeburner went to Callao for a guano cargo, making the run South in 43 days.   The old skipper was noted for the masterly ease with which he handled his big ship, and, in spite of the fact that Callao was crowded with over 20 deep-watermen besides other vessels, he took his ship right into the anchorage under all plain sail with a stiff breeze blowing.   It was not until the very last moment that he clewed up and hauled down his light sails, then, rounding on his heel until the topsails were aback, he stripped the *Great Republic* of her canvas whilst she was losing way, and when the order to let go was given the hands were on the lower yards making a harbour stow of it.

Loading at the Chinchas, the *Great Republic* sailed to Queenstown for orders, where Captain Limeburner again roused the admiration of seamen by sailing his big ship right up to the anchorage.   The guano was discharged in the Thames, and after a 27-day passage across the Western Ocean the *Great Republic* paid off at New York in May, 1864.

It was Captain Limeburner's last voyage ; the grand old seaman retired after handing over the vessel, which he had commanded so well through such difficult times, to Josiah Paul.

The following is the epitome of the *Great Republic's* last outward passage to San Francisco :

Left New York	October	24	1864	
Crossed the Line	November	20	1864	.. 27 days out
Crossed 50° S. Atlantic	December	20	1864	.. 57 ,,
Crossed 50° S. Pacific	December	29	1864	.. 66 ,,
Crossed the Line	January	27	1865	.. 95 ,,
Arrived San Francisco	February	15	1865	.. 114 ,,

Her last passage home in 120 days was nothing remarkable, but it was said that she had a weak and indifferent crew.

She was now laid up in New York until 1866, when she was bought by Captain J. S. Hatfield of Yarmouth, Nova Scotia.   Two years later, in 1868, she was sent across to Liverpool and made the run from St. John in 14 days.   At Liverpool the Merchants' Trading Company bought her for £3500, and disguised her under the name of *Denmark*.

The end came on March 5, 1872, when the old ship was abandoned with 12 feet of water in her hold, not far from Bermuda, being bound from Rio de Janeiro in ballast to St. John, N.B.   Apparently a strong nor'west gale which was encountered on March 2 in 32° N. started a bad leak, which, in spite of double-action pumps, could not be kept under.

Thus, like many another famous wooden ship, the *Great Republic* succumbed to the stormy North Atlantic.

The "N. B. Palmer" Sails up to her 'Frisco Wharf.

The American clipper ships of the fifties were unfortunately a short-lived fleet ; and what with hard driving, light construction, and water soaking, not to speak of Confederate cruisers, few survived long enough to take a part in the California grain trade round the Horn.

There was the lordly *N. B. Palmer*, which was only abandoned, sinking in the North Atlantic, in 1892 ; but she was an aristocratic tea ship, being treated like a yacht by her well-known commander, Charles Porter Low, and was never a grain carrier.   Only her first three passages were made to San Francisco, but on his very first, Captain Low succeeded in astonishing every sailorman in that crowded port by sailing his big clipper right up to and alongside her wharf, a truly magnificent piece of seamanship.

It appears that the pilot anchored the *N. B. Palmer* in the Bay ; the agents were anxious to get the ship with her valuable cargo alongside her discharging wharf, but no tow boats were available.   Whereupon Captain Low hove up his anchor on an ebb tide, set all sail to a light beam wind, backed his mainyard to take the way off his ship at the right moment, and berthed her alongside the wharf as delicately and carefully as if she had been a present-day 50,000-tonner.

A big crowd, most of whom were critical seafarers, cheered this feat of sail seamanship with stentorian lungs ; and it was generally brought up in sailing ship fo'c'sles by elderly seamen in order to show the superiority of the old days of wood and hemp over the new days of iron and wire, now, alas, also defeated by steel and steam.

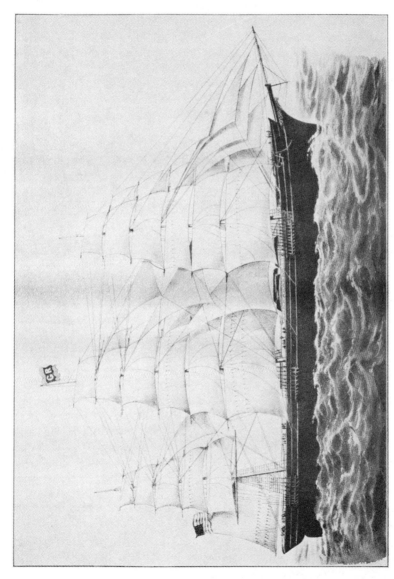

"GREAT REPUBLIC," AS A FULL-RIGGED SHIP.

From the MacPherson Collection.

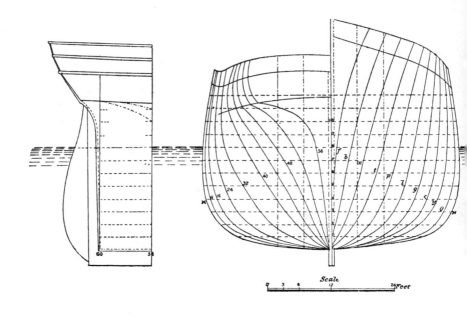

Scale

0   3   6   12   24 Feet

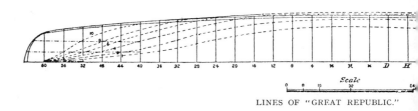

Scale

0   8   16   32   64

LINES OF "GREAT REPUBLIC."

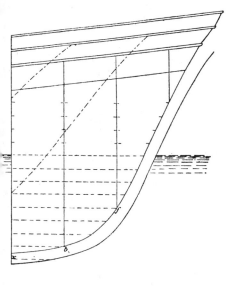

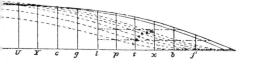

U　Y　c　g　l　p　t　x　b　f

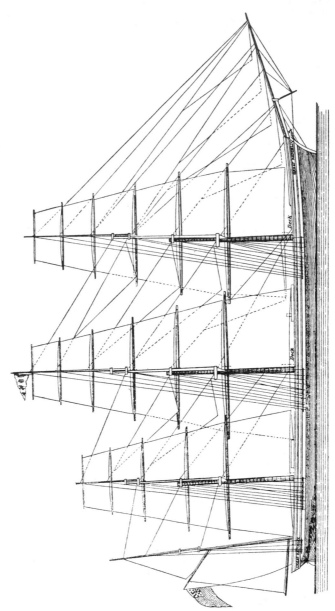

SECOND SAIL PLAN OF "GREAT REPUBLIC."

Other Survivors of the Fifties.

Besides those already mentioned, the following half-dozen clipper-built ships of the fifties survived to a good old age.

Date Built	Name	Tonnage		L'ngth	Beam	Depth	Builder	Remarks
		Old	New					
1851	*Syren*	1064	876	179	36	22	John Taylor Medford, Mass.	As barque *Margarida* of Buenos Ayres in Lloyd's Register, 1920.
1852	*Malay*	868	821	178	33·2	19·1	John Taylor, Chelsea, Mass.	Condemned at Tahiti, October, 1891.
1853	*Dashing Wave*	1180	1054	181·8	39·6	21·3	Fernald & Pettigrew, Portsmouth, N.H.	Stranded in Seymour Narrows, 1920.
1855	*Wild Hunter*	1081	999	178·7	36·2	22·6	Shiverick Bros. E. Dennis, Mass.	Out of Register, 1884.
1855	*War Hawk*	1067	1015	182	35·6	23	Jackman of Newburyport	Burnt at Fort Discovery, April 1883.
1858	*Prima Donna*	—	1529	203·6	42	24	Greenman of Mystic.	Sold to Austrians 1883.

All six were very handsome, well-built vessels, but only two of them, the *Malay* and *Wild Hunter*, were considered out-and-out clippers, the others all being described as medium built.

Though each ship had many records of fine sailing to her credit, that greatest test of speed and endurance, the outward passage round Cape Horn to California, was not amongst them, their best runs on this traverse being :

Syren	.. ..	120 days in	1853
Malay	.. ..	116 ,,	1853
Dashing Wave	..	107 ,,	1858
Wild Hunter	..	112 ,,	1856
War Hawk	..	128 ,,	1855
Prima Donna	..	118 ,,	1858

Syren will be best remembered at Honolulu and New Bedford, for she was employed for many years bringing home the whale oil left at Honolulu by the South Sea whalers.

Malay was one of the last of the Salem East Indiamen, and her figure-head was a very clever representation of a Malay chief.

Dashing Wave and *War Hawk* were famous lumbermen on the Pacific coast, and great rivals. When, at last, the *Dashing Wave* was converted into a barge, it is said that a shot was found embedded in her timbers, which was traced back to the Confederate cruiser *Alabama.*

With reference to the Civil War, the *Prima Donna* mounted a rifled gun on her poop throughout that trouble, just as merchantmen were obliged to do in the last War.

The Cape Horners of the Sixties.

From 1861 to 1865, the period of the American Civil War, there was naturally a severe slump in the building of deep-water merchant ships ; nevertheless the following well-known vessels were sent to sea during the war years :

Name	Tons	Built	Date
Louis Walsh ..	.. 1556 ..	.. Belfast, Maine ..	1861
General McLellan	.. 1583 ..	.. Thomaston ,, ..	1862
Valley Forge ..	.. 1286 ..	.. Pittston ,, ..	1862
Edward O'Brien	.. 1803 ..	.. Thomaston ,, ..	1863
Topgallant ..	.. 1280 ..	.. East Boston, Mass.	1863
Colorado ..	.. 1075 ..	.. ,, ,, ..	1864
Mindoro ..	.. 1021 ..	.. ,, ,, ..	1864

With the exception of *Mindoro,* which has been called the last of the Salem East Indiamen, these were all regular Cape Horners throughout the last period of American square-sail.

In 1865, with the ending of the War, the Down East builders once more took up their tools in earnest and some smart ships were turned out, notably :

Name	Tons	Built	Date
Ivanhoe ..	.. 1610 ..	.. Belfast, Maine	1865
Seminole ..	.. 1438 ..	.. Mystic, Conn.	1865
Bluejacket ..	.. 1395 ..	.. Greenpoint	1865
Corsica ..	.. 1336 ..	.. Thomaston, Maine	1865
Pactolus ..	.. 1204 ..	.. ,,	1865

Then from 1866 to 1868 the following were the best-known amongst the new tonnage :

Name	Tons			Built		Date
William A. Campbell	1538	..	..	Thomaston, Maine		1866
Kate Davenport ..	1248	..	..	Bath, Maine	..	1866
Oneida	1130	..	..	Searsport ..	..	1866
Nonantum	1099	..	..	Newburyport	..	1866
Arcturus	1054	..	..	Kennebunk ..	..	1866
Alice M. Minott ..	1093	..	..	Phippsburg ..	..	1867
Highlander	1352	..	..	Boston ..	..	1868
Two Brothers ..	1382	..	..	Farmingdale ..	..	1868
Prussia	1212	..	..	Bath ..	..	1868
Ringleader	1184	..	..	Boston ..	..	1868
Yosemite	1153	..	..	Portsmouth ..	..	1868
Southern Cross ..	1129	..	..	Boston ..	..	1868
Sovereign of the Seas	1502	..	..	Boston ..	..	1868

Though none of these ships was an out-and-out clipper, many of them had a good turn of speed ; they were all described as medium built, and it is very evident that both builders and brokers were feeling their way after the disastrous effects of the War and were not ready to launch out into big clipper ships until the commercial sky was a good deal clearer.

The fastest of these early post-war ships was undoubtedly the *Seminole*, which had many fine passages to her credit, and, if we are to believe all that was said about her in 'Frisco shipping circles, must have been a real wonder.

This ship, which was built by Maxon & Fish, arrived in San Francisco Bay, March 10, 1866, on her maiden passage, only 96 days out from New York.

Like many another Cape Horner of renown, she spent her old age as a lumberman on the Pacific coast.

The "Sovereigns of the Seas."

The first *Sovereign of the Seas* was the famous Stuart first-rate man-of-war—the ship-money vessel of Charles I., and in the reign of Charles II. a noted fighter against the Dutch under the name of *Royal Sovereign*.

The second *Sovereign of the Seas* was Donald McKay's great

masterpiece—the first clipper ship to run 400 miles in the 24 hours. After her record-breaking maiden voyage this magnificent clipper had but a short and chequered life, in which dismastings, mutinies and strandings all figured. When bound out to China in 1859 she was wrecked on the Pyramid Shoal, Malacca Strait.

We now come to a third *Sovereign of the Seas*, a smaller ship of 1226 tons and Canadian built ; in 1860 this vessel took 80 passengers out to Melbourne from Liverpool in 93 days. On her second voyage she arrived at Sydney on August 31, 1861, with 104 passengers under Captain Cruikshank. Whilst discharging at Campbell's wharf, No. 3 was set on fire by two members of her crew, and in spite of every effort, including scuttling, was soon a charred wreck.

The fourth *Sovereign of the Seas* was well known for many years in the Cape Horn trade under Captain Wood, and at one time the notorious " Glass-eye " Mitchell was her chief officer. She was Donald McKay's first attempt at a grain carrier, and he improved on her design the next year with *Glory of the Seas*. She was built for Lawrence Giles & Co., of New York.

Mr. Hobart Bosworth, an old clipper ship sailor, relates the following interesting experience which occurred whilst he was serving in *Sovereign of the Seas* No. 4 : " I remember once off Staten Land counting fifty-seven ships in sight at one time, all westward bound, from the the fore topgallant crosstress. It was extraordinary because not a sail had we sighted the day before, and not a sail was visible the day after, nor did we meet another vessel until we put into Juan de Fernandez for fresh water."

During the eighties *Sovereign of the Seas* No. 4 was sold to J. D. Bischoff of Bremen, who promptly disguised her under the name of *Elvira*. Then, just before the end of the nineteenth century, she was bought by L. Luckenbach of New York, given back her old name, and converted into a barge.

After being ignominiously dragged about behind a tug for half a dozen years, this fine old ship was lost off Barnegat in 1910.

"N. B. PALMER."

Lent by Thomas W. Ratsey, Esq.

"PRUSSIA."

"GENERAL FAIRCHILD"
in dry dock at Winslow.

Lent by J. P. Graham.

CHAPTER IV.

THE DOWN EASTERS OF THE SEVENTIES.

The " Glory of the Seas."

THROUGHOUT the seventies and the eighties of the nine-teenth century, at a time when every British yard was occupied with iron plates and rivets, the builders along the New England coast clung to their native woods and fought hard to maintain the all-wood square-rigger in the markets of the world. Nor were they vanquished until their rivals of iron and steel were also vanquished by the cheaply-built, cheaply-run steam tramp.

These Down Easters of New England were the result of 100 years or more of shipbuilding experience, and combined all the attributes of the Yankee clippers—speed, seaworthiness, and sail power with larger cargo capacity and greater strength of build. This last attribute is very well shown in the construction of the *Glory of the Seas* :

"She is built of solid oak ; her timbers are 11 inches square and only 4 inches apart ; 6-inch planking outside and 4-inch ceiling inside make an almost solid oak hull 21 inches thick," wrote an American paper, and it goes on to remark : "The *Glory of the Seas* was assuredly well built, so well built that she made a bankrupt of her builder, McKay."

This splendid vessel, the last with the exception of the U.S. sloops-of-war, *Adams* and *Essex*, to be built by the famous Donald McKay, has been called the last of the American clippers, but it would be more correct to describe her as the first of the Down Easters, for she was her designer's conception of a good cargo carrier with a fair turn of speed, specially suited for the Cape Horn trade.

The " Glory " was launched from McKay's famous East Boston yard in November, 1869. Though she was given the McKay bow with its slightly concave under waterlines, her entrance soon swelled out, giving her a look of power, which was considerably aided by 7 feet of sheer. Her dead rise was given as 8½ inches at half floor, and her run was long and clean, terminating in a very neat semi-circular stern, which was far superior in model to the sterns of most of the Down Easters which followed her.

Donald McKay was not the man to rest content with a fiddle-head and scroll, so the *Glory of the Seas* was given a beautifully carved figure-head representing the goddess Athene, in flowing Grecian draperies. This, according to an American newspaper, now adorns the gateway leading to the home of McKay's daughter, near Boston.

The *Glory of the Seas* was a three-decked ship with a height of 8 feet 2 inches between the decks, which were fully planked. Her largest grain cargo, according to the Californian authority, Mr. F. C. Matthews, was 68,149 centals, and in her later years she loaded over a million and a half feet of lumber, her deadweight capacity being in the neighbourhood of 4000 tons.

The timbering of an all-wood ship, such as the " Glory," would have filled the present generation of marine architects with amazement ; the sizes of frames, beams and knees being terrific and occupying a great deal of space, which in an iron or steel ship could be filled with cargo. The " Glory's " deck-beams, lower and main, were 16 inches square, and the upper 16 by 12. She had the usual American ship's half-poop, which was 60 feet long, the cabin-top or monkey-poop being 45 feet long. Her fo'c'sle-head measured 35 feet, and the midshiphouse 54 feet.

The first of the Down Easters was not a three skysail-yarder like so many of her followers, but she crossed the skysail at the main over a single topgallant yard ; she was splendidly sparred with hard pine throughout, her mainyard being 96 feet long.

Mr. Richard C. McKay reckons that her sail area ran to 8000 yards of cotton canvas. She was christened by Donald McKay's daughter, Frances, and sailed from New York with some 4000 tons of cargo on February 14, 1870.

Averaging 161 miles a day to the Equator, she had an uneventful passage of 120 days to San Francisco.

The following is a complete list of her Cape Horn passages :

Date	Captain			Days
1870	Giet	..	New York to San Francisco	.. 120
1870	Chatfield	..	San Francisco to Liverpool	.. 112
1871-2	Josiah N. Knowles		Cardiff to San Francisco	.. 120
1871-2	,,	..	San Francisco to Liverpool	.. 112
1872-3	,,	..	Liverpool to San Francisco	.. 120
1872-3	,,	..	San Francisco to Liverpool	.. 128
1873-4	,,	..	New York to San Francisco	.. 96
1873-4	,,	..	San Francisco to Liverpool	.. 118
1874-5	,,	..	Liverpool to San Francisco	.. 131
1875-6	,,	..	San Francisco to Liverpool	.. 133
1876	,,	..	Liverpool to San Francisco	.. 114
1876	,,	..	San Francisco to Liverpool	.. 103
1877	McLaughlin	..	Liverpool to San Francisco	.. 144
1877	,,	..	San Francisco to Liverpool	.. 107
1878-9	,,	..	Liverpool to San Francisco	.. 153
1879	,,	..	San Francisco to Cork	.. 111
1880	,,	..	New York to San Francisco	.. 118
1880	,,	..	San Francisco to Cork ..	.. 120
1881-2	,,	..	Cardiff to San Francisco	.. 129
1881-2	,,	..	'Frisco to Havre *via* Valparaiso	220
1882	,,	..	New York to San Francisco	.. 128
	(Laid up at the back of Goat Island from December 1882 to February 1885)			
1885	Joshua S. Freeman		San Francisco to Liverpool	.. 117
	,,	..	Liverpool to San Pedro	.. 121

Like others of Donald McKay's ships, the *Glory of the Seas* was built on spec, and at the end of her first voyage her builders sold her to J. Henry Sears of Boston.

On her first grain passage she left San Francisco in July and reached Cork a day ahead of the clipper *Black Hawk*, and two days ahead of the *Charger*.

On her second passage from 'Frisco she left in February, 1872, her chief rivals being the *Young America*, and the smart little Britisher, *La Escocesa*. *Young America* was too fast for the medium-built ship, and arrived in the Mersey in eight days better time, but *Glory of the Seas* defeated the Britisher by ten days.

In 1873 the race home was as follows :

Glory of the Seas	left 'Frisco Jan.	15	Arrived Liverpool		128 days out
John Duthie	,,	,, 18	,,		122 ,,
Montgomery Castle	,,	,, 21	,,	,,	122 ,,

We now come to the best passage of her career, her outward passage from New York to 'Frisco in 1873-4. Here is the epitome :

Sandy Hook to Line	27 days
Line to 50° S.	22 ,,
Horn passage 50° to 50°	.. 11 ,,
50° S. Pacific to Line ..	.. 19 ,,
Line to Pigeon Point ..	.. 16 ,,
	95 days

The best 24-hour run was 300 miles in a strong south-easter off California coast, and her average 169.

Her last day at sea is logged as follows :

January 16, 1874—First part strong breezes from south-east, thick and rainy. At 6 p.m., all sails which had not been blown away were taken in, except lower topsails, and ship was hove-to, judging ourselves near land. At daylight, made land off Pigeon Point, having drifted to southard during night. At noon, was up to the bar. Found pilots all inside and bar breaking. Stood off and on all night ; in morning, stood in, went over the bar, took pilot, and came to anchor.

From anchor to anchor the passage was 96 days.

During February and March, 1874, four grain ships left San Francisco for Liverpool, their times being :

Ericsson	sailed February	20	Arrived June	3	103 days
Glory of the Seas	,,	,, 26	,,	,, 24	118 ,,
Wasdale	,,	,, 27	,,	,, 24	117 ,,
Young America	,,	March 12	,,	,, 23	103 ,,

The heroine of this race, *Young America,* was off Cape Clear on the 98th day out, then had a dead beat up the Irish Channel. She overhauled both *Glory of the Seas* and *Wasdale* on this stretch, her report showing that she passed 20 ships one day and 19 the next, all close-hauled on the starboard tack, the only vessel to hold her being a large skysail-yarder. The name is not given, but apparently the two vessels sailed side by side for 36 hours, with wind slowly increasing and sail being furled until they had to hand the topgallant sails, after which the stranger tacked.

"GLORY OF THE SEAS."

"GLORY OF THE SEAS."

"GLORY OF THE SEAS."
As Alaska cannery ship.

"S. D. CARLETON."

On her next outward passage *Glory of the Seas* left Liverpool on August 13, 1874, in company with Newton's Dale liner, *Langdale*, Captain Jenkinson, which was considered one of the smartest ships in the Cape Horn trade. It was a trying passage for Captain Knowles as his coal cargo got heated and he had to keep the hatches off whenever possible. The coal steamed and was too hot to handle, the ship evidently having a very narrow escape.

In the Straits of Le Maire and off the Horn the two ships were in company on four occasions. Both made long passages, *Glory of the Seas* arriving a day ahead on December 22, 131 days out.

The disgusted Jenkinson objected to Knowles' published account, whereupon the latter responded with the following :

If it will satisfy the captain of the *Langdale* I will say that whenever I raised his ship she was astern of the "Glory," but came up and passed her. When I got to 'Frisco there was no *Langdale*, but as the passages of the ships were 131 and 132 days respectively, I think that is sufficiently long to prevent any discussion as to the great speed of either.

Such a reply clinched the argument and Jenkinson must have retired discomfited. But Captain Knowles produced a further " sock dolager " for the proud Jenkinson, by breaking the record across the Pacific. I give the "Glory's " log in the Appendix; though very crank from want of ballast, she ran from San Francisco to Sydney in 35 days and returned, coal laden, in 53 days.

In 1876-7 the *Glory of the Seas* made her best passage on the 'Frisco-Liverpool run—103 days. Her time, however, was beaten by two vessels which also left 'Frisco in October 1876—the unconquerable *Young America* was only 99 days to New York, and the British composite clipper *Hawkesbury* was just 100 days to Havre.

In 1879 the old ship was beaten on the run home by one of the "Saints," *St. Stephen*, which reached Liverpool on July 28, the same day that the *Glory of the Seas* made Queenstown, the former being 101 days out and the latter 111.

On her next passage the *Glory of the Seas* got aground in October, 1881, as she was making Dublin, and was so badly strained that she had to be docked and repaired. Probably the effect of this stranding was still felt on the following voyage, for in 1881, after leaving San Francisco on July 11, she put into Valparaiso on September 3, with topsides leaking and pumps choked. Five thousand sacks were found to be damaged by water, and were landed and sold ; the ship was repaired, continued her passage and reached Havre on February 16, 1882, 77 days out from Valparaiso.

In 1885 the old ship was bought by Barneson, Hibberd & Co. for the Pacific coast coal trade, her round being from Puget Sound to San Francisco or San Pedro, with an occasional run up to Alaska.

On June 3, 1886, she arrived at San Francisco from Tacoma with 4000 tons on board, but her usual cargo was round about 3300 tons.

Before the San Pedro jetty was finished the old "Glory " had a nasty experience there. Running in before a severe gale, she went clean over the top of the half-built jetty and managed to bring up in the shallow water inside ; then she had a considerable difficulty in getting to sea again owing to lack of water.

In 1909, whilst lying at Ketchikan, Alaska, she was run into by the steamer *Nord-Western*. The "Glory " was a tough old vessel and the steamer had to go into Heffernan dry-dock for repairs to her bow. When the Down Easter was dry-docked in July, 1910, she was found to be as sound and strong as ever. It was at this time that she was bought by Captain McDonnell, an old South Sea Island trader, who planned to take her to the Island of Malekula, New Hebrides, where he intended to get timber concessions. As the natives of that island were reported to be cannibals of the worst description, who, the previous year, had eaten the crew of the French schooner, *Qualite*, and before that a couple of missionaries, Captain McDonnell proposed taking 250 men, well armed, aboard the *Glory of the Seas*, in order to prevent interference with his lumbering operations.

I am afraid that the old " Glory " had no exciting South Sea adventures, for the following year she was sold at public auction in Victoria, B.C., to F. C. Johnstone, President of the Tongass Trading Co. of Ketchikan, to be employed as an Alaska cannery ship.

The old ship's active service came to an end in 1913, when she was stripped to her lower masts, fitted with cold storage plant, and taken to Idaho Inlet from Puget Sound.

In the illustration a curious box-shaped erection will be noticed round her mizen top. This was her wheel-house ! Here the wheel was connected by an endless chain to the steering gear ; the reason for such an extraordinary arrangement was to enable the helmsman to see the tug ahead over the unsightly machinery houses, which had been erected on the Down Easter's spacious maindeck.

Her owners were now the Glacier Fish Company of Tacoma, and every season she was towed to Alaska, loaded with about 10 million lbs. of salmon, and then towed back to Puget Sound.

In 1922 ship lovers in America were roused by the news that her owners had taken the machinery out of the famous vessel and proposed to burn her for the copper fastenings. At once frantic efforts were made from Boston to raise sufficient money to save the *Glory of the Seas* from such a fate. It was proposed to tow her round to the East Coast at a cost of 43,000 dollars, with a lumber cargo which would about pay the towage bill. However, the money was not forthcoming, and in December, 1922, Messrs. Nieder & Marcus put the old ship on a pebble beach called Laurel or Endolyme beach, near Three Tree Point, about five miles from Seattle. Here she was burnt on May 13, 1923.

The following pathetic account of her end, by the artist, W. Francis, appeared in the *Pacific Marine Review* :

That the old ship was to be burned that day was not made public, so that only a few residents, mostly children, saw the end of what was, to them, merely a lot of wood bolted together and called a boat. Had the event been given publicity, probably thousands would have driven there to see the smoke, and to most of them it would have been entertainment. I felt rather badly, but at the same time, superior to the other few spectators in that I knew what it all meant.

The bow of the "Glory" was almost under the trees that grow on the high banks, and when I arrived there the hull had been burning a few hours. However, nothing was left of her but a fire-punctured shell, a section of which would occasionally fall into the water with a dull explosion. The badly charred fore and main masts had fallen alongside, while the mizen was hanging over the port quarter, the whole mixed up with bolts, wire and remnants of another burned hull.

The only spectacular bit I saw was when, from the weight of the bowsprit, the entire bow from catheads to the bobstays fell outboard in one huge chunk. I felt indeed glad that the old goddess figure-head was saved the humiliation of being smashed to splinters by gravel and shallow water in a ship's bone-yard. The former figure-head was an old friend and I had sketched her more than once.

The day was gloomy and threatening, the water calm and silent, and the scene rather melancholy, so that riding home I felt as though returning from the funeral of an old friend.

The " Great Admiral."

Next to the *Glory of the Seas*, the most noteworthy vessel built Down East in 1869 was the *Great Admiral*, which was launched from Jackson's yard for W. F. Weld & Co.

The black horse on the white flag of the famous Weld family has flown over a number of fine ships since William Fletcher Weld, the founder of the firm, built the *Senator* at Charlestown in 1833. But none of them, not even the clipper *Golden Fleece* or the packet *Enoch Train*, was the superior of the *Great Admiral*, whether in looks, speed, seaworthiness, or money-earning capabilities.

The greater number of the Down Easters were content with a fiddle-head and scroll, but the *Great Admiral*, like the *Glory of the Seas*, had a figure-head which was a work of art. She was called after Admiral Farragut, who presented her with a silver speaking trumpet. She came out as a main skysail-yarder; the illustration shows her as a humble timber-droghuer, after her skysail yard had been sent down.

Her original sail area was just under 8000 yards of canvas, her mast and spar measurements being :

MASTS.

Fore lowermast (from heel)	..	88 feet
„ topmast	..	47 „
„ topgallant	..	26 „
„ royal	..	16 „
„ pole	..	7 „
Main lowermast (from heel)	..	90 „
„ topmast	..	48 „
„ topgallant	..	26 „
„ royal	..	17 „
„ skysail	..	18 „

YARDS.

		Main	Fore	Mizen
Lower yard ..	..	80 ft.	85 ft.	62 ft.
„ topsail yard	..	70	75	53
Upper „ „	..	62	67	47
Topgallant yard ..	..	50	55	36
Royal yard ..	..	40	45	28
Skysail yard ..	..	—	38	—

"GREAT ADMIRAL."

"SAVONA" AND "GREAT ADMIRAL."

"LORETTO FISH."

Lent by J. Randall.

"JAIRUS B. LINCOLN."

Lent by J. Randall.

In her construction everything was of the very best with picked wood, copper and galvanised iron throughout, no iron bolts or spikes being used.

During the time that the *Great Admiral* flew the Black Horse house-flag, that is until 1897, she was commanded in turn by four very well-known American shipmasters. These were Captains Isaac N. Jackson, William Chatfield, Benjamin Thompson, and James F. Rowell.

Captain Jackson, who took the *Great Admiral* from the stocks, was often spoken of as " the dandy captain," and it was commonly said that he took enough white linen shirts to sea with him to have a change for each day. He was one of those dignified grandees who have long been extinct at sea.

His first command was the barque *Marmion,* which he took over new in 1847. This vessel he commanded for Chapman & Flint until 1855, when he took the ship *Spitfire* for a couple of years. Then he went master of Weld's *Belvedere,* at that time considered the smartest of the Black Horse fleet.

While homeward bound from Manila in 1863 the *Belvedere* had a narrow escape from being captured by the Confederate cruiser, *Alabama,* which was lurking in the Straits of Sunda on the lookout for homeward bound Down Easters. Luckily for Captain Jackson, he slipped through the Straits on a very dark night without being seen by the *Alabama.*

Captain Jackson commanded the *Great Admiral* until 1873, when he left her to take over the *Spartan.*

Captain Benjamin Thompson, who commanded the *Great Admiral* from 1873 to 1886, was another very superior American shipmaster. During the North and South War his ship, the *Sportsman,* was used as a store ship by Admiral Farragut's squadron, and so it was quite fitting that he should take command of the ship which was named for the famous Admiral. Indeed, he preferred remaining in command of sailing ships to joining the U.S. Navy when Admiral Farragut offered to recommend him for the Service.

Before commanding the *Great Admiral* Captain Thompson was master of Weld's *Peruvian* until 1872, and then made a voyage in command of their big three-decker, *Enoch Train.* The *Enoch Train* was noted as a hoodoo ship, and even such a capable shipmaster as Captain Thompson found it impossible to keep her out of trouble. His outward passage was from New York to Hongkong. Whilst in the China Sea the ship encountered two typhoons, the first of which threw her on her beam ends, carried away her masts, and shifted her cargo, whilst the second all but capsized her. Eventually she was towed into Hongkong by a steamer. On her return to New York she was sold to Glasgow owners, and Captain Thompson then took over the *Great Admiral*.

The following are the best passages made by the *Great Admiral* under W. F. Weld & Co.'s ownership:

New York to San Francisco	111	days
San Francisco to Queenstown	111	,,
San Francisco to Liverpool	113	,,
Philadelphia to Tacoma	111	,,
San Francisco to Hongkong	37	,,
San Francisco to Manila	43	,,
Hongkong to San Francisco	38	,,
Hongkong to San Francisco	39	,,
Newcastle, N.S.W., to Hongkong	37	,,
Manila to New York	89	,,
Hongkong to New York	95	,,
New York to Sydney	90	,,
New York to Melbourne	73	,,
Sydney to London	92	,,
London to New York	24	,,

On her last voyage under the Black Horse house-flag the *Great Admiral* made the following passages:

New York to Melbourne	91	days
Hobart to Gibraltar	90	,,
Gibraltar to Marseilles	8	,,
Marseilles to New York	48	,,

In 1897 Captain E. Sterling of Seattle bought her for 12,500 dollars, and put her into the Pacific lumber trade.

Her end came ten years later, and it is so vividly described by C. Forbes in that wonderful little magazine, *Sea Breezes*, that I have taken the liberty of transcribing it word for word. Mr. Forbes writes as follows:

We left Vancouver December 22, 1907, after loading a cargo of timber at Hastings

Saw Mills, for Adelaide. Having a big deck cargo, we had special rails built to make the braces fast and no sooner had we got clear of Cape Flattery when the old *Barcore* struck one of the worst gales ever experienced off the Sound, one in which several ships came to grief. Losing one side of her deck cargo, the *Barcore* was soon on her beam ends, and to make matters worse, the new rail carried away, leaving the braces washing about the deck. As luck would have it we managed to get the ship under bare poles, and the yards, etc., secured before dark, but I will never forget the night we all put in huddled together on the poop hoping nothing else would carry away, for it was a pitch dark night, snowing, and blowing a living gale, while our lee rail was under water, and timber washing around the decks.

How glad we were when daylight came ! But what a sight ! Ropes and timber washing all over the place, and parts of our torn sails flying about aloft. But we soon forgot our plight when we sighted on our starboard bow what at first looked like a small island. It turned out to be all that remained of the ship *Great Admiral* of Seattle, U.S.A., surrounded by her cargo of timber. Every now and again we could hear her crew's cries for help, and as the huge sea raised them up we could see them waving to us: they had been in the water for 36 hours. The Captain (Sterling) and officers were hanging on to the saloon skylight, and several hundred yards away from them were the forward crowd hanging on to the top of the deck-house. The ship's cargo of timber acted as a breakwater, and so saved them from being washed off. The chief officer's wife was dressed up in a man's suit of clothes, and was nearly dead.

It seemed a long time before we could get the boat out, for it stuck to the skids, and we carried the falls away and had to reeve off new ones. Still, our chief officer was a fine old sailor, and he soon had the lifeboat clear of the ship and kept her head on to the sea, leaving the drift to back them down on to the wreckage.

Before long the boat returned with all the survivors, not one of whom had the strength to climb on board, so every time the lifeboat rose we grabbed whomsoever we could and pulled them in over the rail. The mate's wife looked the most pitiful of all, for she lay unconscious in the water in the bottom of the boat; but I am glad to say after a few days they all revived.

When the weather moderated we got rid of most of our deck cargo, but still had a list. Then we unbent our tattered sails, set others, and made for 'Frisco to land our distressed seamen. But when nearing 'Frisco we encountered the usual fogs, so altered course for Honolulu. At last we sighted the three-masted American barque *Andrew Welsh*, bound from Honolulu to 'Frisco, and, strange to say, Captain Sterling and the captain of her were old friends. After signalling that we had Captain Sterling and his crew aboard, the *Andrew Welsh* hove-to, and once again our lifeboat was lowered, and off went the crew of the *Great Admiral* to the barque, but not before they gave us three hearty cheers, which made us feel quite queer. For the rest of the voyage we were all on short rations on account of the extra food used, for we had them aboard of us for three weeks.

It appears that the *Great Admiral* after leaving Port Townsend bound for San Pedro, California, in December, had struck what was

almost a hurricane when four days were out.   Besides going over
on her beam ends the old ship had strained so that she was soon
full of water and only her cargo kept her up.   Captain Sterling
cut away the main and mizen masts, but these had hardly gone by
the board before the jibboom carried away, and with the head
stays gone the foremast speedily went over the side.   Soon after
this all hands were obliged to take refuge on the cabin top or
monkey poop.   This, along with the deck cargo, was soon washed
clear of the ship.   When finally the ship *Barcore* hove in sight all
hands, including the captain's wife, had been clinging to their frail
raft for two days and nights, during which terrible time the cook
and cabin boy had died from exposure.

The " Loretto Fish " and " Jairus B. Lincoln."

Of the ships built in 1869 the *Loretto Fish*, of 1840 tons,
from the yard of Sam Watts, deserves a mention.   Though she had
no great claim to speed or good looks, she must have been a fine
vessel or the Germans would not have bought her in her old age.

A good story relates to her last voyage under the American
flag.   Her arrival at Queenstown was reported as follows :

United States ship, *Loretto, with fish*, from San Francisco for Dublin, put in with
loss of her fore topmast.

The Germans renamed her *Theodore Fischer*, and she survived
in the barrel oil trade from U.S.A. to Europe for many years before
being overcome by the terrible North Atlantic winter.

The *Jairus B. Lincoln*, of 1769 tons, built in the same year by
Briggs & Cushing, was also German owned in the nineties and
disguised under the name of *Hermann* of Bremen.

Chapman & Flint's " Saints."

The families of Flint and Chapman began building deep-
watermen at Thomaston and Bath away back at the beginning of
the fifties.   The earliest of their ships of which I have any record
was the *Oracle*, of 1196 tons, built at Thomaston in 1853.

The first of their ships which was named for a Saint was the
St. Mark, of 1870 tons, built at Thomaston in 1860.   This ship

left San Francisco on October, 3, 1873, with grain for Liverpool, and on March 26, 1874, 174 days later, put into Cadiz with 14 feet of water in her hold and the pumps choked. She was repaired, and on her next voyage was 18 months at the Chinchas waiting her turn to load guano. Finally she sailed from Huanillos, but was lost on the West Coast of South America in July, 1876.

The rest of the " Saints " were all built at Bath. With the exception of the barque, *St. James*, they were all three-decked ships, though they did not always have the decks laid, but the beams were there. They were typical three skysail-yarders, well built, as was proved by the way they kept going in the hard Cape Horn trade, and most beautifully kept up.

After running in partnership for some years, with their offices in New York, Benjamin Flint and J. F. Chapman parted company, divided their fleet, and Chapman set up an office in South Street, and Flint in Broad Street.

A. G. Ropes joined Chapman in 1880, and when the latter died in 1894 became the sole proprietor of a fine fleet of 11 ships. It so happened that Flint & Co. also had 11 ships at this date.

"St. Nicholas " and "St. John."

The second of the " Saints," the *St. Lucie*, of 1318 tons, was built by Chapman & Flint at Bath in 1868, and eventually came under Chapman's flag. Then came the big 1869-70 ships, *St. Nicholas* and *St. John*. These tough old Bath square-riggers were no less than 30 years in the Cape Horn trade—*St. Nicholas* under Captains Thomas C. Williams, William Tobey, Joy, and C. F. Carver, with Ben Flint's flag aloft ; and the *St. John* under Captains J. F. Chapman and O. H. Falls, with Chapman's colours at the truck.

Neither ship claimed to be anything more than a steady-going full-bodied carrier, yet their captains, by dint of driving, maintained a very steady record. Of the two, I think the *St. Nicholas* had the best sailing reputation. For 15 outward passages to San Francisco she had an average of 138 days, her best westward passages being 125 and 126 days from New York, and 129 from Liverpool. When grain-loaded her best run was 110 days to Liverpool in 1881, other good passages to that port being 117, 119 and 119 days.   This is good work, but not that of a clipper.

St. John's best sailing performance is said to have been a trans-Pacific run from 'Frisco to Sydney and back, fully loaded each way, in 122 days.   This was made under Captain Chapman.

In 1882 Captain Joy of the *St. Nicholas* received a silver coffee and tea service from the British Government for rescuing the crew of the Glasgow barque *Lennox*, Dundee to 'Frisco, with coal cargo on fire.   Captain Joy had stood by the burning ship for 18 hours when at 2 a.m. on October 18 her main hatch was blown sky high and flames went licking up to her mainyard.   After taking off the crew, Captain Joy transferred 10 of them to the British four-mast barque, *Dominion*, which luckily came up at the critical moment, but he had the captain and the rest of the *Lennox's* company aboard all the way to San Francisco, where he landed them two months later.

" St. Nicholas " Caught Aback in a Gulf Stream Squall.

Here is another adventure of the *St. Nicholas,* which happened when Fred Perry was mate of her.

Forty-eight hours out from New York for San Francisco, she ran into the usual Gulf Stream weather.   Whilst Perry had the deck during the first watch the weather looked very threatening, and after one or two sudden bursts of wind out of a lurid sky an electric, but windless, black cloud rushed upon the ship from the west, and anyone who has experienced Gulf Stream squalls will recognise the weather from Perry's able description :

> The thunder rolled and the lightning flashed with such force as to charge the air so strongly with electricity that it ran in streaks along the iron jackstays on the yards and formed balls of fire on the iron bands of the yardarms.   At times it exploded with terrific force and sent dazzling streaks of blinding light out across the sky, intensifying the darkness about us, and so destroying our vision that it seemed as though we were heading straight into a perfect reproduction of Dante's description of the " Inferno."

With the weather looking more and more threatening, Perry furled his royals and hauled down his light staysails before handing over the ship to the second mate at 8 bells.   And he had hardly turned in before he heard the captain's voice on deck, asking : " Who took the royals in ? " and the second mate's answer : " The mate just before he went below ; said he thought the squalls were coming heavier, sir." Then from the "old man" : "Have them reset at once, mister ; I'm afraid the mate's rather timid about carrying sail at night."

Perry had not been asleep long before he was awakened by being hurled out of his bunk as the ship was caught flat aback. All hands tumbled up without a call, and Perry groped his way to the quarterdeck just in time to see his frenzied skipper, axe in hand, cutting the halliards of royals, topgallant sails and topsails from the mizen rigging to the fore fife-rail. Headsheets and staysail sheets were let fly, and courses were clewed up, but the ship went on gradually heeling over and over on to her beam ends, the backed sails keeping the yards from coming down so that the captain's axe-work on the halliards was without effect.

Perry dashed aft and gave the helmsmen a hand, but in vain they hove the wheel hard up and then hard down, it had no effect on the ship's head ; and with the wind booming in her topsails, the blocks of her fore-and-afters thrashing and banging in fury, and cut rope-ends streaming to leeward, the old *St. Nicholas* threatened to turn turtle. Then just as the "old man" was about to sing out for axes to the deadeye lanyards, the wind suddenly died, the ship trembled all over, and crash ! bang ! down the masts came the yards with squealing parrels, as she came upright. The next moment all hands were nearly drowned in torrents of rain.

It was a close call ; Perry does not say whether that skipper set his royals again ; probably he caught his mate's timidity in carrying sail at night, at any rate as long as he was in the Gulf Stream.

In December, 1896, the *St. Nicholas* was sold by Benjamin Flint to George W. Hume & Co., after which she became one of the best known ships in the Alaska cannery trade under the management of the Columbia River Packers Association. Her active career ended in 1923, and on February 23, 1926, she was sold for 2500 dollars to B. F. Lee of Portland, and was broken up for her metal fastenings.

The *St. John* disappeared from Chapman's fleet and the Register about 1900.

The " Samuel Watts."

This big 2000-tonner was the product of the Geneva award, being old Sam Watts' share of the millions paid by Great Britain for the damage done to American vessels by the *Alabama* and other Confederate cruisers. She was a typical full-built Thomaston ship, as splendid a specimen of Down East oak, pitch-pine and hackmatack as was ever launched into the Georges river, but without any pretensions to speed.

Her last captain under the Watts management was Captain Bill Lermond. In November, 1881, he left Liverpool, ballasted with salt for New York, having heard that he was to take over Watts' new ship, the *Joseph B. Thomas*, on arrival. But the westerlies played up hard, and, when half-way across, the old ship brought her spars down about the ears of her crew. Lermond, a superb seaman, soon had jury masts on end, and eventually crawled into New York, but he missed the new ship, for as the *Sam Watts* passed in through the Narrows the *Joseph B. Thomas* towed out on her way to 'Frisco. For his skill in saving the old ship, Captain Lermond was presented with the usual spy-glass by the underwriters, after which he left for the Pacific coast in order to take over the *Joseph B. Thomas*.

The *Samuel Watts* was sold to the Germans as soon as she had run off her class, and was renamed *J. Weissenhorn*. For a number of years after this she was employed carrying barrel oil across the Atlantic to European ports. Later, the Norwegians bought her and renamed her *Souverain*. In 1902 she discharged her last oil cargo at Portishead, and with the Brazilian flag at her peak loaded coal at Barry for Rio, where she was condemned in September, 1902, and converted into a coal hulk.

Ed. O'Brien's Early Ships.

One of the first of Ed. O'Brien's ships was the *Eagle*, of 1715 tons, in which Captain Lermond first went to sea as a boy. This ship was launched in 1859, but did not remain long under American Registry, being bought by C. & E. S. Hill of Bristol fairly early in her career. Her staunch old hull may still be seen doing duty as a coal hulk at Gibraltar.

Others of O'Brien's early ships were the first *Edward O'Brien*, launched in 1863; the *William A. Campbell*, launched in 1866; the *John Bryce*, launched in 1869; and the *A. McCallum*, launched in 1870. All these were big ships for their day and good carriers, being solidly built without any frills. In their sail plans, too, they set no flying kites, being content with royals over single topgallant sails.

The *Little Edward*—as the 1863 ship was called to distinguish her from the later *Edward O'Brien*, which was always known as the *Big Edward*—finished her career, along with the *William A. Campbell*, lumber droghuing on the Pacific Coast.

The *John Bryce* was burnt in the South Pacific, when bound out to Japan, loaded with case oil.

The Escape of the "A. McCallum."

Fire was always the greatest enemy of the all-wood ship and a nightmare which ever worried the nerves of the old-time officer.

The *McCallum*, when she had run off her class as a deep-water ship, also reverted to coal and lumber droghuing on the Pacific coast. One brilliant Sunday morning, having just returned from a coasting trip, she was berthed at Mission Wharf with her long jibboom sticking out over the piles of lumber, which had lately been stacked, when these piles caught fire. The *Alexander McCallum* only had a scratch crew aboard, but they set to with a will, cast off her mooring lines, let go the gaskets of one of the topsails, and mastheaded the yard, then with the sail sheeted home and pressed hard against the mast, managed to back the ship out into the bay clear of the smoke and flames. On the other side of the wharf, the *Oregon*, another old-timer reduced to timber droghuing, was backed out and saved in the same way.

The runners, who, by their strenuous efforts, managed to save these two ships, were rewarded with five dollars apiece, but this did not pay one of them, who had spoilt a new suit of clothes which he had just bought with his coasting trip pay-day.

" Carondelet's " Record.

The *Carondelet*, a smart little 1500-tonner, which was built at Newcastle, Maine, in 1872, when owned by Cyrus Walker of Port Townsend, made her number amongst the trans-Pacific record breakers.

She left Yokohama at midnight on October 8, 1881, under Captain W. F. Stetson, was off the Golden Gate 21 days out, and anchored in San Francisco Bay on October 30, 21 days 18 hours from anchorage to anchorage.   She was in ballast on this passage, and in the unusual trim of 30 inches by the head.

In August, 1885, this passage was rivalled by the 400-ton barquentine, *Quickstep*, of San Francisco, Captain Jackson, which sailed from Yokohama to Port Townsend, anchorage to anchorage, in 21 days.   She was also in ballast, and her time to Cape Flattery was 19 days.

About the fastest passage across the Pacific that I know of was that of the British tea clipper, *Kaisow*, under Captain Davies, in her old age, after she had been cut down and her spars reduced. She sailed from Bangkok to Cape Beale light, Vancouver Island, in 19 days.

The old *Carondelet* was degraded to a Seattle towing barge about five years before the War, after a long and faithful service on the Pacific coast.

Converted Steamers, " Three Brothers " Ex " Vanderbilt."

The American Merchant Marine possessed three famous sailing ships which had once been steamers ; these were the *Three Brothers*, *Ericsson*, and *May Flint*, and of these the *Three Brothers* had the most remarkable record.

In 1856-7 Jeremiah Simonson built the wooden, brig-rigged, paddle-wheel steamer, *Vanderbilt*, at Greenpoint, Long Island, at a cost of a million dollars, and to the order of that great financier, Commodore Vanderbilt.   This vessel, which was always known as " Vanderbilt's yacht," had a tonnage of 3361 tons.   She had a straight stem, two funnels 40 feet high by 8 ft. 8 ins. diameter, two vertical beam engines with cylinders of 90-inch diameter and

12 ft. stroke, and four tubular boilers, all constructed at the Allaire works.

Her length on deck was 331 ft., breadth 37 ft. 6 ins., and depth of hold 24 ft. 6 ins., draft loaded being 19 ft. 6 ins. Her frames were 21 ins., sided 15 ins., spaced 32 ins. from centre to centre, and braced double iron straps 6 ins. by $\frac{5}{8}$ in. She had 4 watertight compartments.

With the *Adriatic* and *Illinois* she ran in the trans-Atlantic trade between New York, Havre, Southampton and Bremen, forming Commodore Vanderbilt's North Atlantic Mail Steamship Line.

In the fifties she was considered the fastest steamship afloat. On her third voyage she broke the record with a run of 9 days 8 hours from New York to the Needles, her best day's work being 350, 370 and 333, distances, by the way, which she easily beat when under sail alone after her conversion.

On the western run in June, 1858, she went from Southampton to New York in 9 days 13 hours, and in 1859 from the Needles to New York in 9 days 9 hours 26 minutes. It was under Captain Edward Higgins that she ran from New York to Southampton in 9 days 5 hours, and beat the then record holder, *Persia*, by half an hour.

Vanderbilt withdrew his ships from the Atlantic service in 1860, owing to lack of support by the American Government, which in 1861 chartered the *Vanderbilt* for a period of three months at 2000 dollars a day. Then in March, 1862, Vanderbilt made a present of his crack steamer to the U.S. Navy, and when taken over her deck-houses were removed, her guards lowered, a battery of 14 guns mounted on the maindeck, and two long Parrott guns on the upper deck.

It appears that when the *Merrimac* was being built out of the remains of the burnt-out frigate *Virginia* at Norfolk Navy Yard, a proposal was made to the Secretary of the Navy to send three warships south to make a combined rush on the *Merrimac* and turn her over, and one of the vessels specially strengthened for this duty, which was afterwards accomplished by the *Monitor*, was the *Vanderbilt*. She was actually sent to Hampton Roads to look out for the *Merrimac*.

In August, 1863, we find her in chase of the *Alabama* under Commander C. H. Baldwin. She just missed the *Alabama* at the Cape, and it is to be feared that she was sent off on a wild goose chase in order to allow the *Alabama* to slip into Table Bay, and when she returned the elusive commerce-destroyer had come and gone. About the only adventure on this cruise of the *Vanderbilt's* seems to have been the salvage of the dismasted and rudderless Dutch barque, *Johanna Elizabeth*, which she towed into Simon's Bay.

On June 22, 1866, the *Vanderbilt* arrived in San Francisco Bay from Hampton Roads, flying the broad pennant of Commodore Rodgers, having convoyed the monitor *Monadnock* round the Horn. She was then commanded by J. P. Sanford, and had a complement of 386 officers and men.

In February, 1873, after lying idle at Mare Island for six years, the famous steamer was put up to auction by the Government, which had previously appraised her at 84,000 dollars. The largest bid was 56,000 dollars, and this was refused ; however, after sharp words from Washington, she was put up again on March 27 and knocked down to George Howes & Co., for 42,000 dollars.

The Howes brothers, George, Henry, and Jabez, immediately set about converting her to a sailing ship, first of all renaming her the *Three Brothers* after themselves. The engines were lifted out of her and sold for 20,000 dollars, and a lot of spare parts, stores, etc., went for another 12,000 dollars, so that the brothers could well afford to spend money on her conversion, which cost altogether 175,000 dollars.

The work was done by Coombs & Taylor at Hunter's Point, San Francisco, under the supervision of the notorious Bully Waterman, and also her captain-to-be, George Cummings, who was called away from the *Young America* in Liverpool.

A very full account of her conversion appeared in the local newspapers. The work was begun on April 13, and the ship was loaded and ready for sea by October 23. First of all her upper works were raised 14 ins. and more sheer given to her, but the flush deck was retained. From plank sheer to bends she was 2½ ft. thick, and below that 3 ft. all solid wood.

"THREE BROTHERS."

From the MacPherson Collection.

"THREE BROTHERS" AT GIBRALTAR.

"MAY FLINT."

Her tonnage and measurements after conversion were as follows :

Tonnage (American Register)		Tonnage (Lloyd's Register)	
Below deck .. 1922·91		Net 2936	
Between ,, .. 967·47		Gross 3019	
Above ,, .. 81·79		Under deck .. 2932	
Total	2972·17		
Length .. 312 ft. 6 in.		Length .. 323 ft.	
Breadth .. 48 ft. 6 in.		Breadth .. 48 ft. 4 in.	
Depth of hold .. 21 ft. 8 in.		Depth of hold 31 ft. 1 in.	

With two such experts on the job as Bob Waterman and George Cummings, one would expect something very special in her sail plan—and such indeed was the case. Her lower masts were said to have been the finest sticks ever put into a ship ; they were specially selected and towed round from Puget Sound ; nor was there a knot or flaw to be found in them.

Here are some of her spar measurements :

	Length Feet	Diameter Inches	
Bowsprit	50	40	at knightheads
Jibboom and flying jibboom	65	19	at cap
Main lower mast	98½	44	at deck
,, topmast	56½	20	at cap
,, topgallant mast, royal and skysail mast in one	70		
,, lower yard	100	29	in slings
,, lower topsail yard	87	20	,,
,, upper topsail yard	78	18	,,
,, topgallant ,, ...	55	13½	,,
,, royal ,, ...	41	11	,,
,, skysail ,, ...	33	9	,,

The fore lower mast was 3 ft. shorter than the main, but all other dimensions on the fore were the same. Her sail area amounted to 15,000 yards of cotton canvas, and there were over 1000 yards in the mainsail. The topsails had save-alls to set underneath them, and there were bonnets to lace on to the staysails, but no stunsails were provided. She had gas-pipe ratlines from the sheerpoles up, and a jacob's ladder from the topgallant cross-trees to the eyes of the royal rigging.   She was a three-decked ship, and there were even beams for a fourth deck in the hold, but it was not laid.

When all was ready the *Three Brothers* loaded 5000 tons of grain, and signed on 60 able seamen, 4 mates, 2 carpenters, 2 cooks, and 2 stewards.   She was by far the largest sailing ship in the world and was expected to be the fastest.

As regards her speed under sail, Captain Post, of New Zealand, who sailed in her as a boy, writes : "I have held the log-glass myself and seen her reel off 18 knots."   Another old seaman writes with, I fear, some exaggeration : "She was known to have done 24 knots."

Friday, October 24, 1873, was her sailing day from San Francisco for Havre, and we are told that at noon precisely the tug *Neptune* left the Pacific Mail Dock, having a party on board consisting of Captain George Cummings and his wife, the Howes brothers, of whom Jabez occupied a cabin to Havre, the Pilot Commissioners, and Nathan, the pilot, several of 'Frisco's leading citizens, and a band of music.   At 1.15 p.m. the tugs *Rescue* and *Neptune*, with their tow-ropes fast, began to turn ahead to the tune of "Good-bye, Eliza Jane," which was immediately drowned by the guns of the clipper ship *Herald of the Morning*, the scream of innumerable whistles, and the cheers from the wharves and the shipping (all the ships in port, by the way, being dressed rainbow fashion in honour of the *Three Brothers*).

Then the steamer *Princess*, with a large excursion party aboard, followed the outward bounder with continued cheers and music as far as Fort Point, where the guns, together with those of an inward bound Revenue cutter, fired a grand salute.   Finally the pilot and visitors left the ship at 5 p.m., by which time she was under all sail, close-hauled, with a fine westerly breeze.

The first passage of the *Three Brothers* showed that she possessed just as good a pair of heels as the mail steamer *Vanderbilt*.   There are not many opportunities for big runs on the eastward passage round the Horn, but on February 5, 1874, the sights showed a run of 314 miles, the wind being strong from N.E. to North.   The *Three Brothers* was off the Horn in 54 days, and on the Equator in the Atlantic on the 86th day ; took her pilot off Falmouth when

108 days 16 hours out, and anchored off Havre at daylight on February 13, 1874, having sailed 16,073 miles in 111 days 12 hours.

Apparently there was a good deal of betting on her passage, but the monster sailing ship won all the bets, vanquishing her chief opponent, the *British King*, by three days.

The following is a complete epitome of her voyages both under the American and British flags :

FIRST VOYAGE.

Left 'Frisco   Oct. 24, 1873. Arrived Havre Feb. 13, 1873.   .. 111 days 12 h*r*s
  ,, New York June 29, 1874.   ,,   'Frisco Nov. 8, 1874.   .. 132 ,,
              (13 days of calm in North Atlantic, light weather passage.)

SECOND VOYAGE.

Left 'Frisco   Dec. 28, 1874. Arrived Liverpool April 17, 1875. .. 110 days
  ,, Liverpool June 12, 1875. Arrived 'Frisco Oct. 24, 1875. .. 134 days
              (Best run 310 miles under all sail ; she frequently logged 15 knots.)
              (36 days to Equator, 19 days off the Horn in heavy gales; 3 days off the Farallones
                in thick fog.)

THIRD VOYAGE.

Left 'Frisco   Dec. 23, 1874. Arrived Liverpool April 9, 1876. .. 108 days
              (Was 13 days 15 hours to Line, and 48 days to the Horn. Best run 318. Crossed
                Equator Atlantic 76th day, then had head winds.)
  ,, New York Sept. 19, 1876. Arrived 'Frisco   Jan. 13, 1877. .. 116 days
              (52 days from the Horn to the Farallones.)

FOURTH VOYAGE.

Left 'Frisco   March 17, 1877. Arrived Liverpool June 29, 1877. .. 104 days
              (19 days to Line ; 52 to Horn ; 77 to Line ; 101 to Fastnet light.   She beat the
                Dale Line cracks, *Patterdale* and *Langdale*, by over a week, and *Benmore* and
                Charger by a fortnight. All these four were noted fast ships.)
  ,, Liverpool Sept. 19, 1877. Arrived 'Frisco   Jan. 9, 1878. .. 112 days
              (Cargo 3473 tons of coal.)

FIFTH VOYAGE.

Left 'Frisco   Oct. 11, 1878. Arrived New York Jan. 30, 1879. .. 111 days
              (Cargo 3258 short tons of barley.)
  ,, New York May 8, 1879. Arrived 'Frisco   Sept. 19, 1879. .. 134 days

SIXTH VOYAGE.

Left 'Frisco   Nov. 24, 1879. Arrived Liverpool April 4, 1880.   .. 132 days

On her arrival in the Mersey, the unpleasant news of the Howes' suspension, and that his ship was for sale, was broken to Captain

Cummings.   The *Three Brothers* was bought by John Williams of Liverpool, a partner at one time of James Baines in the Black Ball Line.   Williams persuaded Captain Mathias to take over the big ship, much against his inclination, as he did not think she could earn money.   His comment upon the ship which appeared a few years back in the *Liverpool Weekly Post* is worth quoting:

> She was very fast, and I do not think could be beaten.   She was a favourite ship at Antwerp, where we loaded general cargo, principally glass, for 'Frisco.   Finally freights got so low for wheat that a great many ships were laid up, so when I arrived in Liverpool in July, 1885, she was laid up and shortly afterwards sold to the Anchor Line to go to Gibraltar as a coal hulk.

By this time the complement of the *Three Brothers* had been reduced to 36 men before the mast.

SEVENTH VOYAGE.

Left Liverpool Mar. 22, 1881.   Arrived Wilmington, Cal., Aug. 3, 1881. .. 134 days out.
    (Discharged 3000 tons coal and took 1000 tons on to 'Frisco.)
  „ 'Frisco   Oct. 15, 1881.   Arrived Antwerp   Jan. 28, 1882 .. 105 days.
    (Her biggest grain cargo—90,435 centals of wheat.)
  „ Antwerp May 2, 1882.   Arrived 'Frisco   Aug. 22. 1882 .. 112 days.
    (In the S. Pacific Captain Mathias caught his foot in the spanker sheet, and his leg was broken.   He set it with the aid of the steward.)
  „ 'Frisco   Oct. 28, 1882.   Arrived Plymouth   Mar. 15, 1883 .. 138 days.
    (Had a very troublesome crew; they refused to weigh the anchor, 6 refused duty the whole passage, and Captain Mathias put into Plymouth owing to their mutinous behaviour.   Having settled matters with his crew, went on to Antwerp.)

Her next passage was equally unlucky.   After leaving Antwerp, the *Three Brothers* put into Rio with her rudder gone.   It took six weeks to fit a new rudder, but the old ship made up for lost time by running from Rio to San Francisco in 72 days, arriving December, 21, 1883.

On her last passage she left 'Frisco March 7, 1885, and arrived Liverpool July 8, 123 days out.

This ended her active service, but she is still doing valuable duty amongst the famous Gibraltar coal hulks, as the illustration, a recent photograph, shows clearly enough.

NOTE.—Since writing the above the *Three Brothers* has been sold by the London Coal Company for £450 to a Spanish firm for breaking up purposes.

The " Ericsson."

A vessel which was almost worthy to be compared with the superb *Three Brothers* was the *Ericsson*, which was built as a steamer in New York as far back as 1852. She was evidently named for John Ericsson, who was afterwards so famous as the designer of the *Monitor*.

The *Ericsson* was a splendidly built vessel of oak throughout, and according to John Boyd, who was mate of her for some years, she was a heeler ; like most converted steamers she was a long ship, with very fine lines forward.

Like so many American deep-watermen she ended her days on the Pacific coast.

The Notorious " May Flint."

The only other converted steamer in the American Merchant Marine of any note was the hideous *May Flint*, which, like the *Three Brothers*, had once been a trans-Atlantic passenger steamer.

As the *Persian Monarch* she ran between London and New York. She was then owned by T. Wilson & Sons of Hull, having been built in 1880 by A. McMillan & Son at Dumbarton.

In 1895 she stranded near New York, was salved and bought by Charles R. Flint & Co., who took her engines out and converted her to a four-mast barque.

As a sailing ship she was notorious for a great many reasons. With her straight stem she was probably the ugliest square-rigger that ever sailed the seas. She was so unwieldy, so unhandy, and top-heavy that she was always in trouble. Her spars were always going by the board; and she figured in the *Red Record* as a more than unpleasant ship to serve aboard of owing to her bucko second mate.

When converted she registered 3340 tons, had 12,000 yards of canvas, and her lower yards were 92 feet long.

Her first passage under sail was from Baltimore to San Francisco. Off the Horn she had the usual severe dusting and lost her mizen topmast and three topgallant masts. Captain Nickels did well in bringing her into 'Frisco in 160 days. It must have been a tough passage for all concerned, and the ship was listed in the *Red Record*.

On August 21, 1897, she sailed from Philadelphia for Hiogo with a cargo consisting of 113,000 cases of refined petroleum, valued at £22,000 ; 3000 cases of mineral ore and 500 cases of paraffin shale. On September 8, when about 400 miles from the Western Isles, the big ship ran right into the centre of a cyclone, in which her fore and main topmasts and mizen topgallant mast went by the board. The steamer *Craftsman* stood by the lame duck until the weather moderated, and then offered the *May Flint* a tow to New York. Captain Nickels refused the tow, but transferred his two passengers to the steamer. He then proceeded to jury-rig his ungainly vessel, having managed to save some of the masts and rigging which were over the side.

A new fore topmast was made from a spare spar, and the stump of an old mizen topgallant mast was sent up as a fore topgallant mast. The *May Flint* had a spare foreyard, the lower topsail yard was unhurt, and the fore topgallant and royal yards were fished out of the wreckage alongside.   Thus only a fore upper topsail yard was missing. Captain Nickels salved the main upper topsail yard and sent that aloft at the fore, thus refitting his foremast completely. At the main it was not so easy, as there was only the broken main-yard left aloft. This Nickels up-ended as a main topmast, but he had no yards to cross on the main, so left the mast as it was.   Though the mizen topgallant mast and topsail yards were more or less damaged, he managed to fish and repair them, and at the end of a fortnight's strenuous work the *May Flint* was fully rigged on the fore, carried only staysails on the main, and had her topsails and crossjack set on the mizen.

Under this lash-up Captain Nickels sailed his ugly duckling back to New York, a distance of 2200 miles, in very good time, making a run of 240 miles in one 24 hours.   It was a magnificent piece of real seamanship, and the captain thoroughly deserved the gold watch which he received from the underwriters, and, what he no doubt valued as highly, the congratulations and applause of his fellow shipmasters.

The unlucky *May Flint* received a complete refit, got out eventually to Japan, and brought home 79,900 bags of sugar from Honolulu to New York.

The very next voyage she was burnt out in San Francisco with a coal cargo. I have mentioned her here because no account of America's last deep-watermen would be complete without her, though she was no more a Down Easter than the slippery *Western Shore*, which I am also unwilling to leave unnoticed.

The Slippery "Western Shore."

This little 1188-ton full-rigger, which was launched in 1874, was the largest vessel that had been built on the Pacific coast up to that date. She was only 186 feet long, but crossed three skysails, and she must have been a very fine model, if we may judge from the sailing records she put up in her very short life.

In 1875 she sailed from San Francisco a few minutes behind the steamer *Oriflamme*, and made the trip to Astoria in $2\frac{1}{2}$ hours less time, being only a little over two days running up the coast.

In 1876 she sailed from Portland (Oregon) to Liverpool in 101 days, and in 1877 went from San Francisco to Liverpool in 103 days and back to California in 110 days.

Unfortunately she was wrecked on July 9, 1878, outside San Francisco, on the Duxbury Reef.

Moon-Blindness Aboard "El Capitan."

The fine De Groot & Peck 1500-tonner, *El Capitan*, had a very curious experience in the early nineties. She was on a passage from Hiogo to New York, when several of her men became moon-blind. Most landsmen scoff at the very idea of moon-blindness, or moon-blink as it is sometimes called, but nearly all sailors of any tropical experience believe it and will always pull a sleeping mate out of the moon's rays. Sometimes the moon screws up the face muscles, but it may strike as it struck the men of the *El Capitan*.

The ship was 44 days out from Hiogo when the first complaints of blindness were made. The weather had been very hot, and some of the men, against the warning of their ship mates, had persisted in sleeping under the rays of an almost full moon. After nine days they began to go blind at night, totally blind, so that they were useless from dark to dawn, though as soon as it was daylight they could see as well as ever. Shortly after this their eyes became inflamed, and ulcers made their appearance, together with a kind of growth on the eyelids.

Captain Humphrey had never believed in moon-blink, and had even gone the length of clapping a man in irons because he declared he was moon-blind and unable to work; but this time he had to acknowledge the scientific fact, as only the men who had slept in the rays of the moon were affected, those who had remained in the fo'c'sle being perfectly well.

Here is another example of moon-blindness, which I quote from Admiral J. W. Domville's *Cruising in Many Waters*. He writes :

I have seen men suffering from moon-blindness with eyes wide open, feeling their way at night, whilst by day their vision was quite clear.

Quincy's " Northern Light," " Triumphant " and " America."

Joshua Slocum, that extraordinary master mariner, who, when his square-rig days were over, amused himself by sailing round the world in a 12-ton boat of his own design and build, writes as follows about the smallest of these three handsome three skysail-yarders :

My best command was that of the magnificent ship *Northern Light*, of which I was part owner. I had a right to be proud of her, for at that time—in the eighties—she was the finest American sailing vessel afloat.

Well, one must allow some exaggeration to a captain when he is writing about his favourite ship, but there is no doubt that George Thomas produced very fine vessels.

The *Northern Light* was not a regular Cape Horner, being mostly engaged in the Eastern trade and making several trips between Manila and Liverpool. She was eventually bought by S. M. Gram of Christiania and renamed *Mathilda*, being employed in the North Atlantic oil sailing and timber droghuing; and in the end the stormy Western Ocean destroyed her, like many another old wooden ship.

Fred Perry, in his *Fair Winds and Foul*, puts the *Triumphant* into a list of nine Down Easters which he says were celebrated for their speed. The other eight were *Young America, Three Brothers, North American, Glory of the Seas, Oracle, Sovereign of the Seas,*

"AMERICA."

"AMERICA."

"ST. PAUL."

THE "BLOODY 'GATHERER.'"

M. P. Grace, and *Levi C. Wade.* Another old Cape Horner would probably produce an entirely different list of flyers, but he would not be able to deny that Perry's list could sail.

The *Triumphant* disappeared from the Register in 1889, but her sister ship, the *America,* launched at Quincy in 1874, was a coal and lumber Californian coaster for many years. She was also fast, though she did not have much of a chance in the Pacific when she had her skysail yards sent down, and was generally loaded to her scuppers with black diamonds.

These grand old wooden ships were mostly reduced to towing barges at the last ; in the illustration, although she has lost her top hamper, her lines and sheer are well shown.

The Two " Graces."

These two Flint ships were fine able skysail-yarders, giving nothing away, whether in speed, good looks, or smartness of upkeep, to any other Cape Horner of their day.

The *W. R. Grace* was called after the head of the firm of New York shippers, W. R. Grace & Co., whilst the *M. P. Grace* was named for Mike Grace, the Irish-American millionaire, who became notorious at one time for sundry escapades in Europe.

In the seventies Captain Black had the *W. R. Grace,* and Captains Wilbar and Bully Williams had the *M. P. Grace.* The *W. R. Grace* did not last over the eighties, but the bigger ship, after a strenuous and somewhat lurid career as a Cape Horner under that hard old nut, Bully Williams, and the still harder De Winter, who got the old ship blacklisted on the *Red Record,* had a lengthy old age as a Pacific coaster. But before the *M. P. Grace* fell to the humdrum coasting she had many a fierce battle with Cape Stiff. On one occasion it blew so hard inside the Falklands that not a shred of canvas would stand, and she was hove-to under bare poles. On another she was 45 days struggling to weather the Horn.

" Grandee " Collides with an Iceberg.

How many ships have been done to death by the dreaded iceberg of the Southern Ocean we have no means of knowing, but amongst the few which have survived this disaster the main skysail-yarder, *Grandee,* may be numbered.

The accident occurred on January 21, 1877, in 49° 25′ S., 2° E., whilst the ship was on a passage to Melbourne. It was on one of those dark, murky nights, when sea and sky appear the same, nor could the ice be distinguished in the gloom even when it was right under the bow. The ship was going along steadily at from 5 to 6 knots when she went head on into the precipitous side of the berg, which immediately tumbled down great blocks of ice from as high as the upper topsail yard, until the topgallant fo'c'sle was hidden under from 5 to 6 tons of ice and snow. The decks, too, were strewed all over with debris from the berg, and it was a wonder no one was hurt.

After a few moments of pandemonium, with ice crashing and cracking both on board the *Grandee* and all around her, the ship went clear. She must have been stoutly built, because, though we are told she was strained, there was no report of extra pumping.

The jibboom was carried away, the figure-head broken, cutwater smashed, and false stem torn out well down below the waterline ; nevertheless the vessel arrived in Hobson's Bay on Saturday, February 25, looking as smart as paint and polish could make her.

The *Grandee* lasted well into the twentieth century.

The Capsizing of the " Alfred Watts."

In 1874 Sam Watts launched another big 2000-tonner and put the name of a well-known New England financier, Abner J. Benyon, on her stern. However, after the ship had been afloat for about ten years, the financier got into difficulties and left many of the Thomaston shipping fraternity with their pockets lightened and decamped across the Canadian border.

After this scandal Watts could no longer keep that man's name on an honest ship's stern, and he renamed her the *Alfred Watts*, a proceeding which is considered to be most unlucky by old salts, and so it proved on this occasion.

The *Alfred Watts* was put on the berth to load case oil for the East. Meanwhile the *Levi G. Burgess* had just been sold on the Pacific coast, and her master, Captain Johnson, was sent for to take over the renamed ship.

The *Alfred Watts* made a flying start from the Delaware breakwater with a fine nor'west wind ; but, as often happened with case oil cargoes, she proved to be very crank for the want of enough ballast. When she got down to the latitude of the Bahamas the hurricane season was in full swing. Sure enough it came on to blow, and the harder the wind the more the ship listed, until at last she lay right down on her side.

The boats as usual were upside down and well lashed on the skids, and could not be launched in time, so that all hands, including the captain's wife, were obliged to take refuge on the ship's channels, which as usual with wooden ships were fairly substantial, the rigging leading outside the bulwarks to the chain plates, not inside, as is usual in iron or steel ships.

The ship, held up by air and case oil, was in no danger of sinking, but every sea swept over her unfortunate crew, and whilst the gale was still at its height both Captain Johnson and his devoted wife were washed away and seen no more.

Nineteen days later the second mate and eight of the men, the only survivors, were taken off by a passing ship, being at their last gasp.

The Hell-Ship, "St. Paul," Shanghaies a Sky Pilot.

The fine Bath ship, *St. Paul*, with Captain Bert Williams in command and an Austrian of the name of Martin as second mate, had a very unsavoury reputation in the eighties, and was one of those hell-ships which had to pay heavy blood-money in order to get any sort of a crew in San Francisco.

About 40 years ago she was lying in the Bay, loaded with grain for Liverpool, and only waiting for a crew, whilst the crimps and their runners hunted 'Frisco for men. But with the *St. Paul* lying in the Bay ready for sea, even the most reckless seamen made themselves scarce, and shanghai-ing had to be resorted to. In their desperation, at last Shanghai Brown and his jackals—or was it Red Jackson and Three-finger Daly?—actually had the temerity to capture and dope a Baptist minister who was innocently walking along Market Street.

Stripped of his clerical garb and rigged out in dungarees, the clergyman did not come to until the *St. Paul* was making sail outside the Golden Gate, and then he was roused by a kick in the ribs by that tough customer, Bucko Martin, and the order, "Minister or Saint—hell! up you get and work!" And before the *St. Paul* was down to Cape Stiff that sky pilot was an adept at furling the skysail.

The ship made a good passage, 101 days to the Mersey, where the shanghaied minister was sent his passage money by friends and thereupon returned to his flock on the Pacific coast, without a doubt all the better for his experience of life as it was lived aboard a real blood-boat!

The Story of the " Bloody " " Gatherer."

The old *St. Paul* was just a plain " hell-ship " or "blood-boat," where belaying-pins and knuckle-dusters kept a somewhat battered and worn-out fo'c'sle crowd up to a high state of efficiency in the way of sail fisting and ship cleaning, but there was a 1500-ton Bath vessel, launched in the same year, whose decks literally ran blood, aboard of which murder and suicide were rife until the law of the land took notice. This was the " Bloody " *Gatherer.*

In the seventies E. & A. Sewall of Bath built four 1500-tonners, and gave them names which were probably suggested by their Californian grain cargoes.

These were the *Gatherer, Harvester, Reaper,* and *Sower,* all splendid five-topgallant yard ships.

The *Gatherer,* under her first captain, Thomson, was a regular ship in the Cape Horn trade, and only figured in the shipping news columns of the newspapers. But when Captain John Sparks assumed command, and Charlie Watts was mate, the front page of the San Francisco papers began to be full of the doings aboard the *Gatherer.*

Finally, the *Gatherer* arrived at San Francisco after a passage round the Horn, during which two of her seamen committed suicide. The first of these was a Scandinavian who had been driven half crazy by the mate. He climbed slowly to the royal yard whilst shouting down curses and insults upon the two tyrants, Sparks and Watts. The mate chased him up the rigging, but was too late. The man reached the royal yard and, running out along the lee yardarm, leapt into space. A burst of foam showed where he had hit the sea, and that was all.

The other suicide was a man named Swanson, who ran aft and jumped on to the taffrail, stood balancing for a moment whilst he drew his sheath-knife across his throat, and then fell headlong into the frothy white of the wake. For a minute his head and a clenched fist showed in a circle of red, and then he too disappeared, another victim to the " Bloody " *Gatherer*.

A third seaman was shot by the mate on this dreadful passage, at the end of which Captain Sparks was obliged to give up his command and retire into hiding, whilst the mate went to prison, as already recorded.

" C. F. Sargent " with Fidded Royal Masts.

In the days of tall ships the Brooklyn Bridge was a great nuisance to vessels which had to pass underneath in order to discharge or load in the East River. Every ship of any size had to lower her topgallant masts and upper yards in order to negotiate the bridge, and this in wintertime with the thermometer down below zero, and perhaps a blizzard of snow sheeting the rigging in ice, was no pleasant job for the hands working aloft.

It was on purpose to obviate the necessity of striking topgallant masts that some ships were given fidded royal masts. These looked rather heavy and clumsy aloft, but were popular with foremast hands as less of a job to send down.

One of the ships which had these fidded royal masts was the *C. F. Sargent*, named after her builder, C. F. Sargent of Yarmouth, and owned in the eighties by Louis Rosenfeld, and later on by G. E. Plummer of San Francisco in the Pacific coal trade.

In his *Fair Winds and Foul*, Mr. Fred Perry gives a very vivid account of an earthquake at a Peruvian guano port, in which the *C. F. Sargent* was involved.

On the W.C.S.A. it was always usual to celebrate the departure of a loaded ship by feasting and song, until in the days of the nitrate boom, when the West Coast ports were crowded with big sailing ships, a regular ceremony came into vogue.

On the occasion of the earthquake a little 900-ton ship, the

Independence, was to sail at daybreak.   The night before, a supper
was given by the captain of the *C. F. Sargent* to all the masters,
their wives, and chief officers, which was followed by a good old-
fashioned sing-song.   At the stroke of 8 bells midnight the skippers
called for their boats, and only the dip of the oars and a few low
voices broke the hush of a close, sultry night.   Then, of a sudden,
there came a deep moan in the air, and a sudden vibration which set
the sea swirling and the land shaking.   In a moment the stillness
of the night was broken by wild cries ashore and the klink-klink
of cables being payed out afloat.   And whilst the shore community,
men, women and children, cats, dogs, goats, pigs, and even chickens
went " hells-bells," as the old sea expression was, for the mountain
tops, the crews of the anchored ships hastily prepared for the tidal
wave, which soon showed its white, frothing top in the offing.

Unfortunately for the little *Independence*, she only had the
old-fashioned barrel windlass, which would not pay out fast enough.
As the wall of water reached her the chain jammed on the barrel,
her hawse-pipes were torn out, and her bow went under.   The
side-ports for ventilating the 'tween decks of the ammonia fumes
from the cargo had not been closed and caulked up, nor were her
hatches on, so that the ship filled and settled down like a stone.

Captain Johnson only had time to cast adrift the companion
ladder, to which, with the aid of the mate and carpenter, he lashed
his wife, the nurse, and his two little girls, whilst he himself went
overboard with his eight-year old boy on his back, before the ship
made her last dive.

Hardly had the sea quietened down after the passage of the fatal
wave when the boats of the ships were launched in answer to the
cries for help which came out of the darkness.   The boat of the
C. F. Sargent picked up the semi-conscious captain of the *Independence*, with his boy still in his arms, but dead.   For a long time
no signs of the gangway ladder could be found ; it was eventually
discovered floating far out to sea soon after daybreak, but the bodies
of Mrs. Johnson, the nurse and two children lay on the shore amongst
a number of natives who had been caught by the tidal wave.

Mr. Perry relates that when he saw Captain Johnson aboard the
C. F. Sargent on the evening of the day after the earthquake the

"INDEPENDENCE."

"HARRY MORSE."

"SPARTAN."

Lent by Capt. Beavis.
Photo by H. H. Morrison.

"SANTA CLARA."

captain was a nervous wreck, his face pallid and shrunken, and his hair, which had been "as black as a raven's wing," heavily tinged with grey.

After the victims of the earthquake had been buried on the bare hillside the *C. F. Sargent* and the rest of the ships sailed for Callao, where they could repair damages after having their decks swept, whilst, as is always the case, the surviving inhabitants set to work to rebuild their flattened homes out of drift-wood and canvas.

The Captain of the " Spartan."

The *Spartan* was built at East Boston for J. Henry Sears of Boston, Commodore Theodore H. Allen of San Francisco, and Captain Isaac N. Jackson.   Captain Jackson left the *Great Admiral* in 1873 in order to command the new ship, and between 1874 and 1878 he made three very fast round voyages in the *Spartan*, the outward passages being from New York with general cargo to San Francisco, and the homeward from San Francisco with grain to Liverpool.

In March, 1878, the *Spartan*, after being ashore on Long Island, was sold to Henry Cairns, and Captain Jackson retired from the sea.

It was whilst she was a coal droghuer on the Pacific coast in her old age that she had a well-known character as her master—this was Captain Polite ; probably if he had been asked, he would have pronounced himself, as Captain Lermond did, the ideal mixture ; he was not a Redskin Paddy, however, but a Portugee Irishman !   The *Spartan* stranded on one of the Hawaiian Islands in 1905 and became a total loss.

The " Mary L. Stone."

One of the finest of the 1874 ships was the three skysail-yarder *Mary L. Stone*, which was commanded in turn by Captains George Josselyn, Andrew Carver, and William H. Gould.

She was lost on the island of Formosa about 1895.

"Chargers" and "Charmers."

There were two *Chargers* and three *Charmers* in the American Mercantile Marine. These vessels have often been confused with each other.

The first *Charger*, which was built in 1856, was wrecked in the Philippines in December, 1873. Sailing from Manila for Cebu to complete her loading of hemp for Boston this ship ran on a reef when ten miles from Cebu and broke her back, the wreck being afterwards sold for 7,595 dollars.

Then came *Charger* No. 2, built in 1874, which was sold to the Germans in April, 1896, and renamed *Louise*. Eventually she became a barge on the Pacific coast, and foundered under her old name in Karta Bay, Alaska, on October 10, 1909.

The first *Charmer* was built at Newburyport in 1854, a medium clipper of 1024 tons. This vessel had a very striking figurehead, which was a Snake with its tongue hanging out. After making a number of good passages both in the San Francisco and China trades she was sold to Liverpool owners in 1863.

Charmer No. 2, which was built in 1869, was sold to the Germans in 1880 and renamed *Marie*.

Then came *Charmer* No. 3, in 1881. This vessel, under Captain Holmes, became a great favourite with shippers. She was eventually cut down to a towing barge in 1909, and finllay was stranded in Chesapeake Bay on December 3, 1912, and became a total loss.

Soule's "Tam o' Shanter."

The old New England seaboard families were not content with building their own ships, but they spent their more vigorous years in officering and commanding them. Thus we find E. C. Soule of Freeport in command of the first *Tam o' Shanter*, leaving Boston on November 15, 1852, with 11 passengers, whom he landed at San Francisco on March 25, 1853.

This ship was built by Enos Soule in 1849 and registered 777 tons. She foundered off Cape Cod in December, 1853, on her homeward passage. But Captain Soule was not discouraged. Another Soule left Boston in charge of the Newhaven ship, *Uncle Toby*, on April 19, 1853, for the Golden Gate.

Soule's second *Tam o' Shanter* was one of the best known ships in the Down East fleet.

Though most of Soule's ships were somewhat wall-sided and box-shaped, more carriers than clippers, this *Tam o' Shanter* certainly put up some very good sailing records. Her best known performance was in 1892, when she raced the big four-master *Shenandoah* from New York to 'Frisco. The two ships sailed on the same day, carried all plain sail throughout the passage, raced side by side for a week, and eventually arrived in the Bay on July 13, the *Tam o' Shanter* winning by three hours with a passage of 115 days. She was commanded at this time by a hard old nut named Peabody, who managed to get himself logged twice in the *Red Record*. Before his time she was commanded by Captain Prescott, who made some good runs to Liverpool, grain-laden.

Peabody handed over to a Captain Waite about 1894, and just about this time the " Tammy " had a very hard passage out to the Pacific, being 49 days trying to get to the westward of the Horn with her decks full of snow most of the time.

In 1899 we find her under Captain Ballard, taking case oil to China, and I believe it was on this passage that she came to grief.

Perry's " Continental."

Of the *Continental*, Fred Perry. her mate for several voyages, remarks :

> I know from experience that all ships have a personality even as you and I. With their likes and dislikes, their individual characteristics and moods, they must be pampered and catered for just as the best of women are cared for. . . . Such an individual character was fully developed in the good ship *Continental*. . . . Although she was one of the fastest vessels in the fleet, at times she had to be nursed, cuddled, coaxed or chidden, as the case might be, in order to maintain the desired speed.

The *Continental* cost 112,000 dollars to build, and loaded 2500 tons of cargo on a draft of 23 ft. 6 ins. She was heavily rigged with single topgallant sails, but nothing above the royals ; her mainmast from step to truck was 195 ft.; her bowsprit was 20 ft. outboard, and her jibboom 70 feet outside the band ; and her mainyard was 90 ft. long, so she evidently did not want for canvas.

She was commanded for many years by Captain Clark, who Perry describes as a "typical old salt, having spent 45 years of his life in sail, during 35 of which he was master." He had the utmost contempt for steam ships and their officers ; referring to the vessels as " steam kettles," and maintaining that any "old woman " could take one across the Atlantic Ocean, as the only order that had to be given was to tell the quartermaster to head her East-North-East to Liverpool, and West-South-West back to New York.

His inherent belief was that no man should be called a sailor until he had his corns soaked in salt water going around Cape Horn. His record at Lloyd's showed that in 35 years in which he had been ship's master he had never called on the underwriters for a loss. To the passer-by he may have appeared rough and uncouth, and at times even repulsive, but, once the outer surface had been pierced and you came in touch with what lay within, you found a man with a heart as big as an ox, generous, kind and liberal—a credit to the profession he followed.

I have quoted this in full, for it describes a type of shipmaster who is now practically extinct.

The *Continental* disappeared from the Register about 1888.

" Centennial's " Battle with Cape Horn.

The *Continental*, of 1712 tons, must not be confused with the Boston-built *Centennial* of 1286 tons ; the fast *Continental*, according to Perry, was once 171 days on the westward passage round Cape Stiff, but the smaller *Centennial* had a very much longer and harder passage in the early nineties, being 199 days between New York and San Francisco. Three times she had to put back from the pitch of the Horn ; twice she put into the Falklands for repairs, and the third time went back to Monte Video, being afraid to attempt the entrance to Stanley in the furious gale that was blowing.

" City of Philadelphia " Wrecked on the Billy Rocks.

As the *Centennial* ran by, her crew noticed an American ship trying to weather the Billy Rocks at the entrance to the harbour. This was the 1500-ton Bath ship *City of Philadelphia*. She also had put back from the Horn for repairs. She missed stays off the entrance soon after the *Centennial* had passed, struck on the Billy Rocks, and foundered with all hands, including a passenger, who was making the voyage for his health.

Captain Waldo of the "Isaac Reed."

Another fine type of American shipmaster was Captain Waldo of the good-looking *Isaac Reed.* He wore long Dundreary whiskers, but he was none the worse for that.

The old *Isaac Reed* became a Pacific coaster at the beginning of the twentieth century, being bought by J. Jenson, whilst her old skipper gave place to a man named Holmgvist. However, she only lasted a year or two at the coast work.

"North American" and "South American."

Two of the fastest ships ever built at East Boston, or at anyrate since the clipper ship boom of the fifties, were the *North American* and *South American,* which were owned by H. Hastings.

So many ships have been named after the "Americas" that one is apt to mix them up. The *North American* must not be confused with the old *North America,* which was a ship of about the same tonnage, but built at Boston as far back as 1851. The latter, under various names of *Wilhelm, Little Willie, Louisa Canevaro* and *Ema Luisa,* outlasted the former and was still afloat under Chilian colours in 1895. And the *South American* must not be confused with a little Belfast barque, which was built at Glasgow in 1891.

It is hard to say whether the *North American* or the *South American* was the faster ship, but the latter has been credited with the fastest trip round the world ever made under sail.

On November 15, 1893, she left San Francisco for Liverpool, and arrived in the Mersey on the hundredth day out. After discharging she was sent round to Cardiff, where she loaded coal for Hongkong. This passage was accomplished in the splendid time of 88 days ; and from Hongkong she crossed to San Francisco in 41 days, making a total of 229 days for a voyage round the world. This was no fluke, for she had other sailing feats to her credit, such as 97 days from 'Frisco to Cork in 1878. She left 'Frisco on July 5, with 54,984 centals of wheat valued at 96,222 dollars for Havre, and anchored at Queenstown on October 10.

Both the "Americans" had disappeared from the Register by the end of the nineteenth century

" Sachem " in the Ombai Passage.

The *Sachem* was an extremely handsome Boston-built ship
and a very fine example of the medium clipper.   Her entrance
was very sharp with hardly any curve to the cutwater, and there
certainly was no room to swing a cat under her topgallant fo'c'sle.
She also had a good deal of deadrise, and it required 300 tons of
ballast to stiffen her sufficiently, even with a full case oil cargo.

Like all Boston ships she was nicely finished.   Her figure-head
was a full length figure of an Indian chief in full ceremonial dress of
feathers.   She had a graceful sheer, and her crew were always very
proud of her semi-elliptical stern, which they contrasted scornfully
with the square counters of so many Down Easters.

It is curious how the eye alters its conception of beauty.   When
round sterns were introduced into the British Navy by the Surveyor,
Sir Robert Seppings, an attempt was made with false frames to
retain the appearance of the beautiful square stern.

Messrs. M. F. Pickering & Co. were the *Sachem's* managing
owners, and they kept her in the Eastern trade—out with case oil
and home with sugar, hemp, rags and camphor.

The *Sachem* had quite a good turn of speed, and could hold
her own with all except the out-and-out clippers.   With regard
to her encounter with one of these in the Ombai Passage, Mr. A. L.
Putnam, who made the voyage in her in 1885, gives a delightful
account.

After a good passage in which the *Sachem* pleased the young
Putnam (he was scarcely more than a kid) by her prowess in running
the Easting down, she arrived at the southern end of the Ombai
Passage, between Ombai and Timor Islands, which is one of the
usual routes into the Pacific.

Previous to this, whilst running before the westerlies, he
records the ease with which the *Sachem* ran by a big Scottish four-
mast barque which, he says, looked like a submerged reef with
masts and sails sticking out of the froth and foam, whilst thousands
of Cape pigeons and mollyhawks circled and darted around her.
He was therefore surprised when the doughty flyer failed to beat
her way through the Strait.   But this was not surprising, for she
found a strong southerly current between the islands, with no wind

at all except for a few hours every afternoon, when it blew fresh to strong from the north, a dead muzzler for all vessels bound up to China. But for these few hours it was either dead calm or with sudden flurries, willy-waws and rain squalls darkening the sky and ruffling the water.

So here the *Sachem* stuck, along with a number of other vessels awaiting a slant, until at last there were from 20 to 30 ships held up, including the American ships, *Tam o' Shanter, Timour* (an 1866 Newburyport ship of 962 tons), *Joseph B. Thomas* (Sam Watts' 1881 ship), and the *Gloaming*, and the Nova Scotians, *Antoinette* and *Hectonoga*.

It was a case of a dead beat to windward every afternoon until the wind fell with the sun; and in these contests of weatherliness the *Sachem* generally found herself in the windward berth at the end of the day. Not a ship succeeded in getting through the Ombai Straits for 16 days.

On the afternoon of the 15th day a strange ship appeared at the tail end of the fleet—a small rakish ship, showing very little freeboard, and with the brown hemp sails of a Britisher. Young Putnam drew the second mate's attention to the newcomer, whose hull could be plainly seen after she had made a couple of tacks. The second mate of the *Sachem* was an Englishman. After taking a good look at the stranger, he remarked impressively : " I don't know her name, but I know her type, and I can tell you that this bunch of Yankees, Blue-noses, and stockfish-eating Souwegians will now have a chance to see a ship sail and be shown how to get through the Ombai Passage."

"Sure enough," writes Putnam, "in a couple of tacks the stranger came about at the same time as we did, but about a mile to leeward."

It was now 6 bells in the afternoon, and the wind was blowing a good whole-sail breeze, but, as usual, a dead muzzler for the Northbound fleet. In twenty minutes from the time when the two ships came on to the same tack, the British ship was two miles ahead of the *Sachem* and a mile to windward. In passing, the two ships exchanged signals, and the clipper gave her name as the *Northampton* of London, bound from London to Shanghai with scrap-iron. (The *Northampton* was a composite ship of 1174 tons, built by Connell of Glasgow in 1866 for the Merchant Shipping Company.)

When the wind fell in the late afternoon the Britisher was a good 10 miles to windward of the *Sachem*, which in her turn was away to windward of the rest of the fleet. And then it was that Barclay, the skipper of the *Northampton*, did what Putnam calls his " real goat getting trick "—though there was not a ripple on the water, he squared away and ran to leeward to visit and gossip. The *Sachem*, with her yards braced sharp up on the backstays, was lying like a log without steerage way, when the *Northampton* dropped down and backed her mainyard right under the former's counter. Putnam, in commenting on this proceeding, writes : "The backing of that mainyard seemed a positive insult as far as we were concerned, but the *Northampton* had to do it to stop her way." He also remembers the British captain singing out across the water : " If I don't get through here to-morrow I'm going to hunt another hole." So it seems that this phrase did not originate in the late War

After a bit of a game the *Northampton*, which, by the way, was so deeply loaded with her heavy scrap-iron cargo that her maindeck was nearly awash, filled away on her mainyard and went off to visit the next ship of the fleet. To the people of the *Sachem* such ghost-like sailing seemed like witchcraft, as they could not detect the slightest whisper of a draught aloft. Nevertheless when darkness fell the *Northampton* was hull down to leeward where her ship visiting had taken her.

That night there was a furious tropical squall, which blew some of the *Sachem's* sails away, and she was in a pretty mess for about an hour. But this left a wind which did not let go until daylight and was sufficiently to one side to allow long and short tacks up the Strait. While all hands on the *Sachem* were clearing up the decks, the ship being on the long port leg, a pair of sidelights were picked up right astern, then the port light faded out and only the green could be seen. Out on their weather beam the *Sachem's* crew caught a glimpse of a painted port ship with her royals furled, and they were able to identify the *Northampton*, going 2 feet to their one.

"JABEZ HOWES."

"HARVEY MILLS."

Lent by Capt. L. R. W. Beavis.

Putnam declares that there was the sound of a gigantic hiss as the clipper surged by to windward, then she faded into the night like a ghost and was gone for ever from their sight. It was blowing half a gale, and the *Northampton* seemed to be travelling like an express train.

This sea picture is of special interest as showing the difference in sailing between a crack Clyde clipper and a fleet of sturdy Down Easters and Nova Scotiamen ; but we must remember that it was smooth water

"Paul Revere" and her Stunsails.

The *Paul Revere*, a smart Boston ship from the yard of Smith & Townsend, was well known in the Cape Horn fleet for her stunsails, which, it was said, added 1000 yards of canvas to her sail area and put a couple of knots on to her speed.

She was commanded by a Cockney named Mullens, who was a great driver and also gave her the reputation of being a hot ship.

The *Paul Revere* swung her main skysail well into the twentieth century, being laid up and dismantled in August, 1905.

"Indiana" and "Jabez Howes."

There were two other Cape Horners which rigged out stunsail booms as late as the nineties ; these were the five topgallant yard ship *Indiana*, and the three skysail-yarder, *Jabez Howes*.

The best known skipper of the *Indiana* was Captain Colley, one of those shipmasters who sported Dundreary whiskers. After a long steady life she was laid up in San Francisco Bay in 1925.

The *Jabez Howes* was a smart ship, and one of John Rosenfeld's regular traders between New York and San Francisco. On her first grain passage she loaded 29,653 centals at £2 10s.; sailed from San Francisco on August 1 and arrived in the Mersey on November 25, 116 days out. In 1893 she arrived at San Francisco on April 24 only 107 days out from New York.

A voyage or so before this she crossed the Sandy Hook bar 98 days out from 'Frisco after being severely dismantled in the Pacific South-East Trades in about 14° S.

Let me quote the captain's own words :

On this particular day I had specially told the mate not to loose the jib topsail, but when I went below after dinner for a nap the beggar did it. When I went on deck again at four there was a squall making ahead, and I ordered some hands to stand by the skysail halliards, for I didn't know the jib topsail had been loosed. Well, sir, the squall hit us (it was a corker) and snapped off the jibboom ; and, as I ran forward, crack went the fore topmast, then the main topgallant mast, and at last, over went the mizen topgallant mast. In all my goin' to sea I never saw the like of it. . . .

Forrard we were a wreck, with nothing at all above the foreyard, whilst alongside was a fearful mass of gear slamming against the ship, and you know those Trades in the Pacific blow fresh. Well, we cleared up the wreck after hard work, sent up a few of the old yards which weren't too far gone to fish, and crossed Sandy Hook bar 98 days from 'Frisco under jury rig.

I have taken this from that classic passenger's log of Paul Eve Stevenson. This skipper was Captain F. T. Henry, who had the *Jabez Howes* from 1884 for about ten years.

The *Jabez Howes* ended her days on the Pacific coast, being commanded for over ten years, up to within a year or so of the War, by Captain R. C. Clapp.

The Unlucky "Harvey Mills."

When Messrs. Mills & Creighton launched the *Harvey Mills* at Thomaston on Monday, September 4, 1876, experts pronounced her to be one of the finest examples of a New England square-rigged ship ever built.

But, alas, she was baptised in blood, as the expression went ; that is to say, that by a mischance a man was killed at her launch. This has always been considered by such superstitious people as old-time seamen as the greatest disaster in the way of future bad luck that could happen to a ship ; and certainly this was borne out in the case of the big *Harvey Mills*.

She left Thomaston on October 7, 1876, for Port Royal, where she loaded cotton for Liverpool. On December 28 she was loaded and ready for sea when a fire broke out aboard, and before it was finally smothered two of her hands had been suffocated in the chain locker. Many West Indian lawyers make a speciality of holding ships up for heavy compensation on even the flimsiest pretexts, and here was the chance of a lifetime. Thus it came about that the captain of the *Harvey Mills* could not move his ship until he had given a bond to cover all possible claims. At last, on January 27, 1877, he was allowed to up anchor for New York, where the charred and gutted ship was repaired.

From New York the *Harvey Mills* went out to the Pacific coast where she loaded grain, and leaving 'Frisco on September 17, 1877, arrived Liverpool on December 29, 103 days out. This was her best passage and also her luckiest. Henceforward, although she was well-found and liberally run, she was everlastingly in trouble of one sort or another.

On her way across from Liverpool to New York she ran into a real howler of a North Atlantic winter gale, which dismasted her on February 18, 1878. However, she managed somehow to crawl into port and had again to have an expensive refit.

Her next disaster of any magnitude occurred at the end of 1880, when she ran into the barque *Eta* off the English coast, and sank her. Again she was beset by the law, and it cost her dear; and when at last she was able to get away from the British Isles she was caught by the Western Ocean in another of its angry moods, and again suffered a dismasting. This time she put back, and twelve months had gone by before she had at last succeeded in overcoming the westerlies and dropping her hook in her home port.

By this time she was notorious for her misfortunes, and the newspapers picked up the gossip of the ports, so that their columns were soon overflowing with blood-curdling yarns of the "hoodoo" ship. It was even rumoured that the ghosts of her dead haunted the *Harvey Mills*—that grisly spectres appeared on her decks and lent their howls to the crash of collision or roar of the tempest— that gaunt forms of drowned seamen, still adrip with water and festooned with strong smelling seaweed, appeared on the foot-ropes amongst her men when they were handing sail, or trod silently from cathead to cathead on the lookout, showing through the sprays which showered over the topgallant fo'c'le as if lit up by a distant searchlight.

Thus it became a difficulty for the *Harvey Mills* to sign on a crew, so fearfully did her reputation daunt even the most reckless of Cape Horn shellbacks. At last on December 12, 1886, she left

Seattle coal laden for 'Frisco. A few weeks later, whilst returning North in ballast, she foundered off Cape Flattery, taking down 22 of her company with her, the only men to be saved being Cushman (her first officer), and two seamen, who were picked up by the barque *Majestic*, after a terrible experience hanging on to floating wreckage.

The " Frank Curling " Capsizes off the Horn.

Another unlucky ship from the yard of Mills & Creighton was the *Frank Curling*, which, on her maiden passage from New York to 'Frisco, capsized off the Horn.

It was rumoured that her commander and chief owner, Captain Frank Curling, in his eagerness to make a passage, carried on for too long until at last the cargo shifted and the ship turned turtle. Half the crew were lost as well as the ship herself, for only Captain Curling's boat was picked up. He returned sadly to Thomaston, where he presently obtained the command of the *Joseph S. Spinney*, the last big ship built by Mills & Creighton. This vessel did not come to grief, but became well known first in the Cape Horn and Far East trades and finally in the lumber trade between the Pacific coast and Australia.

" Paul Richard Hazeltine " Wrecked on Wollaston Island.

Another Down Easter to fall a victim to Cape Stiff about the same time as the *Frank Curling* was the Belfast-built *Paul Richard Hazeltine*. This vessel, on her maiden passage, had a narrow escape from destruction. When bound with a cargo of deals for Liverpool, she stranded on Cape Sable, August 25, 1876, during a dense fog, but was lucky enough to float off after her deck cargo had been jettisoned, and was able to proceed on her passage.

Eighteen months later, on February 18, 1878, when bound out to San Francisco from New York with a cargo valued at 475,000 dollars, she struck on a sunken rock off Wollaston Island, to the eastward of Cape Horn, and foundered.

Her commander, Captain Edwin Horace Herriman, as in the case of the *Frank Curling*, was her chief owner, having a quarter share in the vessel. He had his wife along with him, and his son was second mate. The boats were all picked up without loss of life. The captain, having his interest in the vessel very poorly insured, formed a wrecking company and made an attempt to raise his ship, but in such a tempestuous locality naturally without success ; indeed the venture ended in tragedy, for the worry of the whole business so unhinged his brain that he never recovered his right mind.

The Big " Eureka."

Next to the *Harvey Mills*, the biggest ship built in 1876 was Jeffey Southard's three skysail-yarder, *Eureka*, an attractive, well-built ship, but with no pretensions to speed.

On one occasion Watts' *Joseph B. Thomas*, which was no great flyer, passed her quite easily in the Pacific S.E. Trades, when bound out to San Francisco coal-laden from Birkenhead. The *Joseph B. Thomas* ran the *Eureka* out of sight astern in a couple of days, and arrived in port about three weeks ahead.

In 1891 the *Eureka* took 117 days with general cargo from New York to Melbourne, but Captain Woodward would not admit that his poor passage was due to the ship's sailing. He declared that he never had a more vexatious passage. After leaving New York on July 14 he had calms all the way to the Equator, which was not crossed until August 26 ; then on the other side of the Cape, the meridian of which was passed on October 2, the weather was so bad that resort was had to oil bags ; also the cargo shifted, and altogether the *Eureka* had a very hard time of it.

"St. Mark" Races "Joseph B. Thomas" for the only Tug on Puget Sound.

Another ship which was bested by the steady-going *Joseph B. Thomas* was the second *St. Mark*. These two ships, which were much of a size and very evenly matched, left 'Frisco together in order to load coal at Seattle.

It was foggy weather up the coast, and they did not catch a glimpse of each other until they opened Cape Flattery and entered the Straits of Juan de Fuca in brilliantly clear weather ; then they found themselves racing neck and neck in a strong fair wind. And there was good reason for racing, as only one tug was to be found at Port Townsend at that time, and whoever got the rope of that tug would be the first to get alongside the only loading berth available at Seattle.

It must have been a beautiful sight, with the mountains of the Cascade range glistening in the bright sunshine, whilst the forest-clad slopes on either side of the Strait were rich with the greenery of early summer. The *St. Mark* was a five topgallant yard ship with a main skysail, whilst the *Joseph B. Thomas* swung a main skysail over a single topgallant sail. With every sail set that would draw, the two vessels kept within a few yards of each other and ran into Port Townsend neck and neck.

As luck would have it, the *Joseph B. Thomas*, in racing parlance, had the inside berth ; the tugboat *Richard Holyoak* being on her side took her line and towed her to Seattle. The *St. Mark* followed, close-hauled under all sail, but did not get to an anchor until late that night. Then the next morning, finding the *Joseph B. Thomas* alongside the coal berth, she up anchored and went on to Tacoma.

"St. Stephen's " Record.

Besides the *St. Mark* there were three smaller " Saints " built in 1876-7. These were the 1500-tonners *Santa Clara* and *St. David*, and the 1400-tonner *St. Stephen*. Of the four vessels, *Santa Clara* had the longest life, and the *St. Stephen* the shortest.

Though she was only afloat ten years the *St. Stephen* made a great name for herself in the Cape Horn trade, and must have been a very fast ship. For seven passages out to San Francisco she averaged 130 days, her best being 113 days from Philadelphia. Homeward her average for five passages was only 113 days, the best run being 101 days from San Francisco to Liverpool in 1879.

The "Wandering Jew " and Uncle Talpey.

The *Wandering Jew* was built by J. Pascal at Camden, Maine, and in her design was an exceedingly interesting vessel. The chief novelty was what might be called her double deck. At the height of the topgallant rail above her maindeck a sort of hurri-cane deck was laid, which was flush fore and aft, with nothing to

"ST. DAVID."

Lent by Capt. Schulze.

"SOOLOO."

prevent one going over the side except a 20-inch teak monkey-rail. This deck, however, had the advantage of being 10 ft. above the waterline instead of about 5, as with an ordinary maindeck. It was also built with a good crown or camber to it, so that any water that came aboard ran off at once, the "Jew" never having the usual deep-waterman's experience of a flooded maindeck, and it was stated that she never lost a man overboard. The only breaks from bow to taffrail in this upper deck were the fo'c'sle scuttle, hatch coamings, cabin skylights and wheel-house.

The *Wandering Jew* was not only finely modelled, but splendidly rigged, with a main skysail, and was considered one of the smartest ships in the American Merchant Marine.

Her first captain was known throughout the Seven Seas as Uncle Talpey. He was one of those jovial, hearty sea-dogs who had a host of friends and was a real good sort. Though most of the ships managed by Carleton, Norwood & Co. were notorious for their hard-hearted, grim-visaged work-'em-up skippers, the "Jew" was a popular ship as long as she was sailed by Uncle Talpey.

But D. E. Nichols, who succeeded him, was a chip of the old Green-heart all right, and Felix Riesenberg puts the following characteristic yarn about him into the mouth of an old shellback :

I was in her out of 'Frisco. They'd just run the crew. We was going over to Shanghai in the " Jew "—a West Coast crowd. The captin's daughter was on board, and one day she sez to papa, that same . . . Nichols: " Papa, why don't you knock them men around the way you always used to ! " " Them men is gentlemen," he replies and goes right below. An' you bet they was gentlemen—gentlemen wot carried shooting irons and bowie knives—an' the " old man " knowed it too. But he worked them all out of her in Shanghai and shipped coolies to Hongkong.

Whilst she was under Talpey the *Wandering Jew* was mostly in the 'Frisco grain trade and made some good passages in the eighties. When Nichols had her—he had a good interest in it— she was more often in the Eastern trade. Nichols was a sail carrier and on one occasion he ran from Hongkong to 'Frisco Heads in 39 days.

In 1895 there was a great deal of interest taken in a race from China to New York between the *Wandering Jew* and *Tam o' Shanter*. Both ships sailed on January 3 and proved to be very evenly matched, actually reaching quarantine at the same hour, so that the race was declared a dead heat and all bets were cancelled.

According to Riesenberg's old seaman, Nichols sailed her till a crew of square-heads burned her up on him in Hongkong harbour—it was the only way they could get even with him. As a matter of fact the " Jew's " last days were spent on the China coast, and she was eventually towed 200 miles up to Yangtze-Kiang to Kinkiang, where the famous Down Easter was condemned to do duty as a landing stage.

The Last of the Salem East Indiamen.

In 1877 the 1200-ton *Panay* was built at Boston for Silsbee, Pickman & Allen of Salem. She was the last of the great East India fleet, which, for over 100 years, had represented Salem merchants and the American flag. She was also one of three ships which were specially built by John Taylor for the Philippine hemp trade. These were the *Sooloo*, *Mindoro* and *Panay*.

The first of the three was the little *Sooloo* of 784 tons, built in 1861. She made 19 successful voyages to the East under the following captains : Charles H. Allen, Jr., Daniel H. Hutchinson, John H. Shatswell, and W. Frank Powers. On her nineteenth voyage she was run into off South Shoals lightship by the schooner *Messenger*, and was so damaged in spars and hull that she was with difficulty worked into Vineyard Haven. Subsequently she was towed to Boston, where she was sold and converted into a coal barge. In November, 1892, whilst under tow and deeply laden with coal, she foundered on the Pollok Rip Shoal.

The *Mindoro* was launched in 1864, registered 1065 tons, and cost 123,607 dollars. Her first captain was also Charles H. Allen, Jr., who had her for three voyages. He was followed by the following captains : B. O. Reynolds, S. P. Bray, Jr., Henry Gardner, D. H. Hutchinson, W. Frank Powers, Charles Beadle, J. W. Luscomb and B. C. Creelman. The *Mindoro* sailed regularly to the East until 1893. On her arrival back at Boston in that year she was towed to Salem and laid up alongside Derby wharf until April, 1894, when she was sold and towed to New York, where she was converted into a coal barge.

The *Panay* registered 1190 tons and cost 74,580 dollars to build. Like the other two, she was considered a lucky ship. She sailed out of Boston to Manila until the nineties without breaking any records, but with steady consistent passages.

Pictures, photographs, and the lines of these three ships can be seen at the Peabody Museum, Salem.

The Barque "Amy Turner."

Another little Eastern trader built at East Boston in 1877 was the smart little barque *Amy Turner*, which came from the yard of Smith & Townsend. During her prime she was owned by C. B. Brewer & Co., the Honolulu merchants, her masters being Albert W. Newell and Charles A. Johnson.

Not long ago Dr. L. Vernon Briggs published an account of his trip as a passenger out to Honolulu in 1880. He gives a glowing character to Captain Newell. "I learned to know him as a man of rare abilities, and as a seaman he was unsurpassed. His noble character was plainly marked on his face." After the usual battle with Cape Stiff, the little *Amy Turner* arrived at Honolulu, 139 days out from Boston.

Her quickest passage was from Hongkong to Baltimore in 1895, when W. A. Pendleton was in command. After a quick run down the China Sea, she anchored off Anjer on Christmas Eve for 22 hours; she was off the Cape in 42 days, 53 days to St. Helena, and 66 to the Equator, whcih was crossed in 34° W. Her time from Hongkong to Baltimore was 87 days. Her outward passage, from New York to Honolulu was also a quick one, and the whole voyage was accomplished in 11 days under the year.

Amy Turner finished her active career under the "stars and bars " in 1912; she was then reduced to a barge and towed up and down the Pacific coast until 1916, when she was refitted as a barquentine and went to sea under the Red Ensign. A year later she caught fire and sank in Wellington harbour, but with ships worth their weight in gold she was raised, and in 1918 was once more sailing the seas rigged as a barque.

She finally succumbed to a typhoon in 1923, when bound with coal from Newcastle, N.S.W., to Manila. By this time the

Amy Turner was feeling the effect of her forty-six years of hard service, and the typhoon so strained her and opened her seams that at last pumping could not cope with the leaks.

A course was laid for Guam in order to gain shelter, and apparently during the worst of the storm the barque was actually within sight of the wireless station, though her rockets and other distress signals went unnoticed.

By this time the *Amy Turner* was almost unmanageable, with 15 feet of water in the hold, and every sea made a clean breach over her. By the following morning the bulwarks had gone, and the spare spars, breaking adrift, played havoc on the maindeck. Lastly the main hatch was stove in and the ship began to sink.

Only the two after boats had escaped destruction, and with incredible difficulty these were swung out and lowered. But by this time the ship already had her head under, and as she gave one of those sickly lurches which foretell the last moments of a sinking ship, the port boat caught in the rigging and turned over; the starboard boat, however, floated clear with two men in her, and two others were picked up as she drifted to leeward, half full of water and quite unmanageable in such a sea and wind, which, in spite of their frantic efforts, soon swept the boat out of sight of the sinking ship.

When last seen, the rest of the crew, including the captain, who was supporting his wife, were clinging to wreckage, whilst the ship's boy, Holland, went under striving to the last to cut the capsized boat free from the sinking ship.

Of the four men in the water-logged boat, one named West was the possessor of a master's certificate. He at once took command of the situation, with the other three men, Cornish, Tracey, and Lindholm, most loyally obeying him. His first endeavour was to reach Guam, but as the report said, "The elements were averse." Mackenzie Island, which was next steered for, was also missed. Whereupon the undaunted four decided to steer for the Philippines, 1600 miles away. And after 23 days of incredible hardship and suffering Maws Island, Mindanao, was finally reached. In its report, the Naval Court congratulated West and put on record the fact that the others owed their lives to his skill and energy.

During the seventies wooden barques of the type of the *Amy Turner*, and ranging from 500 to 1000 tons, were very popular. Indeed, there was hardly a port in Maine or Massachusetts that did not build and own several fast sailing barques.

One of the smartest was the *Harvard*, built by Atkinson & Fellmore at Newburyport in 1878. She was owned by Foster & Pray of Boston, and her last and best known commander was Lincoln A. Colcord. This barque was wrecked on Turk's Island in 1898.

Here are a few more worthy of a notice: *Cassandra* (Adam), 1127 tons, from Seabeck, Washington; *H. G. Johnson*, 1080 tons, from Newburyport; *Penobscot*, 1133 tons, from Bucksport, Maine; *Freeman*, 1197 tons, from East Boston; *Grace Deering*, 733 tons, from Cape Elizabeth; *Sarah S. Ridgeway*, 869 tons, from Wilmington; *Joseph A. Ropes*, 711 tons, from N. Weymouth; *Coryphene*, 811 tons, from Millbridge, Maine; *C. D. Bryant*, 929 tons, from Searsport; *Great Surgeon*, 908 tons, from East Boston; *Hiram Emery*, 799 tons, from Kennebunk.

All of these and many more were far more graceful and pleasing to the eye than any vessel of their size to-day, and far more efficient.

The Wreck of the "Alfred D. Snow."

The *Alfred D. Snow*, built and owned by Sam Watts of Thomaston, bore a close resemblance to his previous ships, the *Samuel Watts* and the *Alfred Watts*, and she was considered to have a very fair turn of speed. She was called after one of the partners of the New York shipbrokers, Snow & Burgess, in South Street, who usually did most of the business for the Thomaston shipowners.

The *Alfred D. Snow* went the usual round of American ships during the seventies and eighties, namely, general cargo from New York or Boston to San Francisco, and grain from San Francisco to Europe, or case oil to the Far East, and then home from either the Philippines or the West Coast.

On her last voyage, in 1888, she loaded in Sutton & Beebee's Line with general cargo from New York for San Francsico.

The old-time seaman who served in the square-rigger has many a beautiful sea picture stored up in his memory, which it is one of the consolations of his old age to recall with the aid of a good pipe of tobacco. The name *Alfred D. Snow* at once drew such a sea picture out of the smoke wreaths when mentioned to an ex-officer of the Down Easter *Joseph B. Thomas.*

The *Joseph B. Thomas* was lying in San Francisco Bay one summer evening, when the *Alfred D. Snow* came sailing up to the anchorage in a stiff breeze. Her black sides, wet with spray, sparkled and glittered in the sunshine, whilst her gleaming cotton canvas glowed with a rosy blush as it was touched by the golden beams of the setting sun. As she approached the anchorage she began to take in her sails, and as each was clewed up in the fresh breeze its rounded folds took on all the colours of the rainbow as the transparent pink of the sun's backstays mingled with the green reflections from the water and the pure azure of the upper sky. As the golden ball of the sun sank beneath the western horizon the *Alfred D. Snow* rounded-to under her mizen topsail, and anchored close to the *Joseph B. Thomas.*

The two ships were very chummy during the few weeks that they were in San Francisco together. The *Alfred D. Snow* loaded wheat for Liverpool, whilst the *Joseph B. Thomas* took in general cargo for New York.

The *Alfred D. Snow* was commanded by a Captain Willey, a rather slightly built man of some forty-five years of age, with jet black hair, moustache, and side whiskers. An old sailor, writing in the magazine *Sea Breezes*, thus describes Captain Willey :

I was very well acquainted with Captain Willey of the *Alfred D. Snow*, which was a fine ship of 2000 tons, but very cranky. She would not stand up unless she had 800 tons of ballast in her. Captain Willey had one ambition : that was to make a passage. He had a ship that could sail and he knew it. He was only 80 days out when he piled her up on Dunmore Head.

He was a very venturesome man. He was known to run seven days on dead reckoning without a sight until he was abreast of Holyhead. I should say it was a bit of luck on his side. He made a remark one time that that would be the way he would end his days. He was picked up warm on the beach.

This character for recklessness, and the time of 80 days given for the *Alfred D. Snow's* passage, are by no means agreed to by my friend who was aboard the *Joseph B. Thomas.* He declares that he had never heard Captain Willey spoken of as a reckless sail carrier, either before or after the wreck of the *Alfred D. Snow*. According to his version, the *Alfred D. Snow* was at least 140 days out when she went ashore, for the *Joseph B. Thomas* had arrived at New York about 120 days from San Francisco, was discharged and paid off, and he had arrived at Bristol, having caught the Cunard *Servia* to Liverpool, and been home several days when the gale which finished the *Alfred D. Snow*, and incidentally a number of other craft, blazed its way across the British Isles.

The *Alfred D. Snow* was lost with all hands, and the officer of the *Joseph B. Thomas* crossed to Ireland and was able to identify the bodies of Captain Willey, John Lermond the carpenter, and several others ; and he afterwards had the sad duty of handing the few personal belongings found upon the bodies to their sorrowing relatives at Thomaston.

There is just one other point I should like to refer to in regard to Mr. J. C. Leydon's remark about the *Alfred D. Snow* being cranky. Only an excessively prudent man would put 800 tons of ballast into one of Watts' ships, and that only with a clean-swept hold and for a trip in wintertime. It was quite usual for the captain of one of these skysail yard Down Easters to be content with 350 tons of San Francisco soapstone for a run up the North-West Coast in ballast, and 500 tons was considered sufficient to give a good sailing trim in a hard beam wind.

The Virtues of the Tar Pot.

Another big Down Easter built at Thomaston in 1877 was the *Baring Brothers*. In naming this ship Edward O'Brien aimed to pay a compliment to the British firm which shipped so many cargoes in Thomaston craft.

For many years this vessel was commanded by Captain Dick Thorndike. He was eventually succeeded by another well-known Thomaston shipmaster, Captain Ed. Masters. Captain Masters was an enthusiastic believer in the virtues of what used to be called the "good old British paint "—namely, tar—and when he took over the command of the *Baring Brothers* he had all the beautiful white paint scraped off her deck-houses, bulwarks, etc., and soaked the whole ship in Stockholm tar until she was black as a coal pit inside and out. Her topsides were tarred down to the copper, and on deck even her water-ways received a good coating.

The conversion from spotless white to glistening black took place at Mission Street Wharf, San Francisco. The enthusiastic Captain Ed. Masters had to put up with some very nasty remarks on his artistic tastes from his friends and brother seamen in the port, but he countered their sarcastic sayings by pointing out the saving in his paint bill.

Luckily perhaps for Captain Masters, the *Baring Brothers* never returned to her home port, Thomaston, or he may have had to put up with further opinions on the enormity of his conduct in desecrating a beautiful ship in such a way.

The " Alex Gibson."

The next ship after the *Baring Brothers* on the O'Brien stocks was the *Alex Gibson*, another big full-rigger of over 2000 tons. She was, I believe, named after the head of the firm who acted as agents for O'Brien's vessels in Liverpool.   Like all the Thomaston ships she was a good money-maker throughout the seventies and eighties, and she lasted well into the nineties, finishing her days in the lumber trade between California and Australia.

"Vigilant," a Hot Ship.

One of the most beautiful and also the fastest ships built in 1877 was the 1800-ton *Vigilant*.   Under Captain Gould she was known as a hot ship, and, as usual with vessels of that reputation, she was most beautifully kept up.

According to a writer in *Sea Breezes* she was very crank, and although extremely fast in light weather could not carry sail in hard winds without very careful watching.

The *Vigilant* must have made some fine sailing records in her time, but I have not been successful in unearthing any of them.

She was still in the Register under the ownership of Edward Laurence of Boston in 1900, but was out of it the following year.

The Mystery of the " Pharos."

The following passage from Paul Eve Stevenson's *Deep-water Voyage* points to a sea mystery of the *Mary Celeste* type.

The big clipper, *Pharos,* was found adrift in the Doldrums without a man aboard her. Everything was in its place, and not a boat lowered. Even the dishes lay upon the table with the food rotting in them, but there was not a soul to tell how she came to be unmanned.

She was an unlucky ship, for on her next voyage out she stayed. No one has seen plank or spar of her for twelve years, but the skipper and mate, who left her adrift in the Guinea current, were well known deep-watermen.

I have been unable to find out anything further about this strange event of the high seas. The late Captain N. G. Hatch, however, tells an amusing story about Captain Collyer, who was master of the *Pharos* for so many years.

The present day American no longer bears the least resemblance to the Uncle Jonathan as usually depicted by cartoonists, and possibly many people may think that the typical Jonathan, or Uncle Sam as he used to be called, was purely imaginary. This, however, is not true. The cartoonist's American was far from being a caricature, and was in fact a most common type, especially in the Southern States, throughout the greater part of the nineteenth century ; and the captain of the *Pharos,* in his speech, his manners, and his appearance, was a very fine example of this almost extinct American type, with his long, lean body, long, lean, shrewd face, humorous twinkling eyes, short goatee beard, and thin black cheroot.

When Captain Hatch first met the captain in the seventies it was to apply for the position of chief officer of the *Pharos.* Hatch, however, was refused the job as " old man " Collyer calculated that he might die on the next passage, and that if he slipped his cables he was not willing to entrust his ship to anyone who had not a master's ticket.

Some ten years later Captain Hatch, then in command of the coolie ship, *Boyne,* found himself moored in the Hooghly in the same tier with the *Pharos,* and at his ship chandler's, in the captain's room, he discovered the old skipper lolling back in the usual Indian chair and smoking his usual cigar. He astounded the old man by the following greeting, "How are you, Captain Collyer ? I am glad to see you have not yet slipped your cables." This, of course, led to a long yarn between the two skippers, and afterwards the "old man" of the *Pharos,* whose goatee was now snow-white, presented the *Boyne* with two barrels of apples, which had probably been picked from some Southern homestead of the real Uncle Sam pattern.

The big Maine built 2000-ton *Pharos* must not be confused with a British steel barque which was built at Grangemouth in 1891.

The Dismasting of the " Sintram."

This five topgallant yard ship, which was commanded for many years by Captain Woodside, and in her last days was a common sight on the West Coast of North America, coal droghuing between British Columbia, Puget Sound, and San Francisco, was a victim of a very curious dismasting when off the West Indies and homeward bound from the East.

The weather was fine with a clear sky, and only a four-knot breeze was blowing when, without any warning, all the ship's top hamper came tumbling down about the ears of her crew. The *Sintram* had been struck by a sudden whirlwind in the upper air which was not felt at all on deck. This storm, which came and went in a few seconds, must have been of the tornado type.

Another instance of such a whirlwind in the upper air was experienced by the Down Easter, *Reaper*, when in the North Pacific, homeward bound round the Horn. Although there was only a very light wind blowing on deck, a sudden gust aloft whipped all the light sails off the ship.

The sky at the time, as in the case of the *Sintram*, was quite free from cloud, except for a few wisps and feathers of white.

A Smart Passage by the " Florence."

This Goss & Sawyer three skysail-yarder must not be confused with the medium clipper which was launched by Sam Hall in 1856, owned by the well-known Captain R. B. Forbes, and commanded by the equally well-known Captain Philip Dumeresq.

The latter vessel continued to sail the seas until 1888, when she was stranded in the North Atlantic timber trade and became a total loss.

"SNOW AND BURGESS."

"FLORENCE."

"C. D. BRYANT" HOVE DOWN.

"STANDARD."

The later *Florence,* which was also a very smart ship, once made the run from Newcastle, N.S.W., to Honolulu in 35 days, the record for this trip being 34 days made by the *Marion Chilcott.*

"Levi G. Burgess" and "Snow & Burgess."

These two 1600-tonners, both of which were built by Samuel Watts at Thomaston, were amongst the longest lived of the Down Easters. The former was named after one of the partners, and the latter after the firm of Snow & Burgess, the New York shipbrokers.

Both vessels ended their days on the Pacific coast, the *Levi G. Burgess* in the salmon cannery trade, and the *Snow & Burgess* as a timber droghuer. The latter was converted into a five-mast schooner some years before the War, and changed owners several times.

On March 14, 1921, she arrived in Puget Sound after a long passage from Manila, having suffered considerable damage by heavy weather. After lying idle at Seattle throughout that summer she was sold by her owner, C. Henry Smith, at a public auction, for a breaking up price.

The *Levi G. Burgess* was still doing duty as a salmon cannery tender and looking as good as ever in 1924.

"Red Cloud."

One of the finest vessels built in 1878 was the 2000-tonner *Red Cloud.* She was also one of the fastest. For instance, on March 13, 1882, she arrived in Liverpool under Captain Taylor, only 99 days out from San Francisco. This is the best passage of which I have record, but there were probably many others quite as good.

The *Red Cloud* was a main skysail-yarder. After sailing in the San Francisco wheat trade throughout the booming eighties, she was later transferred to the oil trade from Pennsylvania to the East. She was eventually bought by the Germans, and became the *Carl Friedrich* of Bremen. She was stranded in November, 1893, and afterwards condemned.

A Floating Pigeon Loft.

One of the prettiest of the 1878 ships was C. V. Minott's *Standard,* a very smart little three skysail-yarder.

All her blocks were painted white, and old John Boyd, who was mate of the *Joseph B. Thomas*, which happened to be anchored close to her in San Francisco Bay on one occasion, was very sarcastic about the white paint and nicknamed her the "floating pigeon loft."

The *Standard* was still afloat, owned by the North Alaska Canning Co., when War broke out in 1914.

The Hell of a Ship, " L. Schepp."

The Chapman & Flint three skysail-yarder, *L. Schepp*, will be chiefly remembered amongst the Down Easters for the very stale joke which was made about her name, and in which seamen took a childish delight. For instance, the most common question put to those who served in her was : " What the hell of a ship do you belong to ? "

The best known commander of the *L. Schepp* was Captain Kendall.

In 1902 this ship was bought by T. J. Scully of New York, converted into a barge, and renamed *White Band*.

" John A. Briggs."

The biggest ship built on the Down East Coast in 1878 was the *John A. Briggs* of 2110 tons. She carried a main skysail over six topgallant yards, and was considered a smart sailer.

Most of the Down Easters gravitated to the Pacific coasting trade in their old age, and the *John A. Briggs*, under the ownership of G. Plummer of San Francisco, ran in the Californian coal trade for many years.

In 1902, when bound across from Newcastle, N.S.W., to San Francisco, she put into Auckland, N.Z., leaking ; but was patched up, and it was not until about 1907 that she suffered the fate of so many stoutly built American deep-watermen. She was then sold to the Seaboard Transportation Co. and converted into a towing barge.

" C. D. Byrant " Hove Down.

One of the smallest of the Down Easters built in 1878 was the little barque, *C. D. Bryant*, which registered under 1000 tons.

With the exception of the still smaller *Mabel I. Meyers*, the *C. D. Bryant* was the last square-rigger built at Searsport, the great home of the American sea captain.

Built by Josiah C. Dutch, and commanded by Jasper N. Nichols, she also had a long life, being still afloat, San Francisco owned, in 1914.

The illustration shows her hove down at Colon after being sold for 500 dollars.

" Manuel Llaguno."

The smartest ship launched in 1879 was Chapman & Flint's *Manuel Llaguno*. This vessel was designed and built by John McDonald at Bath. John McDonald was a pupil of Donald McKay's, with the result that about half a dozen of the finest Down Easters ever built came from his board, such as the *Manuel Llaguno, A. J. Fuller, St. Frances, St. James,* and *Henry B. Hyde*.

The *Manuel Llaguno* was one of the few ships which were given fidded royal masts. This was in order to allow her to strike them easily before going under Brooklyn Bridge.

She was a tall ship, crossing three skysail yards, and was considered a very smart sailer. As late as the nineties she was making good passages in the Cape Horn trade; for instance, 102 days from San Francisco to New York in 1895, and again in 1897.

She is said to have been the last sailing ship to load at Singapore for Boston. On this occasion she made the run in 100 days. The record for this passage was held by a ship called the *Charles C. Leary*, which, under Captain Baker, took 50 hours to Anjer, was seven weeks under all plain sail, and arrived at Boston 81½ days out.

The best known commander of the *Manuel Llaguno* was Captain Stackpole.

About 1910 this fine ship was bought by E. F. Luckenbach of New York and cut down to a barge, her name being changed to *Washington*.

O'Brien's " J. B. Walker."

This ship was named after the well-known Dr. Walker of Thomaston. Throughout her life under the O'Brien ownership, from 1879 until 1902, the *J. B. Walker* was most successfully commanded by Captain John E. Wallace, who retired from the sea when his ship went to D. B. Dearborn of San Francisco.

Captain Wallace, it will be remembered, was under twenty years of age when he took charge of the *J. B. Walker*, being easily the youngest shipmaster in the American Mercantile Marine.

After being sold, the *J. B. Walker* did not remain long in active service on the Pacific coast, being converted into a Luckenbach towing barge in 1904.

"Solitaire " and the "Red Record."

This five topgallant yarder was quite a smart vessel—a typical well-kept Cape Horner, " with masts and yards which shone like silver," but she had a very bad name amongst foremast hands as a hell-ship, and I fear that this was well deserved whilst she was commanded by Captain Sewall.

Captain Sewall was quite a young man when he had the *Solitaire*. With a mouth full of gold repaired teeth, with well-kept moustache and goatee beard, he was something of a dandy skipper, and it was evident that he had no mean opinion of himself. There is no doubt also that he was a smart shipmaster, but woe betide the unfortunate who fell foul of him for that man's lot was sure to be a sorry one.

Captain Sewall had the unenviable distinction of figuring more often in the *Red Record* than any other American shipmaster, with the exception of Merriman, of the *Commodore T. H. Allen*.

This is how the *Red Record* comments upon Captain Sewall :

Captain Sewall is one of the most notorious brutes in charge of an American ship. This is his fourteenth appearance in the *Red Record* in less than seven years. Well sustained charges of murder have been made against him, but he has gone scot-free every time. Once in Philadelphia in 1889, when he was in danger of conviction, he disappeared for a time, and afterwards healed the wounds of the complainants with a small consideration in cash.

Captain Sewall left the *Solitaire* in 1891 in order to take over the *Susquehanna*. He was succeeded on the former ship by Captain E. H. Thompson. Before the end of the nineties the *Solitaire* was converted into a Luckenbach barge.

"LEADING WIND."

Lent by Capt. Schutze.

"GRANITE STATE" ASHORE ON CORNISH COAST.

Photo by Gibson & Sons, Penzance.

Sundry Down Easters of the Seventies.

On looking through this chapter I find that there are a number of ships which have escaped mention, and which at any rate deserve a line or two.

I should like to draw attention to the superb photograph of the main skysail-yarder, *Augusta,* lying at moorings in the Hooghly in 1870, which has been reproduced in Lauriat's *Old Sailing Ships of New England.* The photograph shows the *Augusta* with her stunsail booms aloft on both fore and main.

Another fast and beautiful ship which was built in 1868 was the *Highlander,* for which Benjamin W. Stone paid 100,000 dollars in 1869.

The *Matchless,* which rescued the crew of the burning ship *Japan,* was a well-known Cape Horner under Captain Dawes. Whilst bound from Iloilo to Boston in 1883 she struck a rock in the Java Sea and sank on June 16. Her crew reached Anjer the next morning with little more than they stood up in.

A fine painting of this ship will also be found reproduced in *Old Sailing Ships of New England.*

The *Carrie Reed,* launched at Kennebunkport in the same year, 1870, had a very much longer life, being still afloat, under the name of *Adela* and the Chilian flag, when War broke out. This ship, however, did not sail for long under the Stars and Stripes, as she was sold to the Germans in 1876, when her name was changed to *Gustave & Oscar.*

There is one other American ship which was built in 1870 and which is deserving of mention, and that is the barque *Taria Topan,* named after a well-known merchant at Zanzibar. This pretty little barque belonged to Salem and was not a Cape Horner, but traded to the East Coast of Africa. She had a great reputation as a fast sailer, and between 1870 and 1893 was commanded by the following well-known Salem shipmasters, William H. Hathorne, William Beadle, Nathan A. Bachelder, Edward B. Trumbull, and J. Warren Luscomb.

In 1893 the *Taria Topan* was sold and diverted to the South American trade, but was totally lost on Horn Island on October 9 of the following year.

Of the 1873 ships, the big Bath full-rigger *Sterling* should have been mentioned

The pretty little main skysail-yarder *Leading Wind*, which was built at Bath in 1874, is probably still remembered in New Zealand, for she was on fire at Auckland in 1891, when commanded by Captain Francis H. Hinchley, and had to be scuttled, after which she was sold to local owners. Captain Hinchley was a very experienced shipmaster. He was a native of Barnstable, and gained his first command when he was only twenty-one years of age. This was the ship *Ocean Queen*, 829 tons, built by Moses Davenport at Newburyport in 1847. The *Leading Wind* was loading jute when she caught fire. After she had been raised she was bought by a Norwegian firm, who changed her rig to a barque and her name to *Fjord*.

One of the best sailers launched in 1874 was the Stockton-built *Willard Mudgett*. This barque, as late as 1901, sailed from Buenos Ayres to Cape Town in 15 days, which is extraordinary running for such a small vessel, as she averaged close on 300 miles a day for most of the way across the South Atlantic, having first weathered out a pampero. Captain Phineas B. Blanchard, her master, capped this performance by covering the 5400 miles between Cape Town and Barbados in 24 days. On her next voyage, the *Willard Mudgett* ran from Boston to Sierra Leone in 17 days, her daily average being nearly 230 miles. Her next passage was from Konakri, on the French Guinea Coast, to Turks Island, West Indies, in 14 days.

Of the ships built in 1875 which I have not already mentioned, the following should be noticed : *Bohemia*, commanded at one time by Captain Trask, afterwards the well-known San Francisco pilot ; the main skysail-yarder *George F. Manson*, rendered conspicuous by her brilliant red boot-topping ; the *Daniel J. Tenny*, which some say was the biggest ship ever built at Newburyport ; the *Fannie Tucker*, commanded by Captain Greenleaf ; the *Raphael*, commanded by that hard nut, Captain Sherman : the *Elwell*, commanded by Captain Barston ; the Portland ship *Rufus E. Wood*, commanded by Captain Gilkey ; and the *Henrietta*, commanded by Captain Andrew M. Ross ; this vessel is notable as being the only full-rigger ever built at Bucksville, South Carolina. The enterprising

J. C. Nickels of Searsport, instead of having the beams and other timbering for the new vessel shipped north, sent his foreman with a gang of carpenters, riggers, blacksmiths, and joiners, down to Bucksville in order to build the ship there. The *Henrietta* was stranded in a typhoon off Hiogo in August, 1895, and was afterwards condemned.

The *Elwell* distinguished herself in 1896 by breaking the record for the round voyage between San Francisco and Nanaimo, B.C., her times being :

Left San Francisco April 22	Arrived Nanaimo	April 29
„ Nanaimo May 2	„ 'Frisco	May 7

For this feat of sailing Captain J. E. Barston was rewarded by the gift of £110 and a suit of clothes.

The *Granite State*, built at Kittery, Maine, in 1877, should also be mentioned, as she was considered a very smart craft. After a successful career she was wrecked off the Cornish coast in November, 1895. She was the second *Granite State*, the first having been built at Portsmouth, N.H., in 1854 and wrecked in 1868.

In the spring of 1896 the Bath-built *Guy C. Goss*, which had arrived at Auckland, N.Z., with a lumber cargo valued at nearly £10,000, was arrested for debt on Saturday, April 10, whilst berthed at the Central Wharf. At midday a bailiff appeared, and nailed a writ to the mainmast. This had been issued by the Registrar of the Supreme Court, and claimed ship, freight and cargo in default of £1500 owing to the master and crew for wages. This incident shows the straits to which the owners of sailing ships are put in these days of oil and steam-driven vessels.

CHAPTER V.

THE DOWN EASTERS OF THE EIGHTIES.

Boom Years in the Cape Horn Trade.

THE years from 1881 to 1885, as I have already stated, were boom years in the Cape Horn trade, and during these years the finest wooden full-rigged ships ever built in the United States were turned out. American shipbuilders realised that if they were to hold their own against the magnificent fleet of British iron sailers in the San Francisco and European grain trade, it was necessary to produce vessels which were able to combine great carrying capacity with good speed and small upkeep and maintenance charges.

In his *American Marine*, Captain William W. Bates shows up the many difficulties which American owners and builders had to contend against in their rivalry with Great Britain, the greatest of which he states was the discrimination which Lloyd's made in favour of iron ships as against wooden ships. Bates does his best to prove, by many statistics, that the wooden Down Easters had smaller repair bills and fewer accidents to spars and sails than the British iron ships, and the table on next page, taken from one of his tables of statistics, is interesting on this point.

He also gives the statistics of German, Norwegian, French, Italian, Dutch, and Russian ships in the grain trade, but their numbers, as compared with the American and British, are so small (less than 150 all told) as to be not worth mentioning.

With the aid of the above and other tables Captain Bates tries to prove that the wooden Down Easters were superior in speed and efficiency, carried more, were more economical, turned out their cargoes in better order, and, lastly, were more seaworthy than the British iron-built ships.

126

As regards speed, Captain Bates contended that, although the British iron sailing ships had clipper lines, their passages were spoilt because of foul bottoms and overloading, whereas although no wooden Down Easters had been built from clipper models since the North and South War, they were able to do better through their superior all-round efficiency.

A FOUR-YEAR TABLE OF THE COMPARATIVE PERFORMANCE OF FLEETS, CARRYING GRAIN AND FLOUR FROM SAN FRANCISCO TO PORTS IN EUROPE, FROM JULY 1, 1881, TO JULY 1, 1885.

Description of Vessel	No. of Ships	No. Lost			No. in Peril				Accidents			
		Wrecked	Missing	Abandoned	Distress	Sprang a Leak	Jettisoned	Deck Swept	Spars and Sails	Collision	Grounded	Anchor and Chains
American wood ..	418	1	—	1	2	4	—	6	12	9	5	2
British wood ..	198	2	1	1	4	8	4	3	4	4	6	—
British iron	761	2	3	1	2	3	8	27	28	16	8	7

Captain Bates was of course trying his best to help the wooden Down Easter in her fight in the world's markets against the iron-built foreigner, and I think his object would have been helped better if he had devoted more space to descriptions of the beautiful wooden ships turned out in Down East ports during the early eighties rather than to the compilation of endless statistical tables, many of which were undoubtedly misleading.

Throughout the eighties the whole export trade of the North Pacific coast, from San Pedro in the South to Vancouver in the North, was increasing by leaps and bounds, and during this period the bay and water front of San Francisco, the forest-shaded waters of Puget Sound, and the tideway of the Columbia River were crowded with magnificent sailing ships loading the golden grain. Few of these vessels went to their ports of discharge without first putting in to the two famous ports of call, Queenstown and Falmouth.

Thus, the Queenstown anchorage and the Carrick Roads, Falmouth, even as late as the first years of the twentieth century, were often filled up with a fleet of square-rigged deep-watermen such as could not be equalled in beauty and efficiency even by the great convoys of East and West Indiamen which congregated in those roadsteads in the stirring days of the Napoleonic Wars.

"George Stetson " and " James Drummond."

There were no big 2000-tonners launched in 1880, which may be called the year before the boom.   The *George Stetson* of Bath and the *James Drummond* of Phippsburg were, however, noteworthy for their speed.   The *George Stetson*, which was a very fine five top-gallant-yarder, with a good sheer, was commanded by Captain Eb. Murphy, the brother of "Shotgun " Murphy.

The two brothers had a great race from San Francisco to Europe.   The *W. F. Babcock*, Captain Jim Murphy's command, had a three hours' lead of his brother through the Golden Gate, and carried a good breeze down to the Equator.   Here the " Babcock " was becalmed, and whilst she was lying motionless a ship came over the horizon astern, bringing up the breeze.   This turned out to be the *George Stetson*, which came up until she was almost alongside the "Babcock," when she also lost the wind.

Captain Eb. Murphy thereupon paid a visit to his brother, and they agreed to call for orders at Queenstown, unless the wind was more favourable for Falmouth.   Soon after this the ships parted company and did not meet again.

In the end the " Babcock " arrived at Falmouth 109 days out, and the " Stetson " at Queenstown, having been beaten by less than a week.   Captain Jim received orders to discharge at Antwerp, whilst Captain Eb. was sent to Liverpool.   The rivalry between the two brothers still continued.   The *George Stetson* got a quick discharge and sailed for Baltimore well ahead of Captain Jim, whose cargo was handled very slowly at Antwerp.   Thus the "Babcock " arrived off the Chesapeake a day after the *George Stetson* had sailed out with a cargo of coal for San Francisco.   Nevertheless, although Captain Jim had to give his brother such a long start, he managed to drop his anchor in San Francisco Bay just three hours ahead of Eb. Murphy in the *George Stetson.*

The struggle between the two Murphys was interrupted by Captain Jim's appointment to the new Bath four-master, *Shenandoah.*

I think that the *George Stetson's* best grain passage was made in 1895, when she arrived at New York on April 13, 103 days out from San Francisco.

The *George Stetson's* active service came to a finish before the end of the nineteenth century.

The *James Drummond,* in 1888, made the passage from New York to Astoria in 105 days. In 1905 she formed one of the huge fleet which was held up at Newcastle, N.S.W., owing to the coal strike. It was on this occasion that her skipper, H. C. Nason, talked very big about her sailing, and offered to bet any money on her beating the fleet in the race across the Pacific, which was due to come off as soon as the coal strike ended. He even declared that the *James Drummond* could tow the *Cutty Sark.*

Besides a great number of British ships, the following Down Easters were in Newcastle at the time : *W. F. Babcock, S. D. Carleton, A. J. Fuller, Governor Robie, Isaac Reed, General Fairchild, Kauliani,* and the strangely rigged *Olympic.*

When the race did come off, the big Britisher, *Daylight,* with a run of 60 days to San Francisco, was easily first, the pretty little *Kauliani* being second with a passage of 83 days, and I fear the *James Drummond* came in amongst the "also-rans."

This ship, after being owned by the California Shipping Co. until 1908, was then converted into a barge at Seattle, and henceforward operated by the Coastwise Steamship & Barge Co. of that port.

Riesenberg's "A. J. Fuller."

In 1881, the first of the boom years, over a dozen first-class Down Easters were launched. It would be very difficult to say which was the finest of these 1881 ships, for each one represented the best work of a noted builder.

Captain Felix Riesenberg, who gives such a splendid description of his voyage in the *A. J. Fuller* in *Under Sail,* writes as follows about his ship :

The "Fuller" carried a complement of sixteen hands forward, and a "boy," not counting the "idlers"—that is, the carpenter, cook and cabin steward—a small enough crew for a vessel displacing in the neighbourhood of 2500 tons deadweight, a craft 229 feet between perpendiculars, 41½ feet beam and 23 feet depth of hold, ship rigged, with skysails, royals, single t'gans'ls, double tops'ls, and courses. Her mainyard was 90 feet from tip to tip. A crojik was carried as well as a spanker. On her stays she carried flying jib, jib tops'l, jib, and fore topmast stays'l, main t'gallant stays'l, main topmast stays'l, mixen t'gallant stays'l and a main spencer completed her spread of canvas. When on a wind, in a whole-sail breeze, with crojik furled, and spanker set, the ship " Fuller " spread twenty-five kites to the wind.

Whilst she was owned by Flint & Co., the *A. J. Fuller* was commanded by three very well-known Searsport shipmasters. Captain Theodore P. Colcord had her first of all ; then came one of the Carvers, and finally Charles M. Nichols, the latter being in command in 1897 when Riesenberg made his voyage.

At the beginning of the twentieth century the " Fuller " came under the flag of the California Shipping Co. She was then taken over by Captain Dermot. For the next half-dozen years she ran with timber between Puget Sound and the Australian ports. It was about this time that Felix Riesenberg, when second mate of the ss. *Texan,* came upon his old ship at Tacoma. He describes her with such vividness and feeling that I cannot help quoting from his book. He writes :

Always keen for a look at the old ships, I brought my binoculars to bear on a new arrival in the harbour. Something familiar about the craft held my attention as I scanned her point by point, running the glasses along the full length of her sheer. The wheelhouse aft ; the gig, upturned on the cabin trunk ; the gangway bridge from the break of the poop to the gallows frame over the main fife-rail ; the old familiar line of the forecastle-head, and the forward house with long boat and pinnace upturned and lashed to skids ; all were the same, the same but sadly out of tune. A dirty stack rose from an upright donkey boiler. Her paint was grey in the distance. Aloft she fared not quite so well. Her lower spars were painted " mast colour," that sloppy invention of the steamboat seaman. The doublings still retained a trace of varnish, but topmasts and topgallant and royal masts were dull with grease. As for her yards, they were not square and the skysail poles were gone. Still the old precision of her shrouds and backstays, her dead eyes true to a hair with the line of bulwark, these remained. When she swung with the tide, her black transom across the setting sun, I picked out the letters in faded gilt upon her stern, *A. J. Fuller.*

"A. J. FULLER."

" JOSEPH B. THOMAS."

" JOSEPH B. THOMAS."

That night he clambered aboard his old ship. The captain happened to be ashore, but he was welcomed by the mate.

We spent a pleasant hour yarning about the old ship, her points of sailing, her habit of bitterly complaining in a seaway as her timbers creaked and groaned under their load. She still carried her back-breaking bilge pumps, but her main pumps worked by a chain messenger to the winch. When the wind blew hard enough, so he assured me, she gave evidence of splendid speed, even with her cut-down rig.

Soon after this visit of Riesenberg's the *A. J. Fuller* was bought by the Northwestern Fisheries Co. of San Francisco. Just about the end of the War she arrived in Seattle harbour with a cargo of salmon, and she had not been long anchored before the Japanese liner, ss. *Mexico Maru*, came charging into her during a dense fog. The old ship quickly settled down in 40 fathoms, and there she still lies, at the bottom of Seattle harbour.

Chapman's "E. B. Sutton."

This beautiful Bath three skysail-yarder was named after a member of the New York firm of Sutton & Beebee, who were shippers in the New York and San Francisco general cargo trade. After running steadily to and fro round the Horn, the *E. B. Sutton*, like most of her sisters, was cut down into a barge and condemned to the coasting coal trade.

When the Great War broke out, however, she was refitted, and, rigged as a barque, sailed out of New York for the River Plate. She then loaded wheat for Sharpness. Except for her stumpy rig she looked almost as good as when she left the ways, during the short time that she was free of the degrading tow-rope.

"Iroquois," "Arabia," and "Parker M. Whitmore."

These three big carriers were all of very similar appearance. With their six topgallant yards and heavy lines, they looked rather clumsy compared with the typical single topgallant three skysail yard Down Easter.

The *Arabia* was one of the last sailing ships to be wrecked on the Diego Ramirez rocks. She broke up almost at once in the tremendous surf running up on those dreaded reefs, which lie just 18 marine leagues south-west of Cape Horn. The crew of the *Arabia* were most fortunate in escaping with their lives, for another vessel happened to be in the vicinity and succeeded in taking them off the wreck, afterwards landing them at Monte Video.

The *Iroquois* was wrecked in March, 1902, when under the command of Captain C. Thompson.

The *Parker M. Whitmore* had disappeared from the Register some ten years before this date, and I have not been able to find out what was her end.

The Handsome "Tacoma."

This three skysail yard Goss & Sawyer ship was a graceful vessel, with plenty of sheer. During the eighties she was a well-known member of the Cape Horn fleet. Then for a short while she ran in the lumber trade between the Californian coast and the Colonies. Finally, just before the end of the nineteenth century, she became one of the Alaska Packers' fleet, and she was still making her annual passage to the North when War broke out.

The square-rigger, *Tacoma*, must not be confused with the four-mast auxiliary schooner which was launched at Seattle during the last year of the War. This latter vessel sailed on her maiden voyage from Port Arthur (Texas) to Sydney with a cargo of oil, and flying the Norwegian flag. She took her departure in October, 1918, and nine months later put into Moreton Bay with her sails blown away and her Diesel engines out of action. After this she was towed to Sydney, and arrived there exactly twelve months after leaving Texas. At Sydney her engines were removed, she changed her flag to the Stars and Stripes, and her name to *Helen B. Sterling*, and henceforward traded between New South Wales and New Zealand in the coal and lumber trades. At last, in 1922, after being severely battered by a cyclone, she was abandoned between Norfolk Island and the Three Kings.

Captain Lermond's "Joseph B. Thomas."

This vessel was built for Captain Lermond by Watts, but the former, owing to the dismasting of his ship, the *Samuel Watts*, whilst crossing the Atlantic, was too late to take her on her maiden passage, and Captain H. A. Hyler sailed her out to San Francisco, where he handed her over to Captain Lermond, who came overland.

The *Joseph B. Thomas* was a main skysail-yarder with a dead-weight capacity of close on 3000 tons. She was not amongst the clippers of the Cape Horn fleet, but under the skilled guidance of Captain Lermond made a lot of money for her owners whilst keeping singularly free from trouble of every sort.

Captain Lermond commanded this ship for 26 years, until 1908, when she was sold to the California Shipping Co., and throughout this time the *Joseph B. Thomas* sailed to every part of the world, and carried every kind of cargo, without a call on the underwriters. The ship's longest passage was one of 189 days to Kobe, Japan. During this long passage her stock of provisions got very low, and when the pilot boat came alongside one of the Down Easter's hungry boys managed to pinch some of the pilot's potatoes, and, gobbling them up raw, declared that they were sweeter than any apples.

The *Joseph B. Thomas*, under Captain Lermond, was a very happy ship, for he was one of the kindest of shipmasters, and would allow no belaying-pin or knuckle-duster methods of discipline. She had a second mate, at one time, named John Powers, who came from Waterford and considered himself something of a " bucko," but he was not given any chance to show his talents as a crew handler under Captain Lermond's beneficent regime.

The *Joseph B. Thomas* did not remain long in active service after being bought by the California Shipping Co., for in 1910 I find her registered as a barge belonging to Scully's Towing and Transportation Line of New York.

The Hungry "Reuce."

The *Reuce*, which was a very similar ship to the *Joseph B. Thamas*, was one of the few Cape Horners which were noted for bad food. In November, 1889, she arrived in San Francisco with 17 men down with scurvy, one of whom died. Her master and officers, also, had a very hard name, the *Reuce* being twice listed in the *Red Record*. On the first occasion the district court awarded her sick crew 3600 dollars damages. On the second occasion the trouble aboard the *Reuce* seems to have been ill-treatment rather than bad food.

Reuce arrived at San Francisco in January, 1891. One of the seamen, named Blohm, seems to have had a specially unpleasant time. During one night off the Horn he was trussed up to the mizen stay by the two mates, and hung there, with his hands lashed behind his back, for over an hour. Soon after the ship had had arrived in San Francisco this unfortunate tried to escape in a shore boat, but the boat capsized and the man was drowned.

The *Reuce* was sold to the California Shipping Co., at the beginning of the twentieth century, but remained in active service for another dozen years.

The " William J. Rotch " of New Bedford.

This fine five topgallant, main skysail-yarder was one of the New Bedford fleet owned by W. H. Besse. She was commanded by Captain Lancaster until the beginning of the twentieth century, when she was sold to T. Norton & Co., of New York, and was renamed *Helen A. Wyman.*

She continued under sail for the next eight or nine years, but was then cut down to a barge for Scully's Towing and Transportation Line.

The "General Knox."

The fall of 1881 saw the launch of another big ship from O'Brien's yard. This was the *General Knox*, the command of the benevolent Captain Dave Libby.

After voyaging with steady regularity in the Cape Horn trade the *General Knox* caught fire in the nineties whilst at her eastern loading port, and was so badly burnt about the decks that she had to be cut down to her 'tween decks, after which she was sold to Luckenbach to be towed, for the rest of her sea life, to and from the Chesapeake coal ports.

Flint's " John McDonald."

This splendid three skysail-yarder, which was built and owned by Flint, and named after the famous designer, was kept " shining and sailing " by that most capable Captain Storer.

The following story is a typical example of the treatment

"ABNER COBURN."

Lent by Capt. Schutze.

"CHARLES E. MOODY."

Lent by Capt. L. R. W. Beavis.

"I. F. CHAPMAN."

Lent by J. Randall.

of sailors by the crimps and boarding-house runners of San Francisco in the eighties and nineties. One morning the *Joseph B. Thomas* arrived in San Francisco Bay from Liverpool, and anchored close to the *John McDonald*, which, with a cargo of wheat, was awaiting her crew. The anchor of the *Joseph B. Thomas* was hardly on the ground before her fo'c'sle crowd were being plied with the contents of black bottles and offered well paid jobs "up country" or "in a bar" by the runners of Alec. Jackson and Billie McCarty, with the result that they and their bags were soon on their way to the shore in the runners' boats.

It so happened that Mrs. Lermond and Mrs. Storer were relatives, and on the following morning the third mate and two of the remaining hands on the *Joseph B. Thomas* rowed Mrs. Lermond and her children across to the *John McDonald* to visit her relation. The scene that greeted the visitors as they pulled alongside brought the blood to the face of the indignant third mate, for up the gangway of the outward bounder practically the whole of the *Joseph B. Thomas's* late crew were being bundled by the runners. Most of these unfortunate hands were Scandinavians, and were more or less unconscious, drugged or drunk, but two of them, Steve Brodie, of Yarmouth, N.S., and Charlie McDonald, of Prince Edward Island, two superb Blue-nose sailors, were not so far gone, and began to object to the rough handling of the runners, and there and then, in front of Mrs. Lermond and her children, these two fine sailormen had their faces pounded to a jelly with knuckle-dusters and slung shot. Later in the same day Mrs. Lermond waved a sad good-bye to her late shipmates as she went over the side. The *John McDonald* was getting under way, and the men, who had only just arrived after a long passage in the *Joseph B. Thomas*, were walking wearily round the capstan of the outward bounder, and bravely trying to put some warmth into the chorus, " Good-bye, fare you well, Juliana, my dear."

The *John McDonald* had a good reputation for speed. In 1891 she sailed from Yokohama to Port Townsend in 24 days. In 1896 she left New York for San Francisco on March 9, and was spoken a month later in 9° S., 31° W., which is pretty good sailing. On her last voyage under Flint she arrived at Hongkong on December

1, 1899, 159 days out from New York.   At the end of this voyage she came under the flag of the California Shipping Co., but did not last long under the San Francisco ownership, for she has been missing since January, 1901.

The " I. F. Chapman."

It is curious to note the rivalry between the two Bath shipbuilders, Benjamin Flint and I. F. Chapman.   When Flint laid down the *John McDonald* of 2281 tons gross, Chapman laid down a 2146-ton six topgallant, three skysail yard ship, and named her after himself ; and it is a question which was the finer ship of the two. Until 1896 the *I. F. Chapman* was commanded by Captain J. A. Thomson, and was mostly in the San Francisco grain trade.

Captain Thomson nearly got into trouble in July, 1891, on his arrival in New York from San Francisco, for he was arrested on the complaint of his ship's carpenter.   Apparently the carpenter was a " drunken old swab " who more than tried the captain's patience.   At last, Captain Thomson determined to give his useless petty officer a touch of Cape Horn discipline, and he ordered him to be ironed hand and foot and triced up to the spanker boom for an hour, but before the hour was up the soft-hearted man at the wheel cut the carpenter down, whereupon he also was triced up. However, on the case being tried, the Commissioner found that the punishment was not very cruel, and Captain Thomson was acquitted.

He was succeeded by Captain C. S. Kendall.   Finally Captain R. Banfield had the ship for the two or three years before she was cut down to a barge.   Under Captain Kendall she seems to have been employed mostly in the Honolulu sugar trade.

Although the *I. F. Chapman* had many a dusting off the Horn, one of her worst experiences was crossing the Atlantic in midwinter with a salt cargo from Liverpool to New York.   On this occasion with the thermometer below zero she was towed up New York Bay 101 days out from the Mersey.

During the late nineties and the first few years of the twentieth century the *I. F. Chapman*, with a number of other Cape Horners, was engaged in the Hawaiian sugar trade.   On one of these sugar passages, from Honolulu to Philadelphia, she was actually six weeks off the Horn, going east, and during one middle watch pitched the fore topgallant mast clean over the side.

In the spring of 1899 Captain Kendall, whilst loading sugar at Honolulu, agreed to race the *W. F. Babcock* and *St. Catherine* to Delaware Breakwater for a purse of 1000 dollars. The "Babcock" sailed from Honolulu on March 8, and the "Chapman" on the 14th, whilst the *St. Catherine* left Hilo on March 17. After an average passage all three ships arrived off Delaware Breakwater on the same day, July 16. The *I. F. Chapman*, by the way, loaded about 3400 tons of sugar.

During Captain Kendall's regime the ship had a fine pair of mates, Curtis and Darlington, and in 1902, under these officers, she made the run between San Francisco and Seattle in just a week. She was only half loaded at the time, and at Seattle completed with canned salmon. She afterwards made the run home to New York in a little over 100 days.

After being cut down as a Scully towing barge about 1909, the old ship was re-rigged as a barque during the War and was given a steam donkey engine and a Delco electric light plant. As late as 1920 she sailed from New York, coal laden for Rio. Neither her captain nor her mate had had much experience of sail, although her second mate had served in the ship during her palmy days. For a crew, she had 11 A.B.'s and 3 O.S.'s.

The poor old ship, with worn-out gear and rotten sails, was but a ghost of her former proud self, and with insufficient sail aft not only sailed poorly but handled as if she was still a barge. When she was 30 days out the old-timer put in to Barbadoes leaking. Here she lay for six months. Then the coal was discharged and ballast taken in, and finally the *I. F. Chapman* limped back to New York.

Both for man and ship, death or shipwreck in the prime of life is preferable to a neglected and decrepit old age.

"St. Francis."

There was still a third ship built for Chapman & Flint in 1882, and this was the skysail-yarder, *St. Francis*, which came from the board of, and was built by, McDonald. Under that jovial good fellow, Captain Dave Scribner, the *St. Francis* was a very happy ship. She was also a smart sailer, her best performance being in July, 1906, when she left Algoa Bay three days after the tramp steamer, *Ben Vrackie,* had left Cape Town, and arrived at Port Hunter within an hour or two of the steamer. At this time the *St. Francis* belonged to the California Shipping Co. and was commanded by Captain T. Murray.

About four years before the War she was sold to the Alaska Fisherman's Packing Co. of Astoria, which must not be confused with the Alaska Packers Co. of San Francisco.

When War broke out in 1914 the following well-known members of the old Cape Horn fleet were still sailing the seas with Astoria on their sterns : *St. Francis, Reuce* and *W. B. Flint.*

The " Big Edward."

The *Edward O'Brien II* was called the " Big Edward " to distinguish her from the *Edward O'Brien I,* and was a full-rigger of over 2200 tons.

The O'Brien ships, unlike those of Chapman & Flint, carried no such lofty elegances as skysails, nor did they attempt to break records. They were just good, wholesome, solidly built carriers. They could always be distinguished from other Down Easters by their old-fashioned bright line, some six planks immediately under the deck line beading being always kept scraped and varnished. In the twentieth century, when hard competition compelled the strictest economy, the O'Brien bright line was painted varnish colour.

Whilst commanded by Captain D. P. Oliver during the eighties and early nineties the *Edward O'Brien* seems to have suffered from a series of " bucko " mates, and the *Red Record* has the following entries against her :

Edward O'Brien, Captain Oliver, arrived in San Francisco, February, 1890. First mate Gillespie charged with most inhuman conduct. He knocked down the second mate and jumped on his face. Struck one seaman on the head with a belaying-pin, inflicting a ghastly wound, then kicked him on the head and ribs, inflicting life marks. He struck another man on the neck with a capstan-bar, then kicked him into insensibility. Struck the boatswain in the face because the latter failed to hear an order. Gillespie charged and admitted to bail.

"ABNER COBURN" IN SYDNEY HARBOUR.

"HENRY FAILING."

Edward O'Brien, Captain Oliver, arrived in San Francisco, May, 1892. First and second mates, Carey and True, began to "make things lively " as soon as the ship sailed from New York. Crew complained, and the first mate swore he would subdue all hands before they reached Cape Horn. Second mate True offered to fight any three men in the forecastle ; one man accepted the challenge. Second mate retreated aft, seized a belaying-pin, and with the assistance of the cook, steward and carpenter knocked down three men and placed them in double irons. One man, who was knocked senseless, was dragged into the cabin where the second mate kicked him in the face and body as long as he could swing his foot. Captain protested against the brutality, but the mate paid no attention. Men were assaulted with belaying-pins every day. Ship leaking badly off the Horn ; men had to be constantly at the pumps in cold and wet weather. Crew said they would spend all their wages in having the mates punished. Mates disappeared and were not punished.

In 1893 the *Edward O'Brien* was 218 days coming to London from Tacoma. Six years later, when commanded by Captain R. Banfield, this big ship was wrecked in March, 1899.

The Clipper "Cyrus Wakefield."

The *Cyrus Wakefield* was the first Thomaston ship to have double topgallant yards, and with her main skysail she had a more lofty and imposing appearance than the other vessels built at that port. She was also considered to be the fastest ship ever turned out at Thomaston. She does not, however, seem to have made any notable sailing records until young Hibberd took her over in the middle nineties.

It so happened that the *Cyrus Wakefield* and *Joseph B. Thomas* arrived together in San Francisco at a time when grain freights were very low. Sam Watts thereupon decided to lay the ships up and wait for better times. Whilst awaiting a rise in the freight market, Captain Hyler gave up the command of the *Cyrus Wakefield* and went home ill.

Captain Lermond of the *Joseph B. Thomas* at once urged Sam Watts to give the ship to her young chief officer. Watts, who knew he could rely upon the judgment of the master of the *Joseph B. Thomas*, agreed to accept Lermond's advice, and appointed I. N. Hibberd to the command of his crack ship, although Hibberd was barely 25 years of age.

No sooner was the new captain appointed than Captain Lermond persuaded his owner to charter the *Cyrus Wakefield* at 20s. grain for Europe. Captain Hibberd proceeded to drive the *Cyrus Wakefield* from San Francisco to Liverpool and back in 8 months and 2 days, his return passage round the Horn being one of the best ever made, for the ship was only 100 days from Liverpool to San Francisco and sailed through the Golden Gate only 11 days from the Equator.

This was followed by further smart passages. On March 3, 1897, the ship docked in New York only 91 days from San Francisco, and her next voyage from San Francisco to New York was also the best of the year. This time she arrived on January 5, 1899, 100 days out.

The youthful captain of the *Cyrus Wakefield* has been immortalised by Peter B. Kyne in that very entertaining sea story, *Cappy Ricks*.

The *Cyrus Wakefield* disappeared from the Register about 1901, but I believe she was then commanded by a Captain Henry.

" John Currier."

I have only two notes about this fine Newburyport ship. On October 4, 1893, she was towed into Hongkong, having been dismasted in a typhoon. Then on August 9, 1907, she was totally wrecked whilst salmon laden at Nelson's Lagoon, Bristol Bay, Alaska.

The Beautiful " Abner Coburn."

The *Abner Coburn*, which was built by W. Rogers of Bath, was one of the longest lived of the Down Easters, being still in the Alaskan trade in 1926.

Both the illustration showing her under sail and that lying in Sydney harbour with her sails hanging in the buntlines give one a very good idea of the beauties of the old-time wooden ship.

Such a ship and the modern steam tramp might well be compared to Beauty and the Beast, for nothing more beautiful has ever been constructed by man than such a vessel as the *Abner Coburn*, and at the same time nothing more ugly than the steam or oil-driven steel box, with its shapeless bow and stern and forest of derricks.

"Henry Failing."

Another 1882 vessel of about the same tonnage was the *Henry Failing.*

In 1902, when coal laden from Newcastle, N.S.W., to San Francisco, the *Henry Failing* put into Auckland, N.Z., leaking. After this she was cut down to a barge, but she was re-rigged as a barque when War broke out and was sunk soon afterwards.

Minott's " Berlin."

The illustration shows this ship about to load lumber. After running her successfully in the Cape Horn trade until the end of the nineteenth century, C. V. Minott sold her to G. E. Plummer. Then about 1907 the *Berlin* was bought by the Alaska Packers Association of Portland, Oregon, which must not be confused with the Alaska Packers Association of San Francisco.

The old ship survived the War and was still doing duty on the Pacific coast in 1922.

The " W. F. Babcock."

This three skysail-yarder, which was built and owned by the Sewalls of Bath, was named for William Fitzpatrick Babcock, a cousin of the celebrated commander of the *Young America.* W. F. Babcock went to San Francisco as early as 1850 and became one of the managers of the Pacific Mail Steamship Company, of which Captain D. S. Babcock became the president.

For her first eight years the *W. F. Babcock* was commanded by Captain Jim Murphy, and during this time she is said to have paid for herself twice over. Under Murphy, with her jet black hull set off by a gold stripe, her scraped spars shining with varnish, and her tall rig, the *W. F. Babcock* was considered one of the best-looking of the Down Easters.

I have already described her race with the *George O. Stetson.* In spite of her success against that ship, and the fact that in 1897 she averaged 232 knots for a period of 20 days between Honolulu and New York, the *W. F. Babcock* cannot be numbered amongst the fastest of the Down Easters, for I can find no outstanding records to her credit, in spite of the fact that she was so hard driven that in her old age she had to be given a windmill pump as she worked very much in a seaway.

The *W. F. Babcock* had one peculiarity, which gained her the nickname of the " Balky Babcock." Sometimes in heavy weather she would get into the trough of a sea and refuse to move, and nothing her captain or mates could do in the way of sail handling or steering could make her resume her course until she chose. Her balking trick was most often exercised when off the pitch of the Horn, and it sometimes happened when she had a fair wind, to the great annoyance of her officers.

It is probable that a larger or different shaped rudder would have stopped this evil habit of balking.

After sailing the "Babcock" for seven years Captain Murphy handed her over to Captain Robert J. Graham. Captain Graham was one of the best passage makers amongst American shipmasters. He was born in Philadelphia in 1855 and went to sea at the age of sixteen. During his seafaring career he made fifty-two voyages round Cape Horn, retiring from his profession, shortly before the War, to an orchard ranch at Cashmere, Washington, where he died in March, 1929.

Captain Graham commanded the *Babcock* for eight years, during which time she made some astonishing passages for a vessel of her build, two of the best of which were:

Honolulu to New York	.. ..	92 days
Manila to Newcastle, N.S.W. ..	..	53 ,,

The *W. F. Babcock* was considered one of the luckiest ships ever built by Sewall. During the time that she was commanded by Captains Murphy and Graham she never had a bad accident or lost a spar of any size. Captain Graham left her to take over the *Erskine M. Phelps*, and he was succeeded by Captain Colly.

The old ship was very nearly lost when timber droghuing before the War. On January 20, 1910, she left Port Townsend with 1,600,000 feet of timber for Table Bay. Soon after clearing the Straits she had her rudder damaged in a hard gale, and was obliged to put into Honolulu for repairs. On her passage being resumed all went well until she reached Lat. 34° S., Long. 184° W. Here a cyclone was encountered, and the ship very nearly went to

"BERLIN."

"W. F. BABCOCK."

Lent by Capt. Schutze.

the bottom. For six hours she lay on her beam ends, and the whole of her deck cargo, amounting to 200,000 feet of timber, was swept over the side. Oil was freely used, but for some hours the ship's condition was critical, for she was straining and leaking badly.

The weather did not moderate for three days, and then it was found that the foremast was badly sprung; also the foreyard and fore upper topsail yard had been carried away, and in many other ways the ship was so crippled that her captain decided to make for Sydney, N.S.W., instead of rounding the Horn.

At this time the *Babcock* belonged to C. R. Bishop of San Francisco.

Her last passage before being cut down to a barge by Scully was from San Francisco to New York and she was then far from tight, the windmill pump being very necessary to keep her afloat.

During the War she was re-rigged as a barque, and for a short time once more sailed the seas.

The Smart "St. James."

The finest and largest three-mast barque ever built in a Down East port was Flint's *St. James,* designed and built by John McDonald in 1883. Besides being considered one of the smartest sailers under the Stars and Stripes, she was also one of the happiest. This was especially the case under Captain Banfield, who had her during the nineties.

Here is a testimony to her qualities given by a foremast hand in *By Way of Cape Horn* :

"Oh, but she's just a daisy, she is ! Why, she's a square-rigged yacht. And go, I tell you honest, I saw her log 15 knots on that voyage under topsails and foresail between Tristan d'Acunha and the Cape ; and if ever you want to sail with a nice man, you ship with Cap'n Banfield ; there's no better."

The voyage referred to was one of 97 days, made between New York and Shanghai in 1894-5. The *St. James,* which was very lofty for a barque, and crossed two skysail yards, made several fine runs with oil to China and Japan, of which the above was the best.

At the beginning of the twentieth century this beautiful barque came under the ownership of the California Shipping Co., and after ten years on the Pacific coast was cut down, like so many of her sisters, to a barge, and under the flag of the Coastwise Steamship & Barge Co. of Seattle, spent the rest of her days towing up and down the Western American coast.

The Skysail-yarder " S. P. Hitchcock."

If the *St. James* was the happiest of Flint's ships, the *S. P. Hitchcock* was undoubtedly the happiest of I. F. Chapman's. This at any rate was the case during the time when she was commanded by Captain E. O. Gates.

The average deep-water foremast hand's opinion of his officers may usually be relied on for fairness, and I will therefore quote again from *By Way of Cape Horn* to show Jack's opinion of Captain Gates :

"If ever I sign in an American ship again, it will be the *S. P. Hitchcock*. When me and Colman came round from Honolulu in her a little while ago, we did more work in one watch there than we do here in a day, and there wasn't any yelling at all. You never saw Cap'n Gates on the maindeck neither ; he knew his business."

Captain Gates, like Captain Banfield, although he kept his ship shining and drove her hard, would allow no hazing or ill-treatment of the men, and from the above remarks of one of his hands it was evident that his policy paid, and that he could get more work out of his men by kind treatment than a " bucko " officer was able to do with the aid of belaying-pin and boot.

The *S. P. Hitchcock* had a number of smart passages to her credit. Under her first commander, Captain Nicholls, she arrived at Liverpool on June 18, 1886, only 91 days out from San Francisco. In 1898, under Captain Gates, she came home from Honolulu to New York in 92 days. Her best trans-Pacific passage between Newcastle, N.S.W., and San Francisco was made in 1901, when she arrived at the latter port on September 13, 52 days out.

This beautiful ship was thrown high and dry on the Kowloon sea wall during the disastrous Hongkong typhoon of September, 1906.

The " Tillie E. Starbuck."

This vessel was the first full-rigged ship ever built of iron in the United States. She was launched on April 14, 1883, from the yard of Mr. John Roach at Chester, Pennsylvania. The following details of her construction I have taken from the first volume of *The Shipping World* :

She is 270 ft. overall, 248 ft. on the load waterline, 42 ft. beam, 23 ft. depth of hold, and a deadweight capacity of 3750 tons, with a draught of 21 ft. 6 in. Her keel is of the best hammered iron, 10 by 3 in., the stem and stern-post of the same material 10 by 4½ in. Her frames are 6 by 3½ in., spaced 2 ft. from centre to centre. The lower deck beams are 11 in. by $\frac{11}{16}$ of an inch, and those of the upper deck are 10 in. by $\frac{10}{16}$ of an inch. The plating is laid lap-streak throughout, $\frac{15}{16}$ of an inch from the garboard, and $\frac{12}{16}$ above the bends. Both decks are laid in narrow planking of yellow pine. The upper deck, for its whole length, is diagonally braced, while there are diagonals at each partner in the lower deck, and under each mast for a space of 20 ft. is a heavy rider keelson.

She has been built under special survey of the Bureau Veritas, and will receive their highest classification. On deck she will have a low topgallant forecastle, and between the fore and main hatches is an iron deck-house for the crew, and a small engine for hoisting or pumping. She will have a poop-deck about 90 ft. long, beneath which is the cabin. Abaft on this deck is a wheel-house fitted with right and left screw steering gear. An elliptical stern terminates an overhang much longer than is usual, which it is thought will render her easier when passing through the heavy rollers at the mouth of the Columbia River. She has a steel bowsprit, and three hollow masts made from the best fire-box steel, strengthened inside with angle iron. The ship will have double topsail and single topgallant yards, and three standing skysail yards. Her lower yards are 90 ft., and her upper topsail yards on her fore and main are 72 ft. in length.

The *Tillie E. Starbuck* was owned until the end of the nineties by W. H. Starbuck. Her first master was W. A. Rogers, and he handed over in the nineties to Captain Curtis.

It was whilst under Captain Curtis, a noted sail carrier, and with the famous Donald Nicholson as mate, that the *Tillie E. Starbuck* made her best passages. She could not, however, compare as regards speed with many of the wooden ships of her size and date.

After being owned by Luckenbach for a year or two at the beginning of the twentieth century, the *Tillie E. Starbuck* came under the control of Welch & Co. of San Francisco, and her last skipper was Captain W. W. Winn.

In 1905 she got badly ashore and had to have a number of new plates put into her bottom by the Union Iron Works at San Francisco.

The *Tillie E. Starbuck* was lost off the Horn whilst bound out to Honolulu from New York in 1907. Her crew, with the single exception of the mate, were successfully taken off the sinking Down Easter by the British vessel, *Cambuskenneth*, on August 16, and landed at Coquimbo, Chile.

The Hell-ship " Benjamin F. Packard."

This well-known skysail-yarder was built and owned by the Bath firm of Goss, Sawyer & Packard. Two of the partners had already had ships named for them, the *Guy C. Goss* and the *E. F. Sawyer*, and in 1883 Benjamin F. Packard, the third partner, had the honour of seeing his name on the bow of the finest ship in the firm's fleet.

The *Benjamin F. Packard* was commanded for fifteen years by Captain Zachary Allen, one of the toughest customers in the Cape Horn fleet, and at one time he had his own son with him as mate, a 6-ft. " bucko " who also delighted in a " rough house." Both Captain Allen, his son, and the ship's second mate, named Turner, were constantly in trouble with the authorities on arrival in port, owing to their methods of discipline, and their fierce man-handling not only received the attention of the *Red Record* but gained for the ship the curious nickname of " The Battleship of the American Merchant Marine."

Captain Zach, however, managed to make some smart passages in his hell-ship, the best being 83 days from 'Frisco to New York in 1892.

From the early nineties until she was sold to the Northwestern Fisheries Co., of Port Townsend, the *Benjamin F. Packard* was managed by A Sewall & Co.

The Alaska salmon packing trade had the name of being the toughest trade under the Stars and Stripes, the ships being run on the " harshest possible principles "—to quote the words of a West Coast reporter. The men, also, who shipped in the salmon cannery fleet, were probably the hardest lot of sailormen, belonging to every nationality, that ever went afloat. The old " Packard," owing possibly to her reputation as a true hell-ship, was chosen to be the prison-ship of the Alaska fleet, to which all the worst characters in each ship were drafted.

Being an exceedingly well-built ship, and always tight, the

"BENJAMIN F. PACKARD."

From a Painting by C. R. Patterson

"BENJAMIN F. PACKARD."

"B. F. PACKARD."

Benjamin F. Packard sailed year after year to the North until she had outlasted nearly all her contemporaries. The Great War came and went, and still she sailed the seas, until at last, in 1925, she was towed round to New York from the Pacific coast with a cargo of lumber, being then commanded by Captain Dan Martin, with Hans Hanson as his mate. Her arrival at New York aroused a great amount of interest, and the papers gave a good deal of publicity to suggestions as to her being preserved as a marine museum. However, nothing was done, and her owners, growing tired of waiting, sent her back to the Pacific coast. Here she was condemned, and was about to be broken up when Mr. Theodore Roosevelt Pell, a well-known yachtsman, stepped in and bought her in order that she might be preserved as an example of a typical Down East Cape Horner.

The Lovely " Kennebec."

This three skysail-yarder was as shapely a craft as was ever launched in the river from which she took her name. Misfortune, however, overtook her at a very early stage in her career, and she was so badly burnt whilst lying at anchor in San Francisco Bay that she had to be scuttled and beached in Mission Bay. Here she lay for some years, with the tide flowing in and out of her and only the lower masts standing, whilst her solitary foreyard swung idly to the wind.

Then, when the boom in Pacific coast shipping came along in the late eighties, W. A. Boole of San Francisco repaired and re-rigged her. For the next dozen years she played her part on the coast. Then at the beginning of the twentieth century she was bought by G. E. Plummer. Lastly, in 1905, she was cut down to a barge for the Seaboard Transportation Company.

Watts' Last Square-rigger, the " R. D. Rice."

With the exception of the big *Edward O'Brien*, the *R. D. Rice* was the biggest vessel ever built at a Thomaston shipyard. She was Watts' last word on square rig, as after sending her afloat he only built fore-and-aft schooners.

The *R. D. Rice* was commanded by the handsome and athletic

Captain Newton Jordon, a very well-known character at Thomaston who had a great reputation as a lady-killer.

The *R. D. Rice* could sail, and in 1891 beat the famous *Henry B. Hyde* and the British ship, *Dawpool,* in a race from San Francisco to Liverpool.

After being owned for a short while by Flint & Co. the *R. D. Rice* came under the management of W. G. Mighell of the California Shipping Co., but in April, 1901, whilst commanded by Captain C. F. Carver, she was burnt at sea when laden with case oil.

Minott's "St. Charles."

This five topgallant-yarder was a really nice vessel.   Unfortunately her life was a short one as she came to grief by running ashore whilst going into Waterford.

A correspondent sends me two memories of this ship.   The first time that he saw her was when she was bound to Liverpool and snoring through the N.E. Trades, and she made such a sea picture as cannot be duplicated at the present day.

The Trades were strong, and she had every stitch set.   Her cotton canvas gleamed like snow in the brilliant sunshine, whilst her shapely hull flung the spray in rainbow-hued showers as it plunged through the sun-kissed blue of the North Atlantic.

His second memory picture of the *St. Charles* depicts her getting her anchor one calm Sunday morning in San Francisco Bay, when she was bound for Europe, wheat laden.   As her crew breasted the capstan-bars the sweet music of that loveliest of all shanties,

> Shenandoah, I love your daughter;
> Away, you rolling river !

sounded across the peaceful waters of the Bay, to the great delight of the crews of those deep-watermen which were anchored round her.

"T. F. Oakes" Overdue.

W. H. Starbuck seems to have been the only American sailing ship owner to make an effort to introduce iron into the building of American sailing ships.   Hardly had his *Tillie E. Starbuck* been launched before he contracted for another iron sailing ship.

This was the *T. F. Oakes*. Her builders were the American Ship-building Co., which had been recently started by Commander Gorringe of the United States Navy.

The keel of this ship was laid down on May 2, and she was launched on September 29, 1883, having taken less than five months to build.

She had a carrying power of 3200 tons, and with an overall length of 284 ft. drew 22 ft. of water.

The *T. F. Oakes* will be chiefly remembered for her long and disastrous passage home from Hongkong in 1896-7. Three years before this she had taken 195 days between New York and San Francisco, and it is quite evident that she was far from being a clipper.

In June, 1896, this iron Down Easter sailed for New York from Shanghai under Captain E. W. Reed. A month later she put into Hongkong in order to complete her cargo. Six days after leaving Hongkong she ran into a typhoon, which obliged Captain Reed to run away to the eastward.

This "big wind " was no sooner over than an even more violent one fell down upon the ship, and once more Captain Reed found himself compelled to run before the blast.

When this second typhoon at length blew itself out, the *T. F. Oakes* was left bobbing about in calms and baffling airs well out in the Pacific. Captain Reed had intended to take the usual route *via* the Cape of Good Hope, but on working out his position and finding how far he had been driven out of his course he determined to take the other route *via* Cape Horn.

The *T. F. Oakes* made a very long run to the Horn, which was not rounded until she was 168 days out. During this long and weary traverse her crew began to fall sick. On November 2 the Chinese cook had to take to his bunk with what was diagnosed as a severe cold. This, however, quickly ended fatally.

Soon after the death of the cook all hands were attacked with scurvy. On December 26 an A.B. named Thomas King died. He was followed on January 12 by Thomas Olsen, and a few days later by Thomas Judge. Then on February 4 Stephen G. Bunker, the mate, died. He was followed on the 9th by an old seaman named George King. By the time that the ship had got into the Atlantic there was hardly anybody aboard who was fit for duty. On March 1, 1897, Captain Reed, his wife, and the second and third mates were the only members of the ship's company who were still on their legs, and they were in a very exhausted condition.

Somehow or other the ship crawled up the Brazilian coast with the gallant Mrs. Reed doing most of the steering, whilst the three men staggered from brace to brace, from buntline to down-haul.

The ship's way up the South Atlantic was greatly hindered also by nor'west gales and heavy seas, whilst her scanty crew were still further weakened by lack of food and water, it being necessary to cut these down to six ounces of bread and a gulp of water a day per head.

All this time not a ship was sighted, and it was not until the island of Trinidad was abeam that the *T. F. Oakes* was able to gain some relief through the generosity of the *Governor Robie*. This vessel was not able to spare very much, and matters were truly desperate for those aboard the *T. F. Oakes* when her distress signals were picked up one Monday night in March, 1897, by the British oil tank steamer *Kasbek*.

It was thick and misty, and the blue glare of the distress signal could only just be seen by those aboard the steamer, whose course was at once altered to close with the sailing ship. As she ranged up close alongside, those aboard the *Kasbek* stared in amazement, for the *T. F. Oakes* was slowly surging along under lower topsails, and the only person on deck was the man at the wheel.

In reply to a hail from the *Kasbek*, a husky voice shouted back, " Can't heave to—all dead or sick. For heaven's sake stand by and send us a boat." " All right," cried Captain Muir of the *Kasbek* cheerily, "Keep up your hearts, we won't desert you." A boat was then lowered and sent over to the " Oakes " in charge of C. P. Helsham, the chief officer of the *Kasbek*.

Abrams, the second mate of the *T. F. Oakes*, seems by this time to have been the only person besides the captain's wife able to keep the deck, and he begged Helsham to take his ship in tow. The chief officer of the *Kasbek*, with his owners' interests to think of, asked

"ABNER COBURN."

"SERVIA."

how much the captain of the "Oakes" was prepared to pay for being towed into New York. His question drew a cry of distress from Abrams, " For the love of humanity don't stand upon price ! " and he went on to state that Captain Reed was lying in his bunk stricken with paralysis, that Mrs. Reed was at the wheel, and that the eleven other survivors were unable to leave their bunks and were almost at their last gasp, the mate and six men being already dead.

Captain Muir, on hearing this news, at once took steps to get a towing line aboard the sailing ship. With nobody able to help aboard the *T. F. Oakes*, Helsham and his boat's crew were obliged to board the " Oakes " and bend on that vessel's 8-inch Manila hawser to their own line so that it could be hauled aboard the steamer. Unfortunately the slack of the hauling line got caught round the *Kasbek's* propeller-boss, and before this was noticed several turns of the hawser itself became wound between the boss and the stern-post, with the result that the engines could neither go ahead nor astern.

This predicament gave the chief engineer, Stevens, of the *Kasbek*, a chance to show his ingenuity. He first of all uncoupled the shaft, then forced back the after section about an inch, thus freeing the turns of the hawser. Into the inch space left between the two portions of the shaft he fitted a disc of hardwood, through which he bored holes for the coupling bolts. The shaft was thus lengthened by an inch, the propellers were freed, and the engines were able to work again.

This smart piece of engineering only took 10 hours' work, and Stevens ever afterwards boasted that he had towed a ship into port by means of a wooden shaft.

By the time that the *Kasbek's* screw was once more turning, the " Oakes " had drifted out of sight beyond the horizon, and it was dark and also blowing hard before Captain Muir once more brought his vessel alongside the distressed sailing ship, but the weather was too bad for anything to be done through that night or the next day. The *T. F. Oakes* staggered along with the *Kasbek* keeping close under her lee, until at last, about noon on the third day, the wind and sea subsided sufficiently for the chief officer of the

Kasbek to board the *T. F. Oakes* again. He was met by the second mate, Abrams, who was the only person still able to keep on his legs.

For those who have never witnessed scurvy, it is hard to realise the condition of the crew of the *T. F. Oakes*. The man Abrams could hardly speak, and his legs were so swollen that it was a wonder that he could drag himself about the deck, or even stand at the wheel. The captain and the third officer, Eagan, were too helpless to leave their bunks, and Mrs. Reed was almost as bad. Forward, eleven men lay starving and helpless in their bunks ; most of them were toothless owing to the scurvy, and they were so weak that they slid from side to side on their straw mattresses at every roll of the vessel.

Mr. Helsham and three of the *Kasbek's* crew were ordered to remain on board the " Oakes " and navigate her. This time the tow line was successfully passed, and the *Kasbek* set off for New York with the *T. F. Oakes* in her wake. The latter dropped her anchor outside quarantine station on the forenoon of Sunday, March 21, 1897. She was then 259 days out from China, and had already been posted as missing.

Lloyd's showed their appreciation of Mrs. Reed's gallantry in steering the ill-fated Down Easter by presenting her with their silver medal for meritorious service.

The *T. F. Oakes* stranded on the Californian coast near San Francisco in 1901.

The Other 1883 Ships.

The *Governor Robie*, which supplied the *T. F. Oakes* with provisions, was one of four smart vessels owned by the three Searsport captains, Pendleton, Carver and Nichols. These were the *Abner Coburn*, launched in 1882, *Governor Robie* and *Mary L. Cushing* in 1883, and the *Henry B. Hyde* in 1884.

One of the best passages made by the *Governor Robie* was 110 days from New York to Hongkong in 1900. This vessel foundered at sea in November, 1921, after she had been cut down to a barge owned by the Neptune Line of New York.

The *Mary L. Cushing* is said to have been the last full-rigged ship built in Massachusetts. Her last owners were the California Shipping Co., but she disappeared from the Register in 1907.

Other vessels built in 1883 which should receive a mention are Houghton's *Servia*, Kelley's *John R. Kelley* (the biggest of all the 1883 ships), the *William H. Smith*, the *William H. Macy*, and the *E. F. Sawyer*. The first of these to go was the *E. F. Sawyer*, which was lost some time before the end of the nineteenth century. The *John R. Kelley* followed her to Davy Jones' locker in 1901, but the *Servia, Mary L. Cushing, William H. Smith* and *William H. Macy* all ended their days coal and wood droghuing on the Pacific coast, the last survivor of the four being the *William H. Smith*, which was still doing duty as a towing barge owned by the Nelson Company two or three years back.

Wreck of the " Servia."

Of these five the *Servia* was probably the speediest vessel. In 1893 she arrived at New York on May 5, only 97 days from San Francisco, and in 1901 she made one of the best passages across the Pacific, her time from Newcastle, N.S.W., to San Francisco being 55 days. She came to her end November 6, 1907, when she was owned by Captain H. Nelson of San Francisco.

On August 26, 1907, the *Servia* left San Francisco under charter to the Alaska Packers Association with cannery material and supplies for Karluk, Alaska. She was commanded by Captain Anders Aas. After arriving at her destination on October 10 she encountered a series of severe gales whilst moored at Karluk. These culminated in a strong N.E. gale on November 6. Although as much as 90 fathoms were out on one chain and 75 fathoms on the other, the *Servia* laboured very severely all the forenoon.

In spite of 165 fathoms of chain being out there was still more in the locker, but Captain Aas dared not pay it out for two reasons: first of all he feared that it could not be paid out slowly and evenly enough; secondly, the ship was already tailing into shoal and broken water.

About 1.15 p.m. the port chain carried away with a jar that shook the vessel. The only chance now was to beach her in the most favourable spot, which was on the west side of the entrance to

Karluk River.   Captain Aas had steam up in the donkey boiler, and two head sails, two staysails, and spanker all ready to set.   He then commenced slowly heaving in the port chain; but at 2 p.m., when only about 10 fathoms had been got in, the starboard chain carried away and the ship fell into the trough of the sea and began to roll very heavily.   The sails were immediately set, but owing to the chains dragging on the bottom and holding the *Servia's* bow up to windward it was found impossible to get her head off and she began to drift broadside on towards the beach.

Half an hour later the ship struck on a rock which was about 75 feet out from high water mark.   This rock holed her under the mizen rigging and held her broadside on to the surf, which caused a big under tow between the vessel and the shore.   The *Servia,* lying over at an angle of 45 degrees on her port bilge, began to break up almost at once.

The position of her crew was now so desperate that eight men started to swim ashore.   One only reached the beach, three were drowned, and the other four managed to get back to the ship.

Just before 3 p.m. the masts began to go over the side, the main being the first to go, and by 3.30 the wreckage of gear and cargo between the ship and the shore was piled up in such quantities as to form a bridge through the surf to the beach, and by means of this strange bridge the whole crew, with the exception of the three who had been drowned, made a successful landing.

Within two hours of the *Servia* striking the rock she had broken up.

The Famous "Henry B. Hyde."

This magnificent vessel has always been considered the finest and fastest three-masted sailing ship built under the Stars and Stripes since the clipper ship era.   During the greater part of her career, also, she was a notoriously hard ship for foremast hands, who generally referred to her as " that damned Yankee hot-box, the *'Enery 'Ide.*"

The *Henry B. Hyde* was launched from John McDonald's building slip at Bath in November, 1884.   On February 24, 1885, she sailed from New York for San Francisco under the command

of Captain Phineas Pendleton. The new crack was immensely
lofty, crossing three skysail yards, and when she was in the Doldrums,
close to the Equator, both her fore and main topgallant masts went
by the board in a heavy squall. Captain Pendleton, however,
managed to refit his big ship at sea, and rounding the Horn on
the 59th day out reached San Francisco on June 27, 123 days out.

Here the *Henry B. Hyde* loaded 82,234 centals of wheat at the
rate of 27s. per ton, and sailing on October 29, passed Cape Horn
47 days out; crossed the Line 75 days out ; was off Point Lynas
95 days out ; and reached Liverpool on February 2, 1886, 96 days
6 hours from the Golden Gate.

After discharging her grain cargo in excellent condition she
sailed for New York, and made the splendid run of 22 days from
Liverpool to Sandy Hook against the westerlies.

This fast maiden voyage made her reputation in the American
Merchant Marine, and henceforward she was the favourite of the
shippers in the Cape Horn trade.

Captain Phineas Pendleton commanded the *Henry B. Hyde*
for her first eight voyages. He then handed her over to his son,
Phineas Pendleton, Junior. The following are the times of the
ship's Cape Horn passages from 1886 to 1893 :

SECOND VOYAGE 1886-7.

New York to San Francisco	133 days
San Francisco to Liverpool ..	104 ,,

THIRD VOYAGE 1887-8.

New York to San Francisco ..	129 days
San Francisco to New York ..	89 ,,

FOURTH VOYAGE 1888.

New York to San Francisco ..	130 days
San Francisco to Liverpool ..	115 ,,

FIFTH VOYAGE 1889-90.

New York to San Francisco ..	108 days
San Francisco to Liverpool ..	109 ,,

SIXTH VOYAGE 1891.

New York to San Francisco ..	108 days
San Francisco to Liverpool ..	110 ,,

SEVENTH VOYAGE 1891-2.

New York to San Francisco   .. 105 days
San Francisco to New York   .. 94 „

EIGHTH VOYAGE 1892-3.

New York to San Francisco   .. 112 days

Although the *Henry B. Hyde* was a hard ship, this passage was the only one recorded in the *Red Record*. After the ship's arrival at San Francisco the mate was charged with " breaking a seaman's wrist by a blow with a belaying-pin, and otherwise ill-treating him." Although the facts of the case were easily proved, it was dismissed on the ground of "justifiable discipline."

On her homeward passage this year the " Hyde," for the only time in her career, interrupted her passage from San Francisco to New York by putting into a South American nitrate port.

On her ninth and tenth voyages the *Henry B. Hyde* was commanded by Captain Phineas Pendleton, Junior, and her passages were as follows :

New York to San Francisco   .. 130 days
San Francisco to Liverpool   .. 102 „
New York to San Francisco   .. 113 „
San Francisco to Liverpool   .. 111 „

On her eleventh voyage, in 1896, the " Hyde " took 132 days going out to San Francisco with Captain Colcord in command. This was an unusually long passage for her, but Captain Colcord showed that he knew how to drive the big ship by covering the distance between San Francisco and Honolulu in 1897 in 9 days 4 hours 30 minutes.   This was a record, but it was shortly afterwards broken by Captain Rock in the *Roderick Dhu*, who arrived at Hilo from San Francisco on January 29, 1898, only 9 days 3 hours out, thus beating Captain Colcord's record by 1 hour 30 minutes.

On his homeward passage from Honolulu Captain Colcord made New York in the splendid time of 89 days.

On her next outward passage the *Henry B. Hyde* arrived at San Francisco on January 12, 1898, 113 days out from New York, but her return trip was not quite so good as usual, and she had the unusual experience for her of not figuring amongst the best homeward passages of the year.

CAPT. DAVE RIVERS OF "A. G. ROPES."
Receiving orders to load coal for Hongkong.

WRECK OF "HENRY B. HYDE."

It was at the end of this voyage that the ship came under the management of Flint & Co. Whilst Benjamin Pendleton was her owner she was kept clear of the black diamond trade, but on her very first voyage under the new management she loaded coal at Norfolk (Virginia) for Honolulu.

The *Henry B. Hyde* seems to have been very unlucky the only times that she loaded coal, and on this particular occasion Captain Scribner was obliged to put into Valparaiso in December, 1899, with his cargo on fire.

At the beginning of the twentieth century all Flint's ships with the exception of the little *Alice McDonald*, the *Henry B. Hyde* amongst the rest, came under the management of W. E. Mighell and became members of the California Shipping Company's fleet.

The command of the "Hyde " was now given to Captain W. J. McLeod, and the famous Down Easter seems to have kept out of the limelight until the year 1902, when Captain McLeod sailed from Baltimore on May 18 with coal for San Francisco. Once more the coal became heated, and McLeod was obliged to put into Table Bay where 600 tons had to be discharged.

The illustration shows the *Henry B. Hyde* lying off Cape Town before continuing her passage to San Francisco. She eventually resumed her voyage and reached San Francisco on December 26, being no less than 222 days out from Baltimore. Captain McLeod, however, made quite a good run of 82 days from Cape Town, and made the clipper ship time of 15 days from the Equator to the Golden Gate.

The ship was taken over at San Francisco by the well-known Captain Edwin T. Amesbury. Loading a mixed cargo in which such different items as wine, rags, bones, and lead figured, Captain Amesbury sailed from the Golden Gate on July 17, 1903, and arrived at New York on November 5, 111 days out.

This passage was Captain Amesbury's last in active service. On arrival he retired from the sea, after handing over the command of the *Henry B. Hyde* to Captain Pearson.

Sailing from New York on February 11, 1904, the *Henry B. Hyde* was driven ashore on the Damsbek Beach, Virginia, about 10 miles south of Cape Henry, during a heavy gale. She was soon badly sanded up.   However, after some considerable delay, during which she changed hands, the crack Down Easter was refloated on September 23, only to be once more stranded in the same place a few hours afterwards.   This time the grand old ship was abandoned as a total loss.   By October 4 she had broken in two, and the wreck was eventually blown up with dynamite.

The " A. G. Ropes."

The only vessel which could in any way dispute the *Henry B. Hyde's* claim to be the finest full-rigger under the Stars and Stripes was I. F. Chapman's *A. G. Ropes*, which was named after the head partner in that firm.

The *A. G. Ropes* was commanded throughout her career by Captain D. H. Rivers, and under his skilful guidance she not only maintained a wonderful average in her passages out and home round the Horn, but kept singularly free of trouble of every sort.

I cannot find that she made the run from San Francisco to the United Kingdom in under 100 days, but on the other hand she was rarely much more than 100 days out when she docked in Liverpool. One of her best bursts of speed was a run of 24 days from Yokohama to Tacoma when loaded with tea in November, 1887.

So far as I know, the *A. G. Ropes* never had a race with the *Henry B. Hyde*, as their passages never happened to coincide. It is therefore very difficult to give any opinion as to which of the two was the smarter ship, but on the whole American shipping people considered that the *Henry B. Hyde* had just a little the best of it as regards speed.

After having sailed the *A. G. Ropes* with great success to every part of the world, Captain Rivers had at last, in 1906-7, to hand over his beautiful ship to the Luckenbach Transportation and Wrecking Co. of New York, for conversion into a barge.

My last news of her was from a British steamship captain during the War, who wrote that he had passed a barge towing down the Delaware which he recognised as the one-time Down Easter, *A. G. Ropes*.

"Commodore T. H. Allen," Blood-boat.

This vessel, which was the largest ship built in 1884 next to the " Hyde " and the " Ropes," was the last vessel built by T. J. Southard of Richmond. She was named for old Allen, the famous San Francisco stevedore, a leading man in the Forty-nine Society, having taken part in the gold rush of that historic year.

The figure-head of the *Commodore T. H. Allen* was an excellent portrait of the old stevedore, and it was probably the only figure-head in existence which was smoking a cigar.

The *Commodore T. H. Allen* was a beautiful ship, but I fear she had a terrible reputation as a blood-boat. Neither Captain R. L. Merriman, who I believe had the ship throughout her life, nor his son, Robert Merriman, who was his chief mate, were men that any deep-water Jack would care to ship under unless he was contemplating suicide. But when one notes also that big Crocker was second mate, with a " bucko " of equal ferocity as third "blower and striker," one would not be wrong in saying that the *Commodore T. H. Allen* was by far the worst hell-ship sailing the seas.

Between 1889 and 1894 the ship and her officers figured no less than four times in the *Red Record*. The following evidence of some of the seamen who were man-handled aboard her will undoubtedly bring a smile to any old Cape Horner who reads it.

After the *Commodore T. H. Allen's* arrival at San Francisco in April, 1889, a seaman named McDonald reported that "whilst expostulating against the vile language of the third mate he was struck several times by that officer, and thrown against the rail with such violence that his shoulder was dislocated." The captain remarked, when appealed to, "Serves you damn well right," and ordered the mate to confine McDonald in the carpenter's shop. As treatment for his wounds he "was given a dose of salts."

On the *Commodore T. H. Allen's* arrival back at New York in October, 1889, Fred Hall, a green hand, complained of being shanghaied aboard by the San Francisco crimps, and "upon complaining to the first mate and attempting to see the captain, was driven forward with kicks and curses. He was accorded cruel treatment on the passage to New York, and when he asked the captain for his pay was told that there was nothing due to him

—the crimps had received all the advance and blood-money. The third mate gave him 50 cents to pay his ferry across the river."

When the " Allen " arrived at San Francisco in August, 1892, Edwards, the coloured cook, charged the second mate, Crocker, with hitting him on the head with a belaying-pin because he allowed the watch on deck to warm themselves in the galley. Crocker afterwards "tried to gouge out his eyes as he lay on the deck. The first mate, Merriman, kicked him as he lay on the deck, and Captain Merriman made him wipe up his own blood."

On this occasion the captain was admitted to bail, and the mates remained in hiding until the case was dismissed for "lack of evidence," the crew, including the unfortunate cook, having been shanghaied to sea on another ship.

On the *Commodore T. H. Allen's* arrival in New York from San Francisco in June, 1894, Charles Heyne, able seaman, charged Captain Merriman and his son with assaulting him whilst at the wheel. Apparently the mate belaboured him with a rope's end whilst the captain used his fists.

The skipper of the " Allen " was arrested and held in a 1500-dollar bond, but this case also was dismissed for lack of evidence.

In November, 1901, the old hell-ship was condemned after being on fire. She was afterwards repaired and cut down to a barge, being then run by the Baker Transport Company of New York under the name of *Sterling*.

The " Robert L. Belknap."

This ship was a heeler with three skysails over double topgallant yards. On one occasion in the eighties she lay alongside the Oakland wharf with the big steel ship, *British Isles*, Bates' *Kistna*, and the *Crown of Denmark*, and her trucks towered above those of these ships, making them look quite stumpy.

The *Robert L. Belknap* had almost as bad a reputation amongst foremast hands as the *Commodore T. H. Allen*, and when she arrived at New York in December, 1889, the charge of murdering a seaman named William Thomas was preferred against the second mate, who, however, had made himself scarce.

On this passage all hands bore marks of scurvy, and they

"A. G. ROPES."

"A. G. ROPES."

"CLARENCE S. BEMENT."

"HENRY B. HYDE."

complained as bitterly of the bad food as of the violence of the officers.

Soon after this the *Robert L. Belknap* disappeared from the Register.

The " Clarence S. Bement."

This was the second iron ship built by the American S.B. Co. at Philadelphia, but like the " Oakes " I fear she was more notorious for the length of her passages than for the shortness of them.

This ship had a most beautiful figure-head of a white swan with wings outstretched.

In 1901 55 guineas had been paid to re-insure when the *Clarence S. Bement* reached New York, 222 days out from Yokohama. The following year she was sold to G. W. Hume of San Francisco. In 1904 she was burnt at sea when on a passage from Newport News to San Francisco.

The Speedy " Adam W. Spies."

This little 1200-ton barque might almost be said to have been clipper-built, for speed rather than capacity for cargo was evidently the desire of her owner. Built at Newburyport, the *Adam W. Spies* had a tremendously tall sail plan. Whilst loading coal at Newcastle, N.S.W., in December, 1888, she was the tallest ship in port out of a fleet of 151 vessels, most of which registered considerably more than her tonnage.

On this occasion she made the run from Newcastle to Hongkong in 31 days, a record which has only been beaten by the famous tea clipper, *Thermopylae.* She was commanded by the well-known Searsport captain, Clarence N. Meyers.

Another excellent passage was from New York to Mauritius, where she arrived on May 15, 1902, 72 days out. By this time she had been sold by Cautillion to W. R. Hutching of New York, and a Captain W. Godett was in command.

The *Adam W. Spies* disappeared from the Register in 1906.

" George Curtis."

One of the last of the typical Cape Horners to be afloat and in active service was the *George Curtis.* Her first master was

Captain T. Sproul. Then at the beginning of the twentieth century G. S. Calhoun had her until she was sold to the North Alaska Salmon Co. about four years before the War.

In 1921 she was still afloat under the command of Captain J. Nelson, and owned by Libby, McNeil & Libby of San Francisco.

The "Frederick Billings."

This was the first of the big wooden four-mast barques, and the only one built by Carleton, Norwood & Co. She was indeed an impressive ship to look at, with her long full poop, massive Oregon pine lower masts, terrific spike bowsprit, heavy double topgallant yards, and three skysails.

The newspaper reporters gave a great deal of publicity to her launch in August, 1885, and as she was the first American four-master since the *Great Republic* others besides shipping people were interested in her performances.

" Old man " Sherman, with his shaggy whiskers, left the *Raphael* in order to take Carleton, Norwood's new ship. Like most of their skippers, he was a real hard nut and a nigger driver. He was succeeded in 1889 by Captain H. A. Williams, late of the *St. Paul*. He was another hard nut, and on the ship's arrival at San Francisco in March, 1892, twelve of the *Frederick Billing's* foremast hands charged him with cruelty.

The big ship had had a very rough time off the Horn, and during a severe squall some of her yards were carried away and six of her men were lost overboard. One of the charges was that the captain had pushed one of the drowning men out of the mizen chains with a boat hook ; but the chief complaint was that he had made no effort to rescue the men who were overboard. The case was dismissed, the complaints being considered trivial by the Commissioner, though he seemed to think that the captain should have made some effort to rescue the seamen. It is probable that the weather was far too bad for a boat to be lowered, in which case there was nothing that the captain or anyone else could do.

On her homeward passage that year the *Frederick Billings* reached New York 93 days out from San Francisco.

On the very next voyage she went to Caleta Buena from San

Francisco to load nitrate. When nearly loaded she was burnt to the water's edge whilst at anchor, and the origin of the fire was reported to be incendiary or malicious. It was thought at the time that some of her crew were taking their revenge for the ill-treatment or hazing which they had received from her officers, but it was always necessary to be extremely careful in loading a nitrate cargo owing to the danger of fire, and this was specially the case in a wooden ship.

The Good-looking "Francis."

One of the handsomest of American wood ships was the *Francis* of New Bedford. During her first years she was owned by W H. Besse, and then Captain F. H. Stone had her.

This fine ship, however, did not have a very long life, having gone to Davy Jones' locker before the end of the nineteenth century. Her last commander was, I believe, Captain A. Doane.

Besse's "Hotspur" and Other 1885 Ships.

This 1200-ton three skysail-yarder was a very handsome little ship, but unfortunately had a very short life, being out of the Register by 1889.

There are three others amongst the 1885 ships which should be noticed. The first of these was the *Willie Rosenfeld*, which was the first of Sewall's big ships. The *Willie Rosenfeld* had a very fair turn of speed, and on May 8, 1892, arrived at San Francisco only 113 days out from New York. She was commanded at this time by Captain W. H. Dunphy. She was lost a few years later.

The *George R. Skolfield*, which was built at Brunswick, Maine, and was owned by G. R. Skolfield, became a barge of the Coastwise Steamship Co. at the beginning of the twentieth century.

The barque *Wallace B. Flint*, launched at Bath in 1885, was the smallest of Benjamin Flint's fleet with the exception of the little *Alice McDonald*. At the beginning of the twentieth century she went to San Francisco owners, and for the next eight years was commanded by Captain C. A. Johnson. Then about five years before the War she was bought by the Alaska Fisherman's Packing Co. of San Francisco.

The Slump of the Square-rigger and the Rise of the Fore-and-after.

A severe slump in building of the typical Down Easter set in in the year 1886, and, so far as I know, not a single square-rigged ship was launched in Down East ports between 1886 and 1889. It must not be supposed, however, that wooden shipbuilding in the ports of Maine and elsewhere was at a standstill. This was far from being the case. The American coasting trade was steadily increasing, but both owners and builders had satisfied themselves that the fore-and-aft rig was the most economical for work on the American coast. Thus we find that by 1889 three and four-mast schooners were doing the work which used to be done by square-riggers.

The size of these schooners gradually increased. The largest of the four-masters built in 1886 was the *King Philip* of 1224 tons, launched at Camden. Bath produced three four-masters of over 1000 tons, namely, the *Eva B. Douglas, Cassie F. Bronson*, and the *Benjamin F. Poole*, and in 1887 sent the *Lucy H. Russell*, of 1166 tons afloat.

This year Camden excelled itself by producing the smallest as well as the biggest four-mast schooner afloat. The first was the *Bertie & Maud* of only 191 tons, her big sister being the *Pocahontas* of 1382 tons. In 1888 two five-mast schooners were built. These were the *Louis* of 831 tons, launched at North Bend, Oregon, and the *Governor Ames* of 1778 tons, launched at Waldoboro'.

In 1889 two other big four-masters were built at Bath. These were the *Massasoit*, 1377 tons, and the *Tucumseh* of 1658 tons. These big schooners did not prove themselves as efficient as the square-riggers in the turbulent waters of Cape Horn, but they were no doubt very satisfactory for running up and down the East Coast, where beam winds are the rule.

By the year 1889 the British iron full-riggers and four-masters seem to have collared the greater part of the grain trade from the Pacific ports to Europe. For instance, in 1889, 234 ships, aggregating 387,091 tons, sailed grain laden from San Francisco. 213 of these ships were bound to Europe, 167 of which, totalling 278,885 tons, were British; 30 of 58,601 tons American; 11 of 14,551 tons

German ; 3 of 3277 tons Italian ; 2, of 2891 tons Swedish and Norwegian. The average rate of freight paid to foreign ships was also in excess of that paid to the Americans, the rates being :

American ships	.. ˙	£1 10 6
British ,,	..	1 15 3
German ,,	..	1 14 6
Norwegian ,,	..	1 18 3
Italian ,,	..	1 16 8

Of 30 ships which sailed with flour that year, 21 were British, 3 American, 4 German, 1 Norwegian, and 1 carried the Hawaiian flag. Finally, in December, 1889, 24 British ships sailed from San Francisco with grain for Europe, with a tonnage of 40,221, compared to 4 American ships with a tonnage of 8722, and 1 German ship of 1178 tons.

From these statistics it seems evident that Down East owners were abandoning their competition with the British iron ships in order to take part in their own fast-growing coastal trade, which, of course, was barred to foreign ships. However, with the coming of the nineties there was all-round recovery in the world trades in which sailing ships were still able to compete, besides which the new American export of kerosene oil was calling every day for more sailing ship tonnage.

Thus we find the wooden American square-rigger given a new lease of life, chiefly, it must be confessed, owing to the enterprise of Arthur Sewall of Bath.

However, Sewall's famous four-masters are deserving of a chapter to themselves.

The Mutiny of the " Frank N. Thayer."

I will finish this chapter with an account of one of the most extraordinary mutinies in the whole annals of the sea. This mutiny took place aboard the American ship *Frank N. Thayer*, 1600 tons, in January, 1886, when she was homeward bound from Manila with a cargo of hemp for New York.

On the night of Saturday, January 2, the ship was sailing quietly along in the steady South-east Trade about 700 miles from St. Helena. The watch had been called, and the port watch had gone below, whilst the starboard watch, as was usual on such a night, had coiled themselves down to sleep in various corners where the rays of the moon could not get at them. The first and the second mates were sitting chatting on the booby hatch, whilst Captain Clark, his wife, and child were asleep below.

Suddenly into the moonlight stepped a couple of young Manila men, one of whom belonged to the watch on deck and the other to that below. This latter murmured that he felt sick, and this seems to have been a signal, for before either of the mates had time to answer they were attacked with knives by the two coloured men. Both officers were mortally wounded. The mate staggered forward, where some of the men, aroused from their sleep by a sudden piercing scream, picked him up and carried him into the fo'c'sle.

The watch on deck seem to have given way to panic, for, pursued by the two Manila men, they tumbled head first into the fo'c'sle and proceeded to barricade themselves in. The mate, whom they had carried in with them, died there three hours later. Meanwhile the second mate had dragged himself to the cabin door, where he was only able to call the name of Captain Clark before he fell dead.

Captain Clark had already been aroused by the scream, and hearing a confused babble of voices and a patter of feet along the deck, he rushed out of his stateroom towards the door leading to the companion. As he opened the door the second mate, with a cry of "Captain Clark, Captain Clark!" stumbled down the steps and dropped dead at his captain's feet.

Without a moment's thought, Captain Clark, who was unarmed and in his night clothes, sprang up the campanion-ladder. His idea was that the *Frank N. Thayer* had collided with a ship which she was steadily overhauling at sundown. However, he had no sooner put his head out of the companion than his scalp was laid open by a knife, and at the same time a small muscular hand gripped him by the throat. As he staggered under the blow he managed to catch hold of his assailant, and at the same moment recognised that he was one of the two men shipped at Manila. Quick as a flash he hit out with all his force, and caught the man between the eyes, half blinding him. But in spite of this the latter struck out

"HENRY B. HYDE."

From the Painting by Charles R. Patterson.

"SAM SKOLFIELD."

Lent by Capt. Schutze.

with his knife, which he dug into the captain's side. Captain Clark, despite his wounds, continued to use his fists with effect, until at last the pair of them fell down the companionway.

Captain Clark was badly shaken by this tumble and faint from loss of blood, and he fell headlong into the cabin. His assailant, thinking that he had killed the captain, at once retreated to the deck. Captain Clark, however, had still some fight left in him, and crawling inside the cabin door, found a revolver being thrust into his hand by his plucky wife. Armed with this he returned to the foot of the companion and sang out to the man at the wheel to shut the door leading on to the poop. Unfortunately, the man at the wheel was utterly useless from fright. With knees shaking, he had watched the fight between the captain and the Manila man without even attempting to give the alarm, and when the captain called out to him to shut the door he replied in quavering tones, "I can't sir, there is somebody there." "Who?" asked the captain. "I don't know, sir," replied the coward, and, at a loss as to what had happened, and in the belief that the whole crew had mutinied, Captain Clark now returned to the cabin and with the help of his wife locked the doors leading forward and aft out of the cabin.

Hardly had he managed to do this, being now almost too weak to stand, than he heard steps coming down the ladder. Opening the door cautiously, he covered whoever it was with his revolver, and at the same time called out, "Who are you, and what is the matter!" The newcomer proved to be a seaman named Hendrickson, who was so crazed with panic that he could only keep on repeating, "Oh, hide me, captain, hide me!" Turning from this man in contempt, the captain once more locked the door, and believing himself to be mortally wounded and fast bleeding to death, sat down in a corner of the cabin, where he could command the doors and windows with his revolver.

Mrs. Clark now had a chance to dress her husband's wounds. Besides a number of gashes on the head, she found a bad hole in his left side below the ribs, through which the lobe of the lung protruded.

Meanwhile, nine of the men forward had plucked up some spirit, and arming themselves with capstan bars sallied out on to the maindeck ; but they had not got aft of the mainmast before they were suddenly attacked by the two Manila men, who by this time were running amuck with a vengeance. After four out of the nine had been stabbed the remainder fled forward, with the exception of one man, named Robert Sonnberg, who ran aft, and climbing into the mizen rigging took refuge on the crossjack yard. Here he saw them kill Maloney, the cowardly helmsman, who apparently offered no resistance though he begged hard for his life.

After murdering this man the two mutineers attempted to get into the cabin through the skylight, but a couple of shots from the captain drove them off. They then proceeded forward. It was now about 2 a.m., and Sonnberg, from his perch on the yard, saw them murder the carpenter and a man whom they dragged out of the carpenter's shop. After this they started to sharpen a couple of axes. They also lashed their knives to broom-handles. Thus armed they tried to reach the wounded captain through the cabin skylight, but his revolver soon drove them away.

About 8 o'clock in the evening—that is to say, as soon as it was dark—the mutineers decided to try to get the better of the man Sonnberg, who was still aloft on the mizen. The latter, by way of a weapon, had cut a block adrift, which he swung on the end of a gasket. The shaking of the rigging, as the Manila men climbed up it, warned him to look out, and as the first of the mutineers got within striking distance he swung his block at the man, but missed him. Neither of the Manila men, however, cared to face this curious weapon, and descended to the deck, whilst Sonnberg, who was shaking with fright, clambered hastily to the royal yard, where he stayed all night.

Daybreak on Sunday morning found the two Manila men complete masters of the ship ; the captain dared not leave the cabin ; nor could the crew make a sally from the fo'c'sle, for the mutineers had battened them down. About seven bells they hauled the Chinese cook out of the coal locker, where he had hidden himself, and forced him to cook them something for breakfast. After having had a good meal they once more made an attempt to stab the captain and his wife through the skylight, but once again the captain's revolver drove them away.

About midday the mutineers broke open the carpenter's chest and dressed themselves up in his best clothes.

During Sunday afternoon there was not a sound on the stricken ship. The mutineers were evidently waiting for darkness before once more attacking the inmates of the cabin, and the captain was also waiting for darkness before commencing a steady fusilade with his revolver, shooting blind with only the hope of a lucky shot, or of intimidating the mutineers and keeping them quiet: and in this he was successful, for the crazy pair seem to have done nothing during the night; but at daybreak Sonnberg, from his perch aloft, noticed that they were evidently making preparations to set the ship on fire, though they kept a close watch aft.

Whilst they were thus engaged, the Chinese cook, Ah Say, managed to pass an axe in through the fo'c'sle window in order that the imprisoned men could chop down the door and sally out. Sonnberg, also, took his courage in both hands, slid down a backstay, and, getting hold of another axe, started to cut adrift the barricading of the fo'c'sle door. Before, however, he could carry out his object, the Manila men observed him and came forward at the run. However, Sonnberg jumped into the main rigging and once more escaped aloft.

It was about this time that Captain Clark, who, owing to his wife's clever treatment of his wounds, was feeling much stronger, started out to reconnoitre the position. First of all he went into the bathroom, where he discovered the terrified Henrickson crouching on the floor. It was from Henrickson that the captain learnt for the first time that all the mischief had been done by the two Manila men, whereupon he gave Henrickson a revolver.

The mutineers, armed with a harpoon and their knives, now once more advanced to the attack of the cabin. This time Captain Clark was given a good target, and taking careful aim, he shot the first of the pair through the breast. The man flung up his hands, and turning round, ran forward. Here the crew were hard at work chopping their way out of the fo'c'sle, and just as the wounded man approached the door gave way and the crowd of furious seamen burst out.

The case was now desperate for the mutineers, and they evidently recognised this, for the wounded man leapt overboard, whilst his companion dropped down into the 'tween decks. Whilst the hands rushed aft Sonnberg came down from aloft hand over hand, yelling wildly to the captain, who at once came out of the cabin with Mrs. Clark and Henrickson ; but before the liberated men could do anything a wisp of smoke, coming up through the open hatch, advised all hands of the desperate work upon which the remaining mutineer was engaged.

The ship had a jute cargo, and the man was busy firing the jute. Two of the most active of the seamen now jumped below with the captain's revolvers with the intention of hunting out the Manila man. One of them managed to get a sight of him and shot him through the shoulder, but the smoke in the 'tween decks was so thick that the man was able to conceal his movements, and all of a sudden he leapt out on to the deck with a blood-curdling yell, and running to the side, jumped on to the rail and overboard.

Apparently before the first of the mutineers had leapt over the side the pair of them had thrown over a small spar of some sort. There was no wind, and for a few moments the two madmen could be seen clinging to this spar. A fusilade of revolver shots was now directed upon them, and probably some of these took effect, for after a short while both men were seen to sink.

All hands had now to turn to and extinguish the fire in the 'tween decks, but it had evidently been well lit, and it soon became obvious that it had got a good hold on the cargo, and with such an inflammable cargo as jute this meant that the ship was doomed. The captain immediately gave orders for the two boats to be lowered and for provisions to be got on deck. One of the boats capsized alongside, so that the survivors, with rations for about a fortnight, had to stow themselves away into the remaining boat. First of all the wounded were carefully lowered into her, and they were followed by the captain's wife and child. The boat got safely away from the ship's side, but remained close to her all through that Monday night in the hopes that the flames from the burning ship would bring someone to their aid. However, when no sail appeared over the horizon at daybreak, Captain Clark set a course for St. Helena. The boat lacked a sail, but its place was supplied by blankets sewn together.

At midnight on Sunday, January 10, the survivors of the *Frank N. Thayer* safely reached Jamestown, where they were looked after by Mr. J. A. McKnight, the American Consul.

This extraordinary affair on the *Frank N. Thayer* was not really a mutiny but the running amuck of two crazy Manila Indians, who, through their insane blood lust, managed to kill five men, wound five others, master a crew of twenty, and destroy a 1600-ton ship.

CHAPTER VI.

THE DOWN EASTERS OF THE NINETIES.

The Firm of Sewall.

WITH the advent of the nineties, the Bath firm of shipbuilders, Arthur Sewall & Co., who owned the Cape Horners, *Indiana, Iroquois, Reaper, Solitaire, Occidental, Challenger,* and *Willie Rosenfeld,* as well as two four-mast schooners, the *Talofa* and the *Douglas Dearborn,* and the three-mast schooners, *Carrie A. Lane* and *Belle Higgins,* started to build a fleet that was to have the unique distinction of containing the only wooden square-rigged four-masted sailing vessels in the world. These big Sewall ships were a curious mixture of the latest modern labour-saving devices alongside of wooden fittings such as had hardly changed their shape since the days of the Tudors.

There was a great diversity of opinion amongst shipping men all over the world regarding these famous Sewall productions. Some considered that their sea qualities and sailing powers were superior to those of any other sailing ship afloat. Others turned up their noses and declared that they were just plain, big, ugly wooden tubs, which only managed to make passages through the largeness of their sail plans and the driving power of their commanders. At any rate, whether ugly or beautiful, fast or slow, these wooden giants were wonderful examples of the wooden ship-builder's art, and were the very last effort of the wood worker in his struggle to survive against the iron and steel worker with his cheap steel plates and rivets. The Sewalls were indeed one of the last of the big shipbuilding firms where the caulking mallet held its own against the rivetting hammer.

172

The " Rappahannock."

The *Willie Rosenfeld* was succeeded on the stocks by the huge full-rigger, *Rappahannock.* This vessel, which registered 3054 tons, cost 125,000 dollars to build, and her vast wooden hull contained 706 tons of Virginia oak and 1,200,000 feet of pine timber. She was fitted with the first steel bowsprit to adorn the bow of a wooden ship. Painted white from trucks to waterline, she was known as the "Great White Bird."

On her maiden voyage she loaded 125,000 cases of petroleum (200,000 gallons) at Philadelphia for Japan. The command of this mighty ship was given to Captain Dickinson, who had the nerve to run a ship of 5000 tons burden with a foremast crowd of only twenty men. The result was trouble from the very outset of the ship's maiden voyage, which began on February 6, 1890.

Whilst towing down the Delaware the crew complained that the vessel was undermanned. The pilot put Sewall's new ship ashore on the way down the river, and the delay gave the captain an opportunity of disciplining his crew, with the aid of crimps from the shore. This naturally meant a scrimmage, in the course of which one man had his arm broken and another his head smashed. In the end the men were locked up in the fo'c'sle, where they were kept for two weeks on short rations.

During this time a detective managed to get aboard the ship and make inquiries as to the trouble. He was followed by a United States marshal, who took Captain Dickinson back to Wilmington to be examined before the Commissioner. However, the case was dismissed on the ground of "justifiable discipline," and the *Rappahannock* proceeded to sea with twenty sore, half-starved, discontented sailormen in her fo'c'sle.

During the voyage one of these was washed off the jibboom and drowned, whilst another fell from the mizen cross-trees and was killed.

The *Rappahannock*, after discharging her petroleum in Japanese ports, went on to San Francisco for a grain cargo. Here her crew told the usual tales of belaying-pins and pistols.

The ship's next passage was from San Francisco to Liverpool, where she proceeded to load a cargo of soft coal back to the Golden

Gate. Leaving Liverpool on July 29, 1891, Captain Wylie Dickinson had barely succeeded in making the difficult passage of the Horn when the *Rappahannock's* cargo took fire from spontaneous combustion. Dickinson managed to get his ship into Cumberland Bay, Juan Fernandez, but from the first there was little hope of saving her, and the " Great White Bird " was completely destroyed, her crew taking refuge on Robinson Crusoe's island.

Murphy's " Shenandoah."

Sewall's next big ship was the four-mast barque, *Shenandoah*, which was launched on November 26, 1890. The American people were so proud of this remarkable vessel that her picture was reproduced by the United States Government on the registers of all ships flying the American flag, and on the licenses issued to all masters of American sailing ships.

There is no doubt that Arthur Sewall & Co. recognised that a three-masted full-rigger of over 3000 tons was both an unhandy and uneconomical vessel to run, and they, like many other firms with old-fashioned traditions, reluctantly decided to adopt the rig which is called a "four-mast barque" by John Bull but "shipentine" in the United States.

The *Shenandoah* cost 175,000 dollars to build, and spread no less than 2 acres of canvas. Her fore, main, and mizen lower masts were built spars of Oregon pine measuring 38 ins. in diameter, and 90 ft. in length from deck to cap. Her top masts were 56 ft. long, and topgallant masts 68. She was given the usual American rig of deep single topgallant sails and three skysails. It must have taken quite a climb to reach her skysail yards, for her fore, main and mizen trucks were 217 ft. above the deck. All her spars were built of Oregon pine with the exception of the bowsprit, which was of steel, and her mainyard was 94 ft. long.

Captain Jim Murphy was called from the quarterdeck of the *W. F. Babcock* in order to superintend the building and rigging of Sewall's first four-master, and he always claimed that she owed her sailing powers to the fact that under his direction she was " sparred right." He said that her masts were stepped just where they ought to be, and, as every sailing ship man or racing yachtsman

"SHENANDOAH."

"SHENANDOAH."

will tell you, the position of a ship's masts is the first consideration. If these are correctly placed it will make all the difference between a ship that is easy to handle and smart in every evolution, and one which is the reverse.

Captain Murphy used to declare that *Shenandoah* manoeuvred like a knock-about sloop, and that she sailed a full point nearer the wind than the best of her contemporary square-riggers. As a proof of this he used to record how on one occasion she beat up Chesapeake Bay in the teeth of a northerly gale in company with a number of big fore-and-aft schooners, and that she both outfooted and outpointed every one of these vessels.

On his maiden passage Captain Murphy loaded at New York for San Francisco, and made the difficult outward passage round the Horn in 124 days.

Whilst running for the Horn in a strong fair wind, Captain Murphy records how the *Shenandoah* was overhauled and passed by the British ship *Kensington*, which passed so close that her crew jumped into the rigging and cheered as they went by. On the very next day the usual Cape Horn snorter came down on the two ships. Whilst the Britisher was head-reaching under lower topsails and making very heavy weather of it, the powerful *Shenandoah* went foaming by her close-hauled under a press of canvas, clawing out to windward in magnificent fashion, and behaving splendidly in the face of the Cape Horn greybeards. The *Shenandoah* was hardly over the horizon before the *Kensington* had to bear up for the Falklands in order to have her damages repaired. This incident does not quite fit the date, for the *Kensington* was not launched until July, 1891, and it is therefore possible that the ship which ran past the *Shenandoah* was the *Old Kensington,* a very much faster vessel altogether than the *Kensington.*

At San Francisco the *Shenandoah* loaded the biggest grain cargo on record, viz., 112,000 centals (about 5300 tons) worth 175,000 dollars.

Captain Murphy sailed from San Francisco at 10 a.m. on August, 1891, in company with the Down Easters *S. D. Carleton* and *M. P. Grace,* and the two British ships *Strathearn* and *Balkamah* All these ships were bound to Havre with the exception of the *M. P. Grace,* whose port was New York.

The *Strathearn* was the Allan Line clipper built in 1871, whilst the *Balkamah* was a little iron ship of 1397 tons built at Hull in 1866. Neither of these Britishers was expected to hold her own with the powerful *Shenandoah*, but the *S. D. Carleton*, a new full-rigger of Carleton, Norwood's, commanded by Captain E. T. Amesbury, a very experienced master, was expected to make a good race of it.

There was a head wind blowing as they towed through the Golden Gate, and the tugs cast off after dark within hearing of the Farallone whistles. Amesbury tacked the *S. D. Carleton* to the northward, whilst Murphy headed south, but when the logs of the two ships were afterwards compared it was found that they were never more than 50 miles apart all the way down to the Equator in the Pacific. Nevertheless, after splitting tacks they never met again

After averaging 278 knots for 20 consecutive days, the *Shenandoah* reached Havre on November 18, 109 days out. The *S. D. Carleton* picked up a tug off Plymouth on November 21, and docked in Havre that night, 112 days out.

In a modern newspaper report Captain Murphy claimed that he had discharged and sailed before any of his antagonists reached Havre, but in this his memory had evidently played him false, because, as Captain Amesbury said, "If James sailed from Havre before I came in, how was it he used to come aboard the *S. D. Carleton* so often as we lay alongside the dock there, and take hot biscuits out of my cook's oven? We both cleared out before either Britisher hove in sight, he with a cargo of French pebbles to be used in making glass, I with a cargo of chalk."

On this passage to the westward across the Atlantic Captain Murphy had a race with the smart British four-mast barque *Swanhilda*, which he succeeded in beating, although his passage of 36 days was nothing wonderful. It must be noted, however, that the two ships had a hard time getting clear of the Channel, for they were battling for 9 days with furious head gales on the French coast.

It was on her second passage out to San Francisco that the *Shenandoah* raced the *Tam o' Shanter*, as recorded on page 97.

After making such an excellent passage as 111 days from New York to San Francisco, Captain Murphy must have been very disappointed to find that the *Tam o' Shanter* had beaten him by three hours. Apparently the *S. D. Carleton* was also in this race, and the three captains had heavy bets on it. Murphy and Amesbury wagered 1000 dollars on their ships, and Murphy also bet 2000 dollars with Captain Peabody that the *Shenandoah* would beat the *Tam o' Shanter*.

The *Tam o' Shanter* sailed from Baltimore the same day as the *Shenandoah* left New York. The two ships met off Cape St. John, and were afterwards in company for a week off the Horn. On arriving outside the Golden Gate, Captain Murphy was obliged to back his mainyards owing to a thick fog. As the fog lifted, the *Tam o' Shanter* passed in tow of a tug and thus managed to win the wager.

Captain Murphy always contended that his ship was the first to reach the entrance. The one trouble in making San Francisco at certain times of the year is fog, and whilst he was in command of the *Shenandoah* Captain Murphy showed his skill in fog navigation off the Golden Gate on two other occasions.

On the first of these he was approaching the land under all sail. The fog whistle on the Farallones was picked up successfully, and then the whistle buoy on the Bar was heard, but, as is often the case with fog, it was quite impossible to tell from what direction the whistle was coming, with the result that in the end the *Shenandoah* ran right over the whistling buoy. The fog signal on Point Benita was next picked up, but the fog was so thick that Captain Murphy decided, when he could no longer hear the whistling buoy, to stand off-shore, and he therefore gave the order to clew up the royals and skysails ; but as soon as the men went aloft they could see the land right ahead over the top of the fogbank. A moment later Captain Murphy, who was standing on the charthouse, could also see the line of the coast.

Ordering the royals and skysails to be sheeted home again, he at once bore away and, bursting out of the fogbank, found himself right in the middle of the channel well inside the Golden Gate.

As the *Shenandoah* raced in through the Bay, a pilot boat

made an effort to hail her but was left standing.   A while later, as the ship was working up to the anchorage, Captain Murphy was hailed by a tug, whose captain ranged up alongside and asked if he might put a gentleman and his wife aboard, who were anxious to see how a sailing ship was worked.

" I let them come aboard," said Captain Murphy in describing the incident, "but I did not have much time for entertaining visitors, for the harbour was full of moving craft, and I only had three miles to get the sail off the ship—she was carrying everything—and bring her to an anchorage."

All hands were on the jump, and the sharp orders from the *Shenandoah's* skipper were obeyed with such smartness that Murphy overheard the visitor say to his wife, "Isn't he an old pirate !   See how the poor sailors are afraid of him."

On the third fog occasion the *Shenandoah* was standing off and on waiting for the fog to lift, when one of the U.S. transports from the Philippines came by.

" My position is 37° 40'" (the latitude of the Golden Gate), sang out the master of the transport from his bridge.

"My position is 37° 30'," roared Captain Murphy.   The transport commander, satisfied with his own reckoning, kept on, and piled his ship up on the rocks right under Point Montera.   He at once reported that he had passed the *Shenandoah* standing in on a parallel course to his own, and that that ship must have also gone ashore. However, he was entirely wrong in his supposition, for Captain Murphy's reckoning was correct, and when the fog lifted the next day the *Shenandoah* sailed safely into port.

Reverting back to her second voyage in 1892, the *Shenandoah* loaded 4800 tons of grain for Liverpool.   This time as antagonists she had the two British four-mast barques, *Wanderer* and *Bracadale*. The *Wanderer*, sailing 24 hours ahead of the *Shenandoah*, arrived at Queenstown on December 6.   The *Shenandoah* did not reach Liverpool until December 14, and just about the time when she was entering the Mersey the *Bracadale* anchored off Queenstown.

The *Shenandoah's* best passage from San Francisco to Liverpool was made in 1896-7, when she anchored in the Mersey on March 12, 1897, 100 days out.

Her best passage from 'Frisco to New York was in 1898, 98 days. On this occasion she was 15 days from the Golden Gate to the Line, and $44\frac{1}{2}$ days from San Francisco to the Horn.

Her passage in 1897 was spoilt by unfavourable weather in the North Pacific, when the big ship actually took 46 days in making the run to the Equator.

Captain Murphy found himself logged in the *Red Record* for an incident which occurred on his outward passage to San Francisco in 1893. He was accused of making no attempt to save a man who fell overboard from the royal yard. The ship was being heavily pressed on a wind under topgallant sails, and the captain's answer was that the weather was too bad for him to lower a boat.

When the Spanish-American War broke out the *Shenandoah* was on a passage from San Francisco to Liverpool. On making the English coast Captain Murphy was given a friendly warning from a British tramp steamer, which made the astonishing statement that there were hostile torpedo boats on the look-out for his famous ship. Captain Murphy first thought that the tramp must mean tug-boats, but his officers were quite sure that the tramp skipper had said torpedo boats.

A little further on the matter was put beyond all doubt, for another tramp not only warned him of the waiting torpedo boats, but actually towed him up the coast until he was within the three-mile limit, where a Liverpool tug was picked up.

It was after this incident, in July, 1898, whilst the *Shenandoah* was lying in the Mersey, that Captain Murphy received a cablegram from his owners instructing him to insure the ship against war risks, for her passage across the Atlantic to Baltimore. Captain Murphy, who, like all Irishmen, was simply thirsting for a fight, decided that guns were the cheapest war policies, and he accordingly bought two 4-inch guns which he mounted on the deck of the *Shenandoah*, one forward and one aft.

Whilst rounding the South-west Coast of Ireland, four days out from Liverpool, the *Shenandoah* fell in with a Spanish gunboat, which fired a shot across her bows in order to make her heave-to. Captain Murphy, who was logging 15 knots under a tremendous press of sail, not only held on his course but fired two rounds at the gunboat, which, after a fruitless chase, was dropped below the horizon in a matter of four hours.

One of the *Shenandoah's* greatest victories whilst commanded by Captain Murphy was in a race against the White Star four-master, *California*, one of the finest of Harland & Wolff's creations. The *California* left San Francisco 10 days before the *Shenandoah*, and was not overhauled until she was in sight of the coast of Ireland one Sunday morning. The wind was blowing fresh, and the *California* had all three royals furled. The *Shenandoah*, however, ranged up on her beam carrying not only her three royals but her main skysail.

Whilst she was commanded by Captain Murphy the *Shenandoah* gained a great reputation for speed, but this, I think, was entirely due to her master's daring methods of sail carrying, for the *Shenandoah*, though capable of 15 knots under favourable conditions, was not a really fast ship, and certainly no faster than others of Sewall's big four-masters which had not her reputation for speed.

The late Captain Woodget of the *Cutty Sark* has recorded overhauling the *Shenandoah* in 56° 12′ S., 72° 44′ W., on January 25, 1895. As the *Cutty Sark* came up Captain Murphy signalled "What ship is that?" being not only irritated but amazed that any little full-rigged ship should be able to overhaul his great four-master in Cape Horn weather. The *Cutty Sark* was bound to London, and reached that port some days before the *Shenandoah* reached Queenstown.

In 1898 Captain Murphy left the *Shenandoah* and took steam to Santiago de Chile in order to supervise the repairs to the *Kenilworth*, which had put in there in distress. However, he could not say good-bye to his old favourite for ever, and in 1902 he again took her over in San Francisco and sailed her to Liverpool and then back to New York. Finally he was in command during her last passage before she was cut down to a barge in 1910.

Between 1902 and 1910 the *Shenandoah* was commanded by Captain O. E. Chapman.

The *Shenandoah* was, on the whole, a lucky ship, but she had one very unlucky passage, and that was in 1907-8. She sailed from Baltimore on March 30, 1907, with 5400 tons of coal for the

CAPT. EDWIN T. AMESBURY.

"PACTOLUS," "JAMES ROLPH," "B. R. CHENEY" AND "HECLA."

"S. D. CARLETON."

"SUSQUEHANNA."

[To face Page 182.

naval yards of San Francisco. For some reason or other, I believe because he had a very weak and inexperienced crew, Captain Chapman decided to sail to San Francisco *via* the Cape rather than round the Horn. The passage seems to have been without incident until June 28, by which time the *Shenandoah* was some 800 miles to the eastward of the Cape of Good Hope. Here she experienced a very severe westerly gale and strained so much that two days later, when the wind moderated, her sluggish movements aroused the suspicions of her officers, and it was then discovered that she was half full of water and leaking badly.

It was soon found that it was only possible to keep the ship afloat by pumping without ceasing, and Captain Chapman wisely altered his course for Melbourne. Until this port was reached the *Shenandoah's* crew, most of whom had never been to sea before, and who included almost every nationality, had a very hard time of it, for in addition to the constant pumping one storm after another kept them sail handling in their watch below. The contemptuous mates declared that the ship lost seven brand-new sails, blown away or torn to ribbons, through the incompetency of her foremast crowd. Speaking to a reporter, the mate remarked : " Why, some of them did not know one end of the ship from the other, and were more of a hindrance than a help to us ! Had we gone round the Horn with such a lot the ship might have been lost, and when all is said and done we are lucky to be alive."

The *Shenandoah* was repaired at Melbourne and continued her passage. After a long trip across the Pacific she once more got into trouble, by running ashore on the treacherous shoals of the Potato Patch on December 26, 1907. This started all her leaks again, and the water was soon nearly 6 ft. deep in her holds. The pumps, however, got the water under, and the following morning a number of tugs towed her off and took her to Mare Island, where she was pumped dry and her cargo of coal discharged.

After this she was put into dry dock and given an extensive overhaul.

The end of her active service came in 1910, when she was sold to Scully of New York for 36,000 dollars in order to be converted into a coal barge.

She was then out at San Francisco, and Captain J. F. Murphy went out to take the command of his famous ship on her last Cape Horn passage. For a few years she suffered the degradation of being towed up and down the American coast ; then just before the end of the War she finished this dreary service by foundering off Shinnecock Bay, Long Island.

The " S. D. Carleton," Captain Amesbury.

The *Shenandoah's* rival on her maiden voyage, the *S. D. Carleton*, was commanded by Captain Edwin T. Amesbury from her launch until 1906, during which time she put up many fine records.

Captain Amesbury was one of the best known of the latter day Down East skippers.   He was born at North Haven on April 3, 1837, and in 1852, when 15 years of age, he started his seafaring career as a boy on the ship *Borodino*.

In those days the second mate of an American ship received his appointment as much for his prowess in handling men as for his capabilities as a seaman.   He was supposed to be able to lick every man-jack of the crew, and he knew that if he allowed any foremast hand to get the better of him that man would at once be promoted into his place by the captain, whilst he would be returned to the fo'c'sle.   However, Captain Amesbury did not have much trouble in maintaining his position as second mate, for although he was only 5 ft. 5 in. in stature his weight in his prime was 220 lbs.   He was so broad, indeed, that people laughingly said that he was as tall lying down as he was standing up.

This wonderful little skipper enjoyed the most perfect health, and was as spritely, active, and bright-eyed in his 84th year as he was in the days before the Civil War.   He always attributed his health to the fact that he had never taken a dollar's worth of medicine in all his life, and this he delighted to announce, with a characteristic chuckle, whenever he happened to be in the presence of a doctor.

His first job as second mate was in the brig *Tullulah*, after which he went in the barque *Richard* ; then he was mate of the schooner *Snow Squall*.   His first command was of the brig *Katahdin*, after which he was master of the schooners, *C. F. Young, E. J. Talbot, Maine Law, Carrie M. Rich,* and *R. E. Pecker,* and the brig *C. S. Packard,* in the West Indian and South American trades.

His first big ship was the barque *Jennie Harkness,* built at Camden in 1879 and registering 1373 tons, which he had for ten years previous to taking over the *S. D. Carleton.*

The *S. D. Carleton* had a very bad time on her maiden passage round the Horn. According to Captain Amesbury she was perfectly sparred, but she spread some canvas, for her mainyard was 96 ft. long, and, unlike most American ships, she carried double topgallant sails.

On February 10, when she was to the southward of the Horn, her topgallant masts went over the side in a fierce Cape Horn snorter, and Captain Amesbury was a whole month battling to make westing, 50° S. in the Pacific not being crossed until March 11. The Equator was reached on April 14, and then the *S. D. Carleton* had a weary run to the Golden Gate, which was not entered until May 29, by which time the ship was 151 days out. Her homeward passage and race with the *Shenandoah* I have already recorded.

The *S. D. Carleton* made several passages in the Australian trade during the nineties. On May 3, 1894, she arrived in Sydney, having made the splendid run of 73 days from Prawle Point.

In the following year, whilst bound out to Melbourne round the Cape, the *S. D. Carleton* was pooped by a veritable mountain of a sea on June 6. This sea broke in the wheel-house, smashed up the wheel, and carried the compass overboard. Of the two men at the wheel one had his arm broken, whilst the other was badly knocked about, and the mate, George W. Hatch, was killed. Nothing was left of the wheel except the upright standard, the hub and the shaft ; but it was in just such a situation that a captain of Amesbury's experience proved his worth. First of all he clamped two heads of beef tierces over the hub of the wheel, then he cut up capstan-bars and stuck them into the sockets in the hub to be used as spokes. These were strung together by a rope, which formed the rim of the improvised wheel. He next made a steering compass by fixing an old compass card to a spindle on the top of a soap box. The spindle was held in this socket by leather, re-inforced by lead in heavy weather. This queer compass was checked by the tell-tale compass in his cabin, and by its means he was enabled to navigate the 2000 miles which the ship was distant from Melbourne.

In 1896 the *S. D. Carleton* had the misfortune to get ashore on the Panjang Reef, Java, when bound out from New York to Shanghai. Captain Amesbury managed to get off unassisted, but the ship was leaking so badly that he was obliged to put into Singapore.

That year the *S. D. Carleton* sailed in the aristocratic London wool fleet. After loading 1468 bales of wool she left Sydney on September 21 and arrived at London on January 2, 103 days out, thus catching the wool sales without any trouble.

At the beginning of the twentieth century the *S. D. Carleton* became one of the California Shipping Company's fleet, and for the next few years did a good deal of timber droghuing across the Pacific between the American ports and Australasia.

Captain Amesbury retired from the command in 1906, and the *S. D. Carleton's* last master was Captain McNaught.

The name of *S. D. Carleton* disappeared from the Register about 1913-14.

"Susquehanna."

Sewall's second wood four-mast barque was over 500 tons smaller than the *Shenandoah*. She was considered to have the prettiest lines of any of the Sewall ships.

The notorious Captain Joe Sewall commanded this ship until 1901, when he was succeeded by M. T. Bailey. Her last master, in 1905-6, was Captain Watts.

On her maiden voyage, after an average passage out to San Francisco, the *Susquehanna* arrived at Liverpool on September 3, 1892, only 94 days out from the Golden Gate.

On her following passage the *Susquehanna* found herself listed in the *Red Record*. On the passage out to San Francisco from New York things had evidently been pretty lively, and on the ship's arrival in April, 1893, the crew complained of their treatment at the hands of the mate, who seems to have been a real fighting officer, for he actually challenged one seaman to a fight on the maindeck.

DECK OF "SUSQUEHANNA."

Lent by J. Randall.

"B. P. CHENEY," "PACTOLUS," "ST. KATHARINE" AND "HECLA."

From a Painting by C. R. Patterson.

Although the mate said he did this to give the man, who was a "limejuicer," a fair show, the seaman does not seem to have appreciated this concession, complaining that he was first knocked down, then tumbled into the lee scuppers, and finally, as he lay there, jumped upon.

This was a comparatively mild charge against one of Captain Sewall's officers, and nothing of course came of it. But when the ship arrived in San Francisco from New York on November 12, 1895, the mate, Ross, was arrested and charged with brutally beating an able seaman named James Whelan. Captain Sewall was furious at the arrest of his mate, and swore that if his officer was convicted he would have his whole crew arrested on a charge of mutiny. The case was heard before the United States Commissioner, Heacock, but also came to nothing.

The best of her later homeward passages were, I believe, the following :—

In 1903 she took 110 days between San Francisco and New York, and in 1904 took a full cargo of sugar from Honolulu to the Delaware Breakwater in 89 days.

On her next voyage the *Susquehannah* loaded 3558 tons of ore at Noumea, New Caledonia, and sailed for Delaware Breakwater. This heavy cargo, added to some severe straining in bad weather, caused the ship to open up, and at last the leaks through the open seams became so bad that her crew of thirty men were unable to keep the water down in the pump well and they were obliged to abandon her on August 24, 1905.

"St. Katherine" and "Pactolus."

The last two ships built for Flint & Co. were the small handy barques, *St. Katherine* and *Pactolus*, both of which came from the board of J. McDonald.

As usual with Flint's vessels, these two barques were beautifully sparred, with the Down Easter's rig of skysails over single topgallant sails.

The *Pactolus* was taken from the stocks by Captain S. Watts, whilst F. E. Frazier was the first commander of the *St. Katherine*. Though I can find no special sailing records to the credit of the

Pactolus, it will be remembered that *St. Katherine* won a thousand-dollar purse by beating the *W. F. Babcock* and *I. F. Chapman* in a race from the Sandwich Islands to the Delaware Breakwater.

Both vessels ended their days as salmon packers, under the management of F. B. Peterson of San Francisco.

When the sailing ships were finally given up in the Alaska trade *Pactolus* and *St. Katherine* were laid up at Antioch, along with the *B. P. Cheney* and the *Hecla.* Here they were painted by the artist, Charles R. Patterson, and I give a reproduction of his painting on the opposite page.

Both ships have since been broken up.

" Parthia."

The last of the Houghton fleet was the *Parthia,* which next to the *Henry B. Hyde* was the largest wooden three-masted ship ever built. Unfortunately she did not have a very long life, being out of the Register before the end of the nineteenth century.

She was commanded by Captain E. O. Day, and her best passage was the one in 1893, when she made the run from San Francisco to New York in 96 days and beat the *Servia* by a day.

The Gigantic " Roanoke."

With the exception of the *Great Republic,* the *Roanoke* was the largest wooden ship ever built in an American yard, and her builder, Mr. Samuel S. Sewall, declared that with her his firm had reached the limit to which wood could be used in shipbuilding. It is therefore interesting to note the different ingredients which went to make up the hull of this huge vessel. These consisted of :—

> 24,000 cubic feet of oak
> 1,250,000 cubic feet of yellow pine
> 98,000 tree-nails
> 550 hackmatack knees.

With a gross tonnage of 3539 the *Roanoke* measured 350 ft. overall, her length of keel being 300 feet. Her spar and sail measurements were equally impressive :

Bowsprit	..	..	..	65 feet
Foremast (from deck to truck)			180	,,
Mainyard	..	..	..	95 ,,
Main lower topsail yard		..	86	,,
,, upper topsail ,,			77	,,
,, topgallant ,,		..	66	,,
,, royal ,,		..	55	,,
,, skysail .. ,,		..	44	,,

Her sail area totalled 15,000 square yards of canvas, and there were 646 square yards in her four headsails.

The *Roanoke* was commanded by Captain J. Hamilton until 1898 ; then Captain J. A. Amesbury had her.

There is no doubt that she was a big, heavy ship to work, but at any rate in her early years she seems to have had real " bucko" officers, who man-handled her crews to some tune; in fact, the *Roanoke* was twice listed in the *Red Record*.

The first occasion was in April, 1893, on the ship's arrival at San Francisco from Philadelphia, when the brothers Orr, the first mate and bosun, were accused of thumping the men. The mate disappeared, but the bosun was tried in the Federal courts, the case being dismissed on the usual ground of "justifiable discipline."

On the second occasion "Black" Taylor was mate. The ship went out to Shanghai and brought a cargo home from Manila to New York, where she arrived on March 13, 1895. This time Captain Hamilton himself was accused of striking the carpenter, Hansome, on the head with a bottle, afterwards putting him in irons and tricing him up to the spanker boom until he was half dead ; whilst "Black" Taylor was indicted for pounding Frank McQueeney into insensibility with a belaying-pin for being asleep whilst on the lookout

The second mate seems to have been a terror also, for whilst the ship was lying in Shanghai he so frightened Edwin Davis, an able seaman, whilst they were at work aloft, that the man lost his hold, fell from the yard and was killed, upon which the second mate is reported to have said with a laugh that " it served the fellow right as he was too slow to be of any use."

From these reports it would seem that the *Roanoke* was indeed a hot ship whilst under the command of Captain Hamilton.

I think it was during this passage from Manila that the ship was becalmed for fifty days in the China Sea.

So far as I know, her best passage was one of 106 days from San Francisco to Queenstown, where she arrived on November 10, 1899.

Captain J. A. Amesbury seems to have avoided any trouble with his men, having quite enough to do to save his ship from fire and collision. Whilst the *Roanoke* was bound from Honolulu to Mare's Island in 1901 with 3000 tons of coal in her hold, one evening in mid-Pacific a wisp of smoke suddenly rose out of one of her hatches, and it only needed a glance below to show that her coal was badly alight. This would have been a serious matter for an iron or steel ship, but doubly so for a wooden one, and Captain Amesbury immediately altered his course for the nearest land, which happened to be Honolulu, 2100 miles away. Luckily the *Roanoke* was supplied with a steam pump and a windmill.

Captain Amesbury describes the battle to save his ship as follows :

We fought that fire all the way west to Honolulu night and day. With the steam engine we pumped water into the ship, and when it reached a 5-ft. level in the hold we set the windmill pump going and kept it down to that level. For days the water went into the hold at a temperature of 69 degrees and came out at from 93 to 95 degrees. Then we began to get charcoal. We made all preparations to leave the ship, but finally brought her to Honolulu.

Though the fire was eventually put out, 20,000 dollars worth of damage was done to the *Roanoke*.

Four years later Sewall's big ship fell a victim to the flames : her last voyage indeed was a disastrous one. During the summer of 1894 she sailed from New York for Melbourne. Shortly after crossing the Line she came into collision with the British steamer *Llangibby*, both vessels being seriously injured. *Roanoke* managed to reach Rio de Janeiro on August 19 whilst the *Llangibby* made for Bahia. Repairs at Rio seem to have taken a very long time, for the ship did not leave that port until December 3. No more was heard of her until January 12, 1895, when the barque *Tasmania* reported speaking her in 41° S., 30° E., when she had her fore topgallant and royal yards on deck. She eventually arrived in Port Phillip on February 23, 244 days out from New York.

"PARTHIA."

"ROANOKE."

"ARYAN."

"OLYMPIC."

From Melbourne Captain Amesbury went to New Caledonia to load ore. It was whilst in port at Noumea, New Caledonia, that the *Roanoke* was burnt and sunk at her anchors in August 10, 1905.

She was all ready to sail, with 3037 tons of ore on board, when the fire broke out. *Susquehanna*—also loaded for what was to be her last passage—and the three-master, *Arabia*, were in port with *Roanoke*. The three crews, amounting to sixty men, fought the flames under the direction of Captain Jabez Amesbury, but it was no use: the *Roanoke* was doomed.

Her famous captain only survived his ship seven years. He died at Rockport, Maine, in April, 1912.

The Queerly Rigged "Olympic."

The *Olympic*, which was built by the New England S.B. Co. at Bath for Captain W. H. Besse of New Bedford, was described in the Register as a four-mast barque ; I suppose because the Registrar did not know what name to give her rig, which was described by seamen as a "fore-and-aft schooner chasing a brig." Some Americans contended that she should be called a "jackass barque."

Captain S. B. Gibbs, who took the *Olympic* from the stocks, has explained how the vessel came to be rigged in this queer fashion. Apparently Captain William H. Besse wished to run a line of vessels out to Puget Sound, taking general cargo from New York and bringing back spars and lumber. This proposed fleet, of which the *Olympic* was the only one built, he wished to be of such stability that they could sail without ballast, and he suggested to Captain Gibbs, who was to take command of the *Olympic*, that she should be rigged as a four-mast barquentine. Captain Gibbs, who was a square-rig seaman born and bred, declared that he did not care to go to sea in a barquentine ; whereupon Captain Besse said that after the Civil War he had bought a wooden gunboat of over 300 ft. in length, and had rigged her with two masts square and two fore-and-aft. This rig apparently had been quite a success, and he proposed rigging the *Olympic* in the same way.

The *Olympic* was not jury-rigged by any means, for she was fitted with double topgallant yards and a main skysail. In order to prove Captain Besse's contention that she did not need ballast, she was sailed from Bath to New York with clean swept holds. She arrived all safe at New York, where she attracted the attention of every sailorman along South Street.

Captain Gibbs found a heavy cargo waiting to be loaded, consisting of steel rails, iron plates, etc. He was careful to see that the stevedores kept their weights high, and two-thirds of this heavy cargo were placed in the 'tween decks.

The *Olympic* made a good passage out to Portland, Oregon, and behaved very well in the usual Cape Horn weather.

The ship seems to have sailed well from the first, and Captain Gibbs declared that she never made a long passage under him, her best being 113 days from Philadelphia to San Francisco, where she arrived on May 7, 1900.

More than once she loaded heavy nitrate cargoes, and here again Captain Gibbs showed his skill at stowage, for he had the old style platform built across her keelsons, and again carried two-thirds of the weight in the 'tween decks.

The *Olympic* was sold to Hackfield & Co. of Honolulu, being managed by Williams, Dimond & Co. at the beginning of the twentieth century, and then for some years kept steadily in the sugar trade between the Sandwich Islands and the Californian coast.

On one of her passages from San Francisco to Honolulu the *Olympic* was dismasted during a severe gale. It was a pitch black night and there was a nasty sea running. There were two men aloft putting extra gaskets on the fore topsail when all of a sudden her foremast and main topmast went by the board. One of the men was never seen again, but the other, in some extraordinary way, contrived to hang on to the wreckage and was hauled aboard uninjured. Captain Gibbs was obliged to cut everything adrift to prevent the heavy spars from knocking holes in the ship, but he managed to make Honolulu under jury rig.

When the *Olympic* was re-rigged after this dismasting she was fitted, as shown in the illustration, with single topgallant sails and no main skysail.

Captain Gibbs left the sea in 1901 and was succeeded by Captain T. H. Evans.

Sailing ships were cut out of the Honolulu sugar trade a few years before the War by the ubiquitous steam tramp, and the *Olympic* was then put into the lumber trade between the Pacific coast and Australia and New Zealand.   She was kept in this trade throughout the War and earned a lot of money for her owners. By this time she had been bought by Thomas Crowley of San Francisco, and the yards had been stripped off her mainmast, thus converting her into a four-mast barquentine.

Her last commander was Captain T. J. Halcrow.   Like most of America's wooden vessels, after being laid up for a few years when the slump came after the War she was cut down into a towing barge.

Minott's "Aryan."

The last ship built by C. V. Minott at Phippsburg was the 2000-ton skysail-yarder *Aryan*.   This vessel is described as having beautiful lines and was evidently a very handsome specimen of a Down Easter.

When the Cape Horn trade began to languish, the *Aryan* retired to the Pacific coast.   She seems to have had a series of well-known shipmasters in command.   Captain W. R. Dickinson took her from the stocks and had her for about ten years, then one of the Pendletons had her for a voyage or two ; he was succeeded by Captain Dickerson ; then came H. O. Sorenson ; and just before the War Captain A. T. Whittier.

On December 18, 1918, the *Aryan* sailed from Wellington, N.Z., under Captain Larsen with a cargo of flax and tallow for 'Frisco. She had not been at sea more than a few days before a fire was discovered.   The usual effort was made to fight the flames, but it was unavailing, and the crew eventually abandoned the ship in three boats.   Those of the captain and the mate arrived safely at the Chatham Islands, but the second mate's boat was never heard of again.

The Unlucky "Holliswood."

The barque *Holliswood* must have been about the last square-rigger launched from the ways at East Boston.   For the first twelve years of her existence she was owned and commanded by Captain E. M. Knight. She seems to have been one of those vessels that were always in trouble, and she was twice badly dismasted.

The first time was in 1903, when she arrived at San Pedro under jury rig and almost entirely out of provisions. On being refitted she was rigged as a barquentine, and sailed from San Francisco on January 20, 1904, for New York with a cargo of asphalt in barrels. When off the coast of California she was again dismasted, her foremast going by the board, and for the second time she seems to have put in to San Pedro in distress. After this she was re-rigged as a three-mast schooner, and continuing her passage eventually reached New York, 169 days out.

The *Holliswood* was still owned by F. S. Pendleton of New York when War broke out, but shortly after this she was sold, I believe, to a San Francisco firm.

The Mighty " Dirigo."

On February 3, 1894, Messrs. A. Sewall & Co. launched the first steel sailing ship ever built in America. This was the mighty four-mast barque *Dirigo*. In appearance the *Dirigo* bore no resemblance to the Down East type either in the modelling of her hull or in the arrangements of her decks ; but this is not surprising for she was designed by J. F. Waddington of Liverpool, England, who was an old Harland & Wolff apprentice, and there was a distinct look of the Belfast ship in America's first steel square-rigger. Her construction was superintended by her designer, and all her steel plates and frames were provided by Messrs. David Colville & Sons of Motherwell, near Glasgow, and sent across to Bath in the steamer *Buckingham*.

The *Dirigo* was in fact a typical British four-master of the nineties. She was designed to carry 4500 tons of deadweight on a draught of 22 ft. 6 ins. and to stand up without ballast. She was built to Lloyd's scantling and under their survey, her deck plan being entirely British with the usual full poop and topgallant fo'c'sle ; and with the steel houses on the maindeck connected to each end by flying bridges. She was also steered by the Waddington screw steering gear, but the helmsman was protected by a steel wheelhouse open at the forward end.

The *Dirigo* spread 13,000 square yards of canvas and was given the handsome American rig of skysails and single topgallant sails. She was not particularly fast, but under Captain G. W. Goodwin, who took her from the stocks, she made the following good passages :

San Francisco to Queenstown	..	107 days
Honolulu to Philadelphia	..	118 ,,
Shanghai to Port Angeles	..	31 ,,
Seattle to San Francisco	..	8 ,,

She also made one or two longish passages such as 162 days from San Francisco to Liverpool in 1901. On this passage she sailed a dead heat with the French ship *Touraine*, both vessels arriving on April 1 the same number of days out.

Another long passage was from Hongkong to Honolulu in ballast—104 days in 1902. The captain's letter in explanation of this long passage shows the difficulties of beating against the strength of the N.E. monsoon and current for a big barque in ballast. He writes :

We sailed from Hongkong bound to Hilo on January 23, 1902, the ship drawing 12 ft. 10 ins. The first night out we took a fresh gale from N.E. by E. which lasted three days ; at times we could carry reefed topgallant sails. The third day out we were 300 miles south and 100 miles east of Hongkong. The wind then favoured us and we stood in and made Cape Balanhazy, Luzon. Off there I saw a four-masted schooner and also saw the same schooner 25 days later off the South Cape of Formosa.

We worked up the coast of Luzon and nearly out to the Bashee Islands, when we got an E.N.E. gale and picked ourselves up over at Pratas Reef. We sighted the light on Breaker Point twice, the last time when we were 31 days out from Hongkong (Breaker Point is about 150 miles E.N.E. from Hongkong). We got over to the South Cape of Formosa three times and each time it blew from the N.E. and E.N.E., a single reefed topsail breeze, with heavy squalls of wind and torrents of rain. These strong winds would last three days and we would lose all we had gained in the previous ten days.

I signalled the ship *J. B. Everett* from Manila, she out-pointed and out-sailed us and probably got by Formosa where we missed doing so by a few miles.

We rounded the South Cape of Formosa on the 44th day out from Hongkong. During the interval we sailed 4336 miles by log. There was not a day when we had less than 25 miles current, setting S.W. by W. and S.W., and frequent gales would increase it to 40 miles per day. After rounding the South Cape we got into the Kuriosiwo Stream and passed up the east side of Formosa through the Eastern Sea and into the Pacific *via*

Van Dieman Strait. We spent two nights and one very anxious day in the Strait, and I want to say that it is a good place to keep out of with a light ship. However, we drifted through all right and up the coast to Japan, and I did not have the pleasure of steering a course with the yards off the backstays until we were east of Japan.

We crossed the Pacific on the parallel of 42°, and had mostly southerly and easterly winds and torrents of rain, with an occasional spurt from W. to N.W.

I fully realised what I had to go through when I left Hongkong. We wore ship 52 times whilst in the China Sea, and altogether we have had to wear ship 81 times this passage ; owing to the current and sea we were not able to tack once.

The *Dirigo* eventually arrived at Honolulu on May 9.

Another longish passage across the Pacific was from Newcastle to Honolulu in 63 days.

The writer, Jack London, once made a trip in the *Dirigo* from New York round the Horn to San Francisco, and from his experiences on this passage he published a very fanciful blood-and-thunder novel, in which the hero and heroine undergo the most incredible adventures in a hell-ship.

In 1909 Captain D. E. Chapman took over the command of America's first steel sailer. In the spring of 1912 there was some talk of fitting her with auxiliary machinery in order to utilise the Panama Canal, but this was never done.

The *Dirigo* fell a victim to a German submarine in 1917. It appears that she loaded a cargo of barley at Seattle and sailed for Kalmar, Sweden, on October 14, 1915. When off the coast of Scotland after an uneventful passage round the Horn she was stopped by the British patrol vessel *Orotava* on March 2, 1916. It seems that information had been received by the Admiralty stating that the *Dirigo's* cargo had been shipped by a German agent, and that it had been arranged for her to be captured by the Germans as soon as she was inside the Cattegat. The British patrol vessel put an armed guard on board, which took her into Lerwick. Here one of the seamen, who turned out to be a German, was arrested and interned. Proof that the information was correct was also forthcoming, and the *Dirigo* was condemned, her cargo being disposed of by the Prize Court.

With tonnage worth its weight in gold, the crack American four-master, whose smart appearance had been greatly admired

"DIRIGO."

"ERSKINE M. PHELPS."

Lent by J. P. Graham.

"ARTHUR SEWALL."

by the Shetlanders, was speedily sent off on another voyage, but she was submarined before she could get clear of British waters.

This happened on May 31, 1917, to the south-west of the Eddystone.

Sewall's Big Clipper, "Erskine M. Phelps."

From the registered measurements of the *Erskine M. Phelps* it will be seen that she was a pretty close imitation of the *Dirigo*. She was Sewall's first attempt at a steel ship, and though I have not seen her lines it is evident from her performances that she must have been a finer lined model than the *Dirigo*, or else her commander, Captain Bob Graham, must have been a marvel at getting her along.

Here are a few of her astonishing records :

Norfolk (Va.) to Honolulu	.. ..	15,000 miles	97 days
,, ,, Ombai Passage	..	14,880 ,,	77 ,,
New York to Java	.. .. ..	13,000 ,,	80 ,,
Java to Chile	.. ..	11,600 ,,	58 ,,
Chile to Philadelphia	.. ..	10,000 ,,	95 ,,
Chile to Baltimore	.. ..	10,000 ,,	96 ,,
Seattle to Philadelphia ..	.. ..		88 ,,
Port Townsend to Norfolk (Va).	..		107 ,,
From 50° S. to 50° S. round Cape Horn		2,000 ,,	11 ,,
Across the Indian Ocean	.. ..	6,500 ,,	26 ,,
Equator to Cape Hatteras	.. ..	3,000 ,,	18 ,,
Bath (Maine) to Cape Henry ..	..	540 ,,	2½ ,,

On her passage from Seattle to Philadelphia, which was made in 1906, she only had 6 sailors out of the 26 men in her fo'c'sle. Off Staten Island, according to the newspaper report, the log was hove every 30 minutes and 19 knots were taken out.

In 1908 she was in company with the big German five-master *Potosi* off the Horn, *Potosi* being in the lead. At 6 a.m. both ships were abeam of Cape Stiff and by 5 p.m. *Potosi* was hull down astern. The best day's run on this passage is given as 359 miles.

In her run from the Equator to Cape Hatteras her best speed is given as 14 knots, and her best day's work 310 miles. She also covered 1675 miles in six days on this traverse.

During the time that Captain Graham commanded the *Erskine M. Phelps* she was a frequent visitor to Honolulu, where her "old

man" was very much respected.   Captain Graham was exceedingly
dignified and upheld the honour of American shipmasters in every
port where he went.   A very alert and active man, he had the
reputation of being a hard nut to serve under at sea, but anyone
who attempted to drive a big four-master under the conditions
prevailing at sea in the last days of sail had to be able to get the best
out of the poor material generally found in a deep-waterman's
fo'c'sle, and this could only be done by severe discipline.

Mrs. Graham always sailed with her husband aboard the
"Phelps," and many people declared that she was quite capable of
taking charge of the ship herself should the occasion arise.

In days when motors were in their infancy the Grahams always
carried a motor-car aboard the "Phelps," which they found very
useful during their stays in port.

The *Erskine M. Phelps* survived the War and is still afloat, but
she has been refitted as an oil barge by the Associated Oil Company.
She now spends her days behind a tow boat trading out of San
Francisco with oil in bulk.   Her lower masts are still standing and
her owners see that she is well kept up, so that she is likely to be
doing duty in her present humble capacity for many years to
come.

"Arthur Sewall" and "Edward Sewall."

In 1899 Arthur Sewall & Co. launched the two lumping
barques *Arthur Sewall* and *Edward Sewall*.   Captain Jim Murphy
took the *Arthur Sewall* from the stocks, whilst Captain J. E. Sewall
took the *Edward Sewall*.   After making one voyage Captain Murphy
handed over to Captain B. Gaffry, whilst Captain Sewall handed
over to Captain Richard Quick.

On her first passage of the Horn the *Arthur Sewall* very nearly
came to grief.   Whilst she was clawing off Cape Stiff under three
lower topsails in the teeth of a regular hurricane during a pitch
dark night, the mate, whose watch it was, suddenly caught a glimpse
through the rain and driving spray of a faint light under the lee
bow.   He immediately called Captain Murphy who, after peering
anxiously into the darkness to leeward for a few moments, decided
that it was a vessel hove-to on the same tack as the *Arthur Sewall*.

It was soon apparent, however, that the "Sewall" was drifting rapidly down on to the other ship, which was evidently making less leeway than she was. As there was no time to bear away under the stranger's stern, Captain Murphy recognised that his only hope, in order to prevent a collision which would have been fatal to both ships in such weather, was to set more sail, so as to draw ahead of the other ship.

All hands were called on deck and all the fore-and-aft canvas that would stand was quickly run up and sheeted home. Slowly the *Arthur Sewall* surged up abreast of the other ship, which now showed her alarm by sending up rockets and burning flares. For a few anxious moments the two ships hung beam and beam, whilst the *Arthur Sewall* seemed to be dropping bodily on top of the stranger.

At last, when it seemed that the two vessels must collide, being only separated by one sea, the *Arthur Sewall* gave a plunge ahead and drew clear.

On the following morning the stranger was still in sight, and she turned out to be a steel four-master, probably of British or German nationality, and she was bowing the Cape Horn greybeards under bare poles, which accounted for the fact that her leeway was so much less than that of the *Arthur Sewall*.

The latter ship, whilst still under the command of Captain B. Gaffry, fell a victim to the Horn in 1908. She was posted as " missing," but the wreck was found by a sealing schooner off Noir Island, half-way between the Horn and Cape Pillar.

The *Arthur Sewall* had left Philadelphia for Seattle on April 3, with 4900 tons of coal for the American fleet in the Pacific. On August 3 the sealing schooner *Fritjof* arrived in the Straits of Magellan and reported that whilst she was off the southern end of Noir Island she sighted a derelict, which was lying sunk to the height of her topmasts but had her royals still set. It was evident that the wreck was quite a recent one, and so the schooner cruised round in the neighbourhood for some time in hopes of picking up her crew. On Noir Island traces were found of the missing men, and the skipper of the *Fritjof* sent search parties along the shore, but was afraid to allow his crew to leave the coast owing to the hostility of the

Tierra del Fuego natives. Finally the schooner was obliged to abandon the search without discovering any of the missing sailors, who, it was reported, must either have perished from exposure to the weather or else been killed by the hostile savages.

The *Edward Sewall* was commanded by Captain Richard Quick with great success for no less than twenty-one years, during which time she made a number of smart passages and weathered out more than one hurricane. The following are about the best of her passages:

Honolulu to Philadelphia	..	107 days
San Francisco to New York	..	111 ,,
Shanghai to Puget Sound	..	22 ,,
Puget Sound to Honolulu	..	12 ,,
San Francisco to Honolulu	..	10 ,,

The *Edward Sewall* very nearly fell a victim to fire, the dreaded enemy of all Sewall's ships. With a cargo of coal from Newport News for Honolulu, the beginning of February, 1912, found her in the Pacific about 1400 miles E.S.E. of Hilo. The coal in the forehold was then discovered to be smouldering. Captain Quick immediately put all hands to work shovelling the coal away from the affected area and pumping water in upon it.

From the first it was touch and go, and Captain Quick made all preparations for abandoning the ship. The lifeboats on the forward house were brought aft, and each boat was provisioned for thirty days.

Meanwhile the fight against the fire went on night and day. There was no thought of sleep, and the men shovelling the coal often dropped on the deck with exhaustion. Luckily the weather was quiet, with light, fair winds, which carried the ship along at about 100 miles a day.

The seat of the fire was round the foot of the foremast, and this great steel telescope alarmed all hands by suddenly settling down a couple of feet. The heat of the fire had softened the steel at the base of the mast until it had buckled and allowed the whole mass of steel, wire, and hemp, weighing close on 60 tons, to come down with a bump.

The best that Captain Quick could do was to keep the fire more or less under control until he reached Honolulu. For fourteen days the fight went on, and no less than 300 tons of coal were burnt before the flames were extinguished in Honolulu harbour.

The resourceful "old man" of the *Edward Sewall* planned and carried out the repairs to her foremast whilst lying at Honolulu. The operation took 21 days. First of all 700 railroad ties in two piles were placed about the base of the foremast, with 200 8 ins. × 8 ins. 4 ft. blocking and four immense steel trusses on top. Then, by means of two 20-ton hydraulic jacks and four 15-ton screw jacks, the mast was lifted and the buckled section cut off and renewed. This buckled piece of the mast Captain Quick kept aboard the ship as a momento of her narrow escape.

The *Edward Sewall's* worst experience in rounding Cape Horn was during the winter of 1913-14. She sailed from Philadelphia on October 18, 1913, and reached the latitude of the Horn when 60 days out. Whilst head-reaching against a heavy gale in December the bowsprit was broken short off as the ship took a deep plunge, and Captain Quick was obliged to bear away for repairs. He put into Bahia Blanca, Argentina, where the bowsprit was refitted.

Sailing again on January 9, 1914, the *Edward Sewall* had no sooner reached Cape Stiff than the first gale carried away the bowsprit again. Once more the big ship was put back to Bahia Blanca, but this time a new bowsprit was built, and it was not until March 7 that the *Edward Sewall* crossed 50° S. latitude in the Atlantic and once more attempted the passage of Cape Horn.

For the next 67 days she fought her way to 50° S. in the Pacific, which was not crossed until May 9. In 46 days to May 1 Captain Quick was only able to get seven chronometer sights for longitude and five sights for latitude. The usual entry in the ship's log was " Strong gale and heavy sea ; wind W.N.W. to W.S.W. ; ship under water."

On April 20 Captain Quick fell a victim to the rough treatment of Cape Horn, which he thus records in his log :

April 20, 1914.—Fresh breezes and sky overcast and light drizzling rain. 6 p.m., wore ship; whilst rounding the fore yards I got hurt and laid up.

From April 23 to 30 the *Edward Sewall* lay head-reaching in the grip of a Cape Horn snorter. On April 29 the captain wrote in his abstract :

Terribly heavy W.N.W. gale with terribly heavy snow squalls : ship under two lower topsails.   At 10 a.m. main lower topsail blew away although it was a brand-new sail and bent for the first time.   This gale lasted 42 hours at hurricane force with a terribly heavy sea.   I have been on deck all this time and am getting pretty tired.

Then on April 30th he records :

At 4 a.m. the gale moderated and we are back to the Cape again.

On May 2 the *Edward Sewall* lay all day in a Cape Horn calm, the great Cape Horn greybeards running sluggishly by in long ridges which were from 50 to 60 ft. high.   Then from 8 a.m. to 6 p.m. on the 3rd it blew a hard N.W. gale.   On May 4 it was again calm all day with a heavy rain falling without ceasing.   On May 8 the captain records that the decks were dry for the first time in 60 days and the royals were set for the first time for 54 days.   On May 10, the *Edward Sewall* at last got abreast of Cape Pillar.

Some two months later, on July 1, the *Edward Sewall* put into Hololulu for provisions, and she finally arrived at Seattle on August 5, having been out ten months or 293 days.   This was the last westward trip of an American ship round the Horn.

Between 1915 and 1920 the *Edward Sewall* was running to South American ports and the East with case oil under the flag of the Texas Oil Company.

Few ships escape having to face the dreaded cyclone at some time or other in their career, and the *Edward Sewall* was no exception.   Her ordeal came after she had been sold to the Texas Oil Co.   The ship was outward bound from the Mississippi and about 200 miles out in the Caribbean when a typical West Indian hurricane came down upon her.   Captain Quick and his officers had snugged the ship down and made every preparation before the worst of the wind hit her, and for the first thirty hours the *Edward Sewall* weathered it out without serious damage.   Unfortunately she was right in the path of the storm, and at the end of the thirty hours she ran into the centre of it.

As a rule the centre of a cyclone is filled with seas like pyramids tumbling about in an earthquake, and this is the only instance I have come across where the centre of the storm was calm water. Here is the captain's own statement :

The water was as calm as the river to-day (he was alluding to the Mississippi)

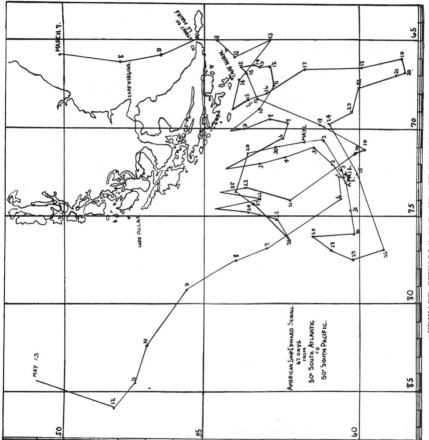

"EDWARD SEWALL." 67 DAYS OFF THE HORN.

Courtesy of F. P. Harlow.

"ATLAS."

"WILLIAM P. FRYE."

and the wind died out completely. The storm centre was filled with birds—scores of varieties, completely worn out from trying to fly in the wind. They fell on the deck in hundreds and they were so exhausted that they would not get out of our way. When the sailors went about the deck they stepped on them. More and more fell on the deck during the three hours that we remained in the storm centre, but we were too excited to pay any attention to them except to see that they were there.

The barometer fell lower and lower—I tell you it was enough to make a man jump overboard just to watch it. Never in my forty years at sea have I seen anything like it. At the end of three hours we reached the other side of the hurricane centre, and within a few minutes from a glassy sea we were in the roughest sort of water.

The hurricane was a quick moving one and left the *Edward Sewall* astern in three hours, but in those three hours it almost tore the vessel to pieces aloft. Steel masts were broken off like carrots, and wire stays carried away as if they had been cut through with an axe.

The *Edward Sewall* managed to stagger into Port Arthur under jury rig, and her repairs to hull and gear cost 136,000 dollars. However, when she was once more sent afloat there was little fault to find with her.

The *Edward Sewall* was one of the few sailing ships which were painted white from the trucks to the waterline, and this gave her a very smart appearance. She was a family ship, for Captain Quick took his wife to sea with him, and both his daughters, Susie and Clarabel, were born aboard, the latter during a night of shrieking wind and raging sea, when the old ship was battling with one of the worst storms encountered during her long career. It must have been a bad time for Captain Quick, who had to watch out for the ship with a heart torn with anxiety for his wife down below.

The following journalist's account of the living quarters aboard the *Edward Sewall*, with its glimpse of peace and comfort, is of interest when contrasted with the hard life both fore and aft that was met with aboard the average Cape Horner :

The living room of the captain and family is 18 ft. square, with Oriental rugs picked up in various parts of the world. There is an upright piano, a music cabinet with popular and classical music—a hymnbook for Sunday—as well as music books from France, Germany, and Spain.

Several easy-chairs stand invitingly about ; a sofa is against the wall. The walls are decorated with Japanese prints. The portholes are covered with white curtains.

There is a sort of charm in the cabin which is hard to define. It seems that the family that lived here was a happy, genial family. Something of the atmosphere still clings, although the family is no longer there, but is living in a big white house in Maine.

Beyond the cabin is the main bedroom with a large bed just like you have ashore, and a smaller bedroom opens from this. This smaller bedroom is where Susie used to sleep, with a whole flock of dolls on her pillow. Why, the captain remembers how Susie used to scold when heavy seas caused her babies to fall out of bed at night, but that was long ago—Susie is older now and no longer plays with dolls.

You go on—there is a large bathroom, and beyond this you can see the stern of the ship and the great iron neck of the rudder, and here in the stern is the captain's tool box and store room : "You know I like to tinker around myself," he said.

Off the living room in the other direction is the dining-room with a large table and a sideboard, and across the passage-way there is a spotless pantry. From this door you go directly to the maindeck, passing the mate's and second mate's quarters on the way or one can go by the stairs, resplendent with shining brass, to the captain's cabin on the poop deck.

This is an office with a roll-top desk and typewriter. The captain must speak to someone—you take a hasty peep at the bookshelves. What does a man read when he is at sea ? Here you find *The North Pacific Directory* and stand aghast at the magnitude of the subject ! Next to it is *Wrinkles on Practical Navigation*, which seems logical enough even to a landlubber like you, and then *Records of American and Foreign Shipping*, and *Nearest the Pole* by Peary. . . . "

The journalist now loses himself in a discussion on the novels of Joseph Conrad, whom apparently the captain had never heard of, and so we will leave him and the *Edward Sewall*.

Captain Quick retired from the sea when the *Edward Sewall* was sold to the Alaska Packers Association at New Orleans in 1922.

The Swift "Kaiulani."

This rakish-looking steel barque, which was built by A. Sewall & Co. for Williams, Dimond & Co. of San Francisco in 1899, was considered one of the fastest square-riggers in the Pacific in the days before the War, and her master, Captain P. Colly, firmly believed that she could sail round anything afloat.

When the port of Newcastle, N.S.W., was packed tight with shipping during 1905, owing to the protracted coal strike, most of the waiting ships were due to load across the Pacific to the West Coast, either North or South. The *Kaiulani* was one of those chartered for San Francisco, and in the betting as to which ship would make the best passage she was a firm favourite. However, she was beaten by the big British oil sailer *Daylight*, her passage being no better than 83 days against the *Daylight's* 60.

A few years before the War the *Kaiulani* became a member of the Alaska Packers' fleet, and under the name of *Star of Finland* is still afloat.

The " William P. Frye."

This huge four-master was the last vessel which Sewall & Co. built for their own use. She was named for the distinguished Maine senator, William P. Frye, who was the foremost champion of American shipping. Captain J. E. Sewall was master of the "Frye" from her launch until 1909, when H. A. Nickerson took her over.

There was a very close resemblance between all Sewall's steel ships, and in her measurements the *William P. Frye* was a sister ship of the *Astral*, *Acme*, and *Atlas*, which Sewall built for the Standard Oil Co. between 1900 and 1902.

About the best passage that I can find was *William P. Frye's* outward run round the Horn in 1903, when she arrived at San Francisco on August 20, 120 days from Cape Henry. After this good run she went across to Honolulu and loaded 5000 tons of sugar. The Sandwich Island sugar trade was booming at that date, and ships often found it difficult to get manned. On this occasion the *William P. Frye* had to fill up her fo'c'sle with Japanese and Kanakas.

On this voyage, by the way, *William P. Frye* was commanded by Captain Jim Murphy, whilst Captain Joe Sewall took a rest. Before taking over the "Frye" Captain Murphy had been suffering badly from rheumatism, but he had not been at sea three weeks before the pain had all vanished and he never had another touch of it.

Captain Murphy made two round voyages in the *William P. Frye*. He then handed her back to Captain Sewall, and finally retired from the sea.

On August 28, 1911, the *William P. Frye* arrived at Philadelphia with a cargo of 90,000 bags of raw sugar, 124 days out from Kahului. The ship was off Cape Horn in midwinter and was held up by strong easterly winds and terrific snow flurries, whilst off the pitch of the Horn itself she was actually hemmed in by bergs and field ice, which covered an area of 18 miles.

The *William P. Frye* was the first American merchantman to be destroyed by the Germans. Bound with a cargo of grain from Seattle to Liverpool, the big four-master ran full tilt into the German merchant cruiser, *Prinz Eitel Friedrich*, in Latitude 29° 45′ N., Longitude 24° 50′ W. The Germans, after removing her crew, blew her up by dynamite bombs on January 28, 1915.

"Astral," "Acme" and "Atlas."

These three sister ships of the *William P. Frye* were built by Sewall & Co., to the order of the Standard Oil Company for their oil trade out to the East. Amongst the British built oil sailers they had the reputation of being very heavy to handle owing to their large sail plans. Their royal yards were actually 56 ft. in length. When they came out their doublings were too short, with the result that their topgallant masts had not much chance when caught aback, and on more than one occasion went over the side.

J. W. Dunham commanded the *Astral* during the years that she sailed under the Standard Oil flag. He left her when she was sold to the Alaska Packers five years before the War, when Captain P. C. Rasmussin took command.

The *Acme's* first commander was Captain R. S. Lawrence, a regular giant amongst shipmasters, both in his stature and his capabilities as a seaman. He was succeeded by Captain McKay about 1906.

The *Atlas* was taken from the stocks by Captain A. F. McKay, and about 1906 he was succeeded by a real hard case Blue-nose skipper who soon gave the *Atlas* the reputation of being a first-class hell-ship. At last this holy terror, as his crew called him, got into trouble over some stowaways and had to give up the command. Nor did the new skipper of the big oil sailer succeed in changing her reputation. On his first passage he was compelled to put into Rio with a mutiny on board. Then, when the *Atlas* resumed her voyage, she managed to run into a Norwegian ship off the Horn and sink her.

The *Atlas* was sold to the Alaska Packers at the same time as the *Astral*, but the *Acme* was not registered in San Francisco until a year or two later, when she became the *Star of Poland*.

CHAPTER VII.

THE LAST OF AMERICA'S SQUARE-RIGGERS.

DURING the last thirty years the surviving Down Easters have mostly found a refuge in the following three trades :
1. The West Coast lumber and coal trade.
2. The Hawaiian sugar trade.
3. The Alaska salmon packers

In the West Coast lumber trade the old square-riggers gradually gave place to big fore-and-afters—four-mast schooners, barquentines, and the like—but in the other two trades square sail remained until the end.

The present flourishing condition of Hawaiian shipping is due almost entirely to the enterprize of five firms, Brewer, Spreckels, Matson, Welch and Williams, Dimond.

C. Brewer & Co.

Messrs. C. Brewer & Co. of Boston were, I believe, the first people to engage in a regular trade between New York and Honolulu. I have already described their *Amy Turner* at some length. Besides this beautiful little barque Smith & Townsend built the following wooden barques for them—*Coringa, Martha Davis, Edward May, John D. Brewer*.

The *Coringa*, commanded by one of the best known captains in the trade, Walter Lyman Josselyn, was wrecked on the Malay Peninsula during a hurricane in 1879. Captain Josselyn, his family, and crew spent four months amongst the Malays before being rescued, the mate, Mr. Weeks, walking across the Peninsula to Penang in order to gain assistance.

Captain Josselyn was the veteran skipper of the firm, with

whom he was connected for forty years. He was born at Duxbury, Mass., in 1841, and was 57 years at sea during the whole of which time he only served in six ships. The *John D. Brewer*, which was one of the six, was wrecked on the coast of Zanzibar in 1897.

The little *Martha Davis* was burnt in the harbour of Hilo in 1903.

Amy Turner and *Edward May*, the last of Brewer's Down East built ships, were sold in 1898, the former to Welch & Co. and the latter to C. Nelson, both of San Francisco.

"Foohng Suey" and "Helen Brewer."

At the end of the eighties, with the Hawaiian sugar plantations beginning to go ahead, Messrs. Brewer & Co. had two ships built of steel at Glasgow. These they were obliged to register under the Hawaiian flag. The first was a beautiful little steel barque of 1060 tons named the *Foohng Suey*. She was launched from the yard of Napier, Shanks & Bell of Glasgow in September, 1888, and with a tall rig topped by a main skysail made quite a reputation as a sailer, one of her best passages being from New York round the Horn to Honolulu 115 days in 1909.

Brewer's second Glasgow built ship was the steel full-rigger, *Helen Brewer*, of 1607 tons. This ship was built by Robert Duncan in 1891, and was also a very handsome main skysail-yarder. The *Helen Brewer* went missing between Sourabaya and the Delaware Breakwater in 1903.

"Iolani" and "Nuuanu."

During the nineties Brewer & Co. bought two little iron barques, the *Thurland Castle*, which they renamed *Iolani*, and the *Highland Glen*, which they renamed *Nuuanu*.

The *Iolani*, which registered 1306 tons, was built by Harland & Wolff in 1876. She did not last very long, being out of the Register by the beginning of the twentieth century.

The *Nuuanu*, which, by the way, was named after the beautiful valley immediately behind the city of Honolulu, registered 1032 tons and was built by Ramage & Ferguson in 1882.

The *Foohng Suey* and *Nuuanu* continued to sail under Brewer's

HONOLULU IN THE FIFTIES.
From painting in smoking room of S.S. *Malolo.*

Courtesy of Matson Navigation Co.

"NUUANU."

Lent by A. Moore, Esq.

house-flag until 1912, in which year they were both sold and the two veteran brothers went out of business on the opening of the Panama Canal.

When the Hawaiian Islands were annexed by the United States in 1898 all vessels with Hawaiian registry were admitted automatically to that of the U.S.A. The *Nuuanu* had the distinction of being the last vessel to enter the port of Honolulu flying the Hawaiian flag, as she was on her passage out from New York when the Islands were annexed.

The *Nuuanu* was commanded by Captain W. L. Josselyn from the date of her purchase until she was sold, during the whole of which time—from 1896 to 1913—the *Foohng Suey* was commanded by Captain J. E. Willett.

Of the two barques the *Foohng Suey* was considered the faster, yet *Nuuanu's* passages were always well above the average, her best from New York to Honolulu being 112 days, and her worst 157 days. Homewards from Hawaii to the Delaware Breakwater her time was generally between 110 and 130 days.

"Nuuanu's" Last Horn Passage.

On her last passage out to Honolulu the *Nuuanu* had a very bad time of it off the Horn. Sailing from New York on August 12, 1911, November 3 found her hove-to under a goose-winged main topsail in Lat. 55° 26′ S., Long. 64° W. The royal yards were down, and with everything about the decks double lashed and well secure, Captain Josselyn was satisfied that his handy little ship was able to cope with the very worst efforts of Cape Horn. However, the squalls came harder and harder, and faster and faster, until from the ordinary Cape Horn snorter the gale had increased to a veritable hurricane, such a blow as the veteran skipper had only seen once in his life before and that during a cyclone.

Gradually the bravely struggling *Nuuanu* was forced down on to her side, until she was almost on her beam ends. Captain Josselyn eased off his main topsail sheet in order to spill the wind in the hopes that this would right his vessel. But the relief was only temporary, and as the wind veered in the squalls from the north-west to the south-west and even to south, the ship was on the wrong tack for the sea running.   An effort was made to wear the ship round on to the other tack, when she would have been heading the seas.   The reefed foresail was somehow set, but almost immediately blew away, and Captain Josselyn had to abandon the attempt. Presently the lee bulwarks began to wash away, and matters looked so serious that the captain ordered the weather topgallant backstays to be cut, in the hopes that the topgallant masts would go over the side.   However, the topgallant rigging held the masts, and it was too risky for any man to go aloft to cut this away.

All this time the thermometer was below freezing point, and the sprays were freezing where they fell, so that the ship's rigging, masts and even the sails, were soon encased.

On the 4th, with the wind at south, it lightened a little, and Captain Josselyn managed to get the fore topmast staysail and jib set.   These helped the ship off the wind until she was running before the wind and sea.   The fore lower topsail was then set although there were no braces on the port side, as they had all been carried away with the bulwarks, which had gone from the fore rigging to the after part of the main rigging.

As usual in such a case, the cargo had shifted down to leeward, and also a great deal of water had got below through the bolt-holes round the broken stanchions.

Setting his main upper topsail Captain Josselyn ran away to the northward in the hopes of finer weather, but it was still blowing a heavy gale, and presently the fo'c'sle was completely gutted, the men losing everything they possessed except the clothes they stood up in.   The galley was also washed out and the stove broken. Luckily it was possible to boil water in the cabin, and until the ship arrived at Port Stanley all hands had to make out on tea, coffee, and hard tack.

The morning of the 5th found the wind at west, thick and rainy.   Soon after daybreak the western end of the Falkland Islands was sighted, and the *Nuuanu* was kept away east in order to make Port Stanley.   As the weather was very thick Captain Josselyn kept as close in as he dared, running from headland to headland under main upper and fore lower topsails.

The *Nuuanu* ploughed through fields of kelp and, Captain

Josselyn was very anxious, as he did not trust his chart very much in that locality, yet he had to keep close in for fear of missing Port Stanley.

The lighthouse was sighted at noon on the 6th, and the *Nuuanu* hauled close in with a distress signal flying and the pilot flag up. The topsails were now taken in, and under his fore-and-aft canvas Captain Josselyn ran in as far as he could, then let go an anchor. Presently the harbourmaster came out in a launch, and without coming very near sang out to give her 90 fathoms of chain and have the second anchor ready, as the tug was laid up.

About 4 p.m. the steamer *Columbus*, a coaster, came down to the *Nuuanu*, and by 9 p.m. the barque was safely moored in Port Stanley.

The gale which the *Nuuanu* had come through was considered to be one of the worst ever known in the Falklands. Three other vessels managed to put back to Port Stanley. The first was the old British four-mast barque, *Albion*, now a Russian. She had struggled in from the longitude of the Horn. The second was the British ship, *Claverdon*, homeward bound from Australia. She had lost sails, had her bulwarks washed away, and an apprentice drowned. The third was the Shire Line four-mast barque, *Kinrossshire*, which had had to jettison a portion of her cargo.

The *Nuuanu* was found to have 28 inches of water in the well besides a big list to port, and Captain Josselyn reckoned that she had 120 tons of water in her hold.

After some time spent in refitting, the passage was resumed on April 26, 1912, and the *Nuuanu* eventually arrived at Honolulu on July 25, 1912. She was then sold to the General Petroleum Corporation of Los Angeles, who used her for the transportation of fuel oil between San Diego, Southern California and Hilo. After a few years of this a Diesel engine was installed, which was apparently very successful.

She now belongs to the Philippine Vegetable Oil Company of San Francisco, is rigged as a three-mast schooner, and is named *Hai Hong*. She runs regularly between the Philippine Islands and San Francisco carrying cocoanut oil.

Captain Walter Lyman Josselyn.

The ·*Foohng Suey* was sold to the Texas Company of New York in 1912. Her last Cape Horn passage under Brewer's house-flag was 139 days from Honolulu to New York. Captain Josselyn took charge of the old ship under her new owners, but died at New York in 1913 whilst still in command.

Captain Walter Lyman Josselyn was one of the last survivors of that wonderful clan, the Down East master mariners. Born at Duxbury, Massachusetts, in 1841, he was just on sixty years going to sea, and he had actually made sixty trips round Cape Horn.

The old skipper had had many curious and exciting experiences and he was a most entertaining lecturer on all sea subjects. No doubt there are still many people in Honolulu who will remember those delightful lectures of Captain Josselyn.

The Dismasting of the "Foohng Suey."

On the death of Captain Josselyn a Captain Haydn took over the command of the *Foohng Suey*. In February, 1914, she left Philadelphia loaded deep with a cargo of coal, and on her passage to New Orleans ran into a terrific south-west gale. The barometer had given good warning, and the ship had been snugged down to lower topsails. However, at 9 a.m. on February 7 a heavy squall laid her on her beam ends until her port yardarms were dragging in the water.

In an effort to save the ship the weather rigging was cut away, and this allowed the masts to go over the side. Several men were injured in the process, and it was impossible to cut the rigging clear on the lee side owing to the vessel's position. All hands were thereupon taken below in order to trim the coal over.

After a hole had been cut in the 'tween decks the coal was shovelled into the lower hold, and this eventually brought the ship on an even keel.

During this squall the *Foohng Suey* was blown as far south as the Virginia Cape, close on 1000 miles, before her crew were able to get her jury-rigged. Eventually, after a weary time, the Scotland Shoal lightship was made, and the lame duck picked up by the tug *Columbia* and towed into Tomkinsville.

CAPT. WALTER L. JOSSELYN.

Lent by A. Moore, Esq.

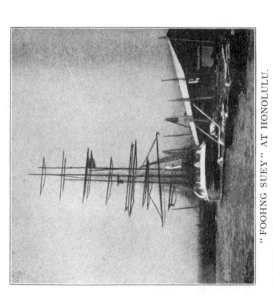

"FOOHNG SUEY" AT HONOLULU.

Lent by A. Moore, Esq.

"ANNIE JOHNSON."

"ANNIE JOHNSON."

On June 24, 1916, *Foohng Suey* changed her name to *Galena* and was rerigged as a schooner.   Just a year later on June 25, 1917, she was torpedoed 70 miles west by south of Ushant by a German submarine.

Captain William Matson.

The founder of the Matson Navigation Company was born at Lysekyl, Sweden, on October 18, 1849.   He first went to sea at the age of ten, but after a year went back to school.   However, in 1863, as a boy of fourteen, he left his native land for good aboard the Nova Scotian vessel, *Aurora*.   Leaving the *Aurora* in New York, his next ship was the *Bridgwater*, which, after the usual voyage round the Horn, landed him in San Francisco in the year 1867.

His next berth was on the old *John J.*, San Francisco and Puget Sound coaster.   Then he went up the coast on the barque, *Oakland*.   Finally he shipped on the schooner, *William Frederick*, which was chiefly employed in carrying coal from Mount Diablo for the Spreckels' sugar refinery on Eighth and Brannan Streets.

In two years young Matson rose to the command of the *William Frederick*.   He commanded one more local schooner, the *Mission Canal*, before launching out on his own.   This was in 1882, when he built the schooner, *Emma Claudina* of 200 tons, which he commanded himself and ran between San Francisco and Hilo, Sandwich Islands.   His outward cargoes consisted almost entirely of stores for the sugar plantations on the island, which were then in their infancy.   At first there was very little return cargo, but by 1886 the Islands were steadily increasing their export of sugar, and Matson being a man of vision, like all those who have built up big businesses, saw his opportunity and took it.

After persuading two friends, the late John A. Scott and C. C. Kennedy, to join him in partnership, he placed an order with the shipbuilder, Matthew Turner of Benicia, for the wooden brigantine, *Lurline*, of 359 tons, which was launched in the spring of 1887. The *Lurline* was a smart little vessel, with a tremendously long jibboom and very high masts, with six yards, including a skysail on her foremast.   She carried 640 tons of sugar, and together with the *Emma Claudina* may be said to have laid the foundations of Captain Matson's fortune.

The present commodore of the Matson Navigation Co., Captain Peter Johnson, left the Islands schooner, *Dora Bluhm*, in order to take command of the *Lurline* on January 1, 1889. The *Dora Bluhm*, by the way, was one of the many vessels chartered by Captain Matson to carry the sugar crop from Hilo, at that time the main port of the Sandwich Islands. Another chartered ship was the brig, *Selina*, but she was wrecked entering Hilo harbour on her second trip to the Islands.

There are many stories of Captain William Matson at this date. He had the reputation of being the best dressed man on the San Francisco water-front. He was also very fond of horses, and always drove down to the wharf in an old-fashioned buggy behind a fast, high-stepping mare.

Captain Matson was naturally a very hard worker, and like all successful business men he saw to it that his employees were equally hard working; but unlike some employers he was a large-hearted man and looked after those under him. One of his slogans was "Feed them well, and make them work."

Like all shipmasters turned owner, he took a great pride in his ships and they were always beautifully kept up; and when he began buying ships he soon proved, as we shall see by his purchases, that he had a real seaman's eye for a good vessel.

In 1890 Captain Matson bought the wooden barque *Harvester*, of 754 tons, built at Newport in 1871. Captain Peter Johnson was placed in command of this vessel, whilst Captain C. P. Matson went to the *Lurline*. In April, 1892, Captain Matson determined to sell the *Harvester*, which was no doubt getting a bit old and leaky. However, so great was his consideration for his captain that he refused to sell the vessel to her new owners unless they would continue Captain Johnson in the command.

In 1894 William Matson went to London and purchased the beautiful little steel barque, *Santiago*, of 978 tons, which had been built by Harland & Wolff in 1885 for Thomas Ismay of the White Star Line, and which had been employed in the nitrate trade.

The *Santiago* was loaded with cement and sent out round the

Horn to San Francisco. She could not, of course, gain American registry, and thus for the first year or two under Matson's house-flag she flew the colours of the Hawaiian Islands.

Another purchase about this time (in 1897 to be exact) was that of the famous clipper ship, *Roderick Dhu*. Although Captain Matson stripped her of her mizen yards, she soon proved herself to be one of the fastest ships in the sugar trade, besides being one of the handsomest. She was also very popular with passengers, a full load of whom she frequently carried between San Francisco and the Islands.

On January 29, 1898, under the command of Captain Rock, she arrived in Hilo harbour in the record time of 9 days 3 hours from San Francisco. Only a short while before, the famous Down Easter, *Henry B. Hyde*, had set up the record of 9 days 4 hours 30 minutes between 'Frisco and Honolulu.

In 1899 Reid's famous old clipper, *Antiope*, came under the Matson house-flag for a few years, but she was sold in 1905 to her captain, P. J. R. Mathieson.

Then in 1900 Matson bought the barque, *Annie Johnson*, the ship *Marion Chilcott*, and the well-known four-mast barque, *Falls of Clyde*, the pioneer ship of the famous Glasgow Falls Line.

The last two obtained their American registry through being under the Hawaiian flag at the date of the annexation, but the *Annie Johnson* had had a most romantic history before being bought by William Matson.

The " Annie Johnson."

She was originally the *Ada Iredale*, built as far back as 1872 for Peter Iredale of Liverpool, a stout little iron ship of 997 tons. On October 15, 1876, she was abandoned about 1900 miles east of the Marquesas Islands in Lat. 13° 30′ S., Long 107° 45′ W., with her coal alight whilst on a passage from Ardrossan to San Francisco. Her crew, 23 in number, managed to reach the Island of Hivahoa on November 9, only one man succumbing to the hardships of the long boat voyage. On November 23 they left Hivahoa in the Tahitian sloop *Proxler* for Nukahiva, where they obtained a passage in the Nicaraguan schooner, *John Bright*, leaving Nukahiva on December 6 and reaching the port of Papeete on December 12. After drifting on the equatorial current for eight months, *Ada Iredale* was towed into Papeete on June 9, 1877, by a French gunboat *Seignelay* with her cargo still burning. Apparently this extraordinary coal fire was not extinguished until May, 1878. After this the almost burnt-out shell of the *Ada Iredale* was offered at public auction and bought for 1000 francs by the enterprising American captain, J. E. Thayer.

Captain Thayer was a real handy man. With a few blacksmith's tools and a small pair of rolls he started in to repair the battered *Ada Iredale*. With only native labour, he faired up and re-rivetted over 100 plates, straightened out warped and twisted frames and deck beams, rebuilt the iron lower masts, and finally sailed the vessel to San Francisco, where her refitting was completed and she was given American registry.

From this date until she was bought by Captain Matson the *Ada Iredale*, under the name of *Annie Johnson*, sailed with steady success under the command of Captain Marcus Hall of Cape Cod.

Captain Hall made thirteen voyages round Cape Horn in the *Annie Johnson*, his best being 117 days from Liverpool to Portland, Oregon, which was within four days of the record. On this occasion the ship was becalmed for several days outside her port, otherwise she should at least have equalled the record. Off the Horn on this passage she was only 11 days between 50° S. and 50° S. After being purchased by William Matson she ran with equal steadiness in the sugar trade between San Francisco and Hilo, her first commander being C. P. Matson. Her best passage was made in 1903, when she ran from the Golden Gate to Diamond Head, Honolulu, in 8 days 9 hours.

Being one of the few iron sailing ships owned in America during the eighties, it will have been noticed that she made the best grain passage for an iron ship, of 118 days between July, 1881, and July, 1885.

The *Annie Johnson* was the last of all Matson's sailing ships to survive. Before the end she was converted to a four-mast schooner and given a Diesel engine. Finally, in 1926, she was sold to Captain Ozanne of Tahiti for the copra trade. She is still voyaging about the Pacific under the name of *Bretagne.*

"Marion Chilcott."

This fine iron full-rigger of 1738 tons was built by Russell of Glasgow in 1882 as the *Kilbrannan.* Under the Matson house-flag and the command of Captain Weedon she soon made a name in the Pacific as a good passage maker, about her best performance being a run of 34 days between Newcastle, N.S.W., and Honolulu.

Besides being a pioneer in the Islands sugar trade, Captain Matson was a pioneer in the Southern California oil industry, and was the first to introduce oil as fuel for the machinery on the sugar plantations. This oil he transported from the Californian port of Gaviotta, and the *Marion Chilcott* was one of the vessels converted into oil tankers.

"Falls of Clyde."

None of Matson's ships was slow, but the *Falls of Clyde* was unusually fast. Built by Russell of Glasgow in 1878 for Wright, Graham & Co. she came out as a four-mast ship. Captain C. Anderson, who commanded her under her Scottish owners, always declared that she was one of the fastest ships afloat and made no fuss at 15 knots. Employed at this time in the Calcutta jute trade, she was never very lucky in her passages.

Though he reduced her to a four-mast barque, Captain Matson was very proud of the *Falls of Clyde* and always liked her to be hard sailed.

Her first commander was Captain C. P. Matson, and her usual run was carrying oil between Gaviotta and Honolulu, which distance she generally covered in about a couple of weeks.

The *Falls of Clyde* continued to run regularly carrying oil from Lower California until two or three years after the War, when the General Petroleum Corporation converted her to a barge at Los Angeles.

"Monterey " ex "Cypromene."

This well-known ship came under Matson's flag in 1905 after a stranding in October, 1903. Matson repaired and re-rigged her as a four-mast schooner and fitted her to carry oil in bulk.

The *Monterey* survived the War, and I believe is still sailing the seas rigged as a barquentine and owned by the Fife Shipping Company.

The Welch Fleet.

In 1908 Captain Matson bought the Welch fleet of San Francisco lock, stock, and barrel. This consisted of the Down Easters, *George Curtis, St. Katherine, Amy Turner, Gerard C. Tobey*, and *Mohican*, also the smart little barque, *R. P. Rithet*, of 1097 tons, which was built by Connell of Glasgow in 1892, and the *Andrew Welch*, an iron barque of 903 tons built by Russell in 1888.

All these sailing ships were run regularly between San Francisco and the Islands, generally carrying a few passengers as well as cargo, the passage rate to and from San Francisco being, in those days, 40 dollars in one of the Welch sailing ships, as against 75 dollars charged by the steamers.

On the outward passage the run was made in from 10 to 14 days according to the strength of the North-East Trade, but coming back it was a steady beat the whole way, and three weeks was considered an excellent passage.

The vessels bought by Matson in 1908 were only a few of the regular traders between the Pacific coast and the Hawaiian Islands, and right up to the date of the War, and even later, there were several very smart four-mast barques running between Honolulu and New York and Philadelphia, such as the *John Ena, Hawaiian Isles, Manga Reva*, and *Fort George*, which last went "missing" on the Cape Horn passage about 1907 when a member of the Welch fleet.

"John Ena."

This steel four-mast barque, which many seamen considered to be the fastest vessel in the Hawaiian trade, was built by Robert Duncan in 1892 and registered in Honolulu under the ownership of the San Francisco Shipping Co. She was named after a prominent Chinese merchant in Hawaii, and was a big ship, registering 2842 tons.

"R. P. RITHET."

"HELEN BREWER."

"JOHN ENA."

Lent by Capt. Schutze.

The following are a few of her more noteworthy passages :

1895	Newcastle, N.S.W., to San Francisco	..	**51 days**	
1900	,, ,, ,,	..	60 ,,	
1902	New York to Hiogo ..	..	.. 125 ,,	
	San Francisco to New York	..	.. 106 ,,	
1905	Shanghai to Hilo	..	.. 22 days 22 hrs.	
1906	Delaware Breakwater to Hilo	..	.. 96 ,,	
1911	Honolulu to Philadelphia ..	..	.. 84 ,,	
1912	Hilo to Philadelphia ..	..	.. 114 ,,	

Her run in 1911 has only been beaten once, so far as I know, and that was by the American clipper, *Sovereign of the Seas,* which in 1853 ran from Honolulu to Sandy Hook in 82 days.

During the *John Ena's* passage her master, Captain Lorenz, died whilst the ship was off the Horn, and she was taken on to her destination by the mate. The dates of this wonderful run were :

Left Honolulu April 28, 1911. Arrived Philadelphia July 21

Amongst the masters of the *John Ena* were C. Schnauer, M. A. Madsen, Olsen, and R. Lancaster. Captain Madson, the present harbour pilot at Honolulu, was master of the *John Ena* from December, 1895, to April, 1910. One of these skippers (I think it was the last) was fond of a very peculiar triangular mainsail, which he was accustomed to set in strong winds.

The *John Ena* had the distinction of being the first big sailing ship to pass through the Panama Canal; this was on January 22, 1915. Her last passage through the Canal was in 1926 on what was to be her last voyage. In this voyage the old ship seems to have come to grief in every way possible. Off Cape Hatteras she lost her main, mizen, and jigger masts from the deck up in a severe Atlantic gale. In addition to the fury of the elements her scanty crew of 16 men had to fight a fire in the galley and a bad leak in the hold. The first was conquered, but the second very nearly did for the *John Ena.*

Three schooners managed to get hold of the lame duck and made an attempt to tow her into San Pedro, but they either broke loose or had to let go the tow-ropes in a hard blow on the Nicaraguan coast.

Somehow or other the *John Ena* survived, and she finally

arrived at Los Angeles on April 6, 1926, in tow of the lumber steamer, *Santa Inez*. Whilst coming to an anchor her single remaining mast nearly caused a disaster, for it fouled the high tension wires of the Southern California Edison Company, which were strung across Long Beach Channel. These were carried away and the mast acted as a lightning conductor to the current.

After this disastrous passage the old ship was towed round to San Francisco in order to be cut down to a towing barge for use in the lumber trade.

The slump, however, in that trade condemned the old ship to idleness. She now lies moored in Oakland Creek, San Francisco, along with eighteen other derelict square-riggers.

"Hawaiian Isles."

This steel four-mast barque was built by Connell in 1892 for A. Nelson of Honolulu. Though not as fast as the *John Ena*, she was a good passage maker ; for instance, in 1909, just before she was sold to the Alaska Packers Association, and was still flying the Welch house-flag, she made the following passages :

> Kahului (Hawaiian Isles) to Philadelphia .. 108 days
> Delaware Breakwater to Honolulu   .. 128 „

She is now disguised under the name of *Star of Greenland*.

The Romantic Story of "Manga Reva."

The story of how the burning *Pyrenees* was beached on the coral strand of Manga Reva has been told by the late Jack London in his *South Sea Tales*. I have added a few particulars of her subsequent salvage by Captains Thayer and Porter in my *Last of the Windjammers*. Her service under the Stars and Stripes, which lasted until 1916, is worthy of being told in some detail.

After being thoroughly reconditioned the *Pyrenees*, under her new name of *Manga Reva* and commanded by Captain H. C. Townsend, sailed from San Francisco in the early spring of 1905 under charter to the Sugar Factors Company of Honolulu. With 750 tons of ballast in her hold she made the splendid run of eight days to the Hawaiian Islands. Sugar was loaded at Honolulu and Kahului, and she made the passage round the Horn from the island of Maui to the Delaware Breakwater in 107 days, which was the best time made by a Hawaiian sugar ship that year. She next loaded a full cargo of blacksmith's coal at Philadelphia for the Navy yard at Cavite, Manila. With this dangerous cargo, and sailing during the most unfavourable time of year for the monsoons, the *Manga Reva* arrived at Manila by way of the Ombay Passage on the 127th day out. It was found as soon as her hatches were opened that the coal was quite warm in places, and it only needed the friction of a shovel to set it on fire. Luckily there was a good stream of water available at the naval station where the ship discharged, and during the unloading the coal was kept wet.

Retaining 1000 tons of coal as ballast, the *Manga Reva* crossed to Honolulu for her second sugar cargo. Her Horn passage this time was made in 114 days. At Philadelphia the ship again loaded coal, this time for San Diego, California. The difficult outward passage round the Horn was made in 124 days. The ship was then ordered across to Honolulu to load sugar once more. Most of her crew, however, had run in San Diego, and the difficulty was to get sailor-men. In the end Captain Townsend and his mate, Mr. Moran, were compelled to man their big four-master with prune pickers, bar-tenders, baseball players, and a bunch of college boys who were out for a lark. With this mixture in her foc's'le, the *Manga Reva's* passage to the Hawaiian Islands was by no means a pleasant one, friction between officers and crew being the order of the day.

Interviewed by journalists, the mate declared disgustedly:

All that the crew do is to sit around and discuss the chances of the various teams in the different leagues to win pennants. Every man is nothing but a baseball fan.

These same baseball fans complained bitterly of the hard life in a sailing ship. They could not understand why they were not allowed ashore in port; they complained of not being treated with sufficient respect; that the names they were called were "positively shocking"; that the food was not fit for any human being to eat and was insufficient in quantity. Their final complaint was that the brutal Captain Townsend had advised his officers to use a club on these make-believe sailormen.

However, in spite of there not being a single A.B. in her foc's'le, the *Manga Reva* made a good run of 12 days to Honolulu; this was in 1907. There was nothing worthy to record about her sugar passage this year. However, in the summer of 1909 the ship loaded a cargo of scrap iron in San Francisco and made the run home to Philadelphia in 100 days.

On her next voyage she made the usual outward passage round the Horn from Philadelphia to San Francisco with coal. She was then chartered by the Alaska Packers Association and proceeded to Bristol Bay, Alaska, where she loaded 105,107 cases of salmon, the largest cargo taken out of Alaska at that date. Following this charter, the *Manga Reva* had the indignity of being towed for three round trips between San Francisco and Panama. Although her topgallant masts were left ashore the ship often had to reduce sail in fair winds in order to avoid running down the tugboat.

After this the *Manga Reva* was chartered by the Californian Atlantic S.S. Co. on time charter—a most unusual thing for a sailing vessel. This charter was to carry general merchandise around the Horn to New York and return to San Francisco. During her return passage the company failed, and the ship was then chartered by Arthur Chesebrough, also for the Horn passage to New York and on time. With such items as 10,000 bags of asphaltum and 13,000 cases of California wine on the manifest, Captain Townsend made a good passage home, and astonished the New Yorkers by sailing right into the harbour before accepting the services of a tugboat.

In the autumn of 1913 the notorious mutiny aboard the *Manga Reva* occurred whilst the ship was returning to San Francisco from New York. The following account of the mutiny I have taken from the captain's letter to his owner, Mr. J. E. Thayer.

The *Manga Reva* went to sea from the Delaware on October 12 with a favourable wind. All went well and there was no trouble until October 25. Up till then the weather had been unsettled, stormy, and cold, and the crew had had little to do but work the ship and get the chafing gear aloft. For three days before the mutiny occurred Captain Townsend had been confined to his cabin suffering from a severe chill and fever. Twice during the night of the 24th the captain heard someone moving about in the cabin, which he took to be the mate. As a matter of fact it was members of the crew removing the fire-arms.

"FALLS OF CLYDE."

"MANGA REVA."

HONOLULU IN THE EIGHTIES.

Courtesy of Matson Navigation Co.

On the Saturday morning a little before eight bells Captain Townsend, although very weak, crawled up on deck to take sights for longitude. It was the mate's watch from 8 a.m. till noon, and soon after eight bells whilst he was forward he noticed four or five men running aft to the poop. This warned him that something was wrong and he also came aft on the run, but he was met by the mutineers with pointed revolvers and had to submit to being handcuffed and ironed. The captain was caught in his bathroom and also handcuffed.

It seems that the mutineers had expected the second mate to throw in his lot with them, but, finding that he would not do so at the last moment, they were compelled to put him in irons also.

The mutineers ordered the captain to navigate the ship to Bermuda, but on his refusing they finally permitted him to navigate her back to the Delaware Breakwater. Captain Townsend was only allowed out of his cabin in order to take sights, an armed guard being kept upon him and the two mates, but after the ship lost six sails through the poor seamanship of the mutineers they consented to allow the mate to stay on deck at night, though an armed guard was still kept upon him.

The night the ship made the Capes it was thick weather though the wind was light and sea smooth. Somehow or other, probably by indifferent steering, the *Manga Reva* got down too far to leeward, and when within four miles of the anchorage got ashore at dead low water. This stranding was not serious and the ship came off without any damage. The next trouble, however, was that the coal cargo was heating. There were eight testing pipes leading to the lower hold, the tops of which came above the coal, and by taking the temperature in every pipe Captain Townsend discovered that some fine coal under the after hatch had become very hot. However, men were hired from the shore, and this was dug over and turned, and in this way the danger was overcome.

Whilst Captain Townsend remained in Philadelphia for the trial of the mutineers, which took place in January, 1914, and resulted in seven of the ringleaders getting terms of imprisonment up to 3½ years, Captain Willett, formerly of the *Foohng Suey*, took over the *Manga Reva* and sailed her round to San Francisco in 134 days, arriving on April 10, 1914. The ship was then laid up at Saucelito to await a charter.

On the outbreak of War the *Manga Reva* was chartered to load a cargo of barley at Port Costa for U.K. or Continent. She arrived at Plymouth on January 8, 1915, after a very stormy passage, during which her foremast had been damaged and a good deal of injury had been done to her deck fittings. Captain Willett also was very ill and had to be taken to hospital, where he was operated on, and the mate had to take the ship to her port of discharge.

The *Manga Reva's* next charter was to load a full cargo of case oil at Port Arthur (Texas), for Port Louis, Mauritius, Tamatave, Madagascar, and Beira. Captain Parke, who had been in the Standard Oil Company's ships, was appointed commander. He took the ship across in ballast to Texas and then made a good trip out to Mauritius. Whilst awaiting a charter at Beira the old ship was sold to a Baltimore firm. Twelve months later she was resold at the wartime price of 300,000 dollars.

In 1917 the *Manga Reva* was reported missing on a passage from London to Hampton Roads, and the official report of the United States Commissioner of Navigation, Washington, declares that she was sunk by a German submarine.

"Mauna Ala " ex "Pakwan."

It is probable that very few people knew that the little composite barque, *Mauna Ala*, had once been a well-known British tea clipper, being built at Sunderland in 1863. After running in the tea trade until the end of the seventies, the *Pakwan* then became well known in the Australian trade, being owned in the eighties by J. Gillan of Newcastle, N.S.W. Then in the early nineties she was sold to J. S. Walker of Honolulu and received the name of *Mauna Ala*. She was finally taken out of the Register in 1904.

"Diamond Head."

The *Diamond Head* was almost as old as the *Mauna Ala*, being built as the iron ship, *Gainsborough*, of 974 tons, by Lungley of London, her first owners being the Merchant Shipping Co. She was bought by S. C. Allen of Honolulu in 1899 Then about 1910 she was put into the oil carrying trade under the ownership of Barneson, Hibberd & Co.

I believe she is still afloat and still belongs to the General Petroleum Corporation.

" Coronado " ex " Waikato."

Another well-known Hawaiian trader was the iron barquentine, *Coronado*, owned by Spreckels. She had originally been an iron passenger ship belonging to the New Zealand Shipping Co. Then in the nineties she was bought by Pfluger of Bremen, who cut her down to a barque. J. D. Spreckels bought her in 1901.

The old New Zealand trader foundered in 1921 when owned by W. S. Dwinnell of Minneapolis.

" Archer."

This little iron barque of 789 tons was built by R. Thompson, Jr., of Sunderland in 1876, and owned by Peter Iredale until the end of the nineteenth century, when she was bought by Welch & Co., who turned her into a barquentine.

For many years she was commanded by Captain G. S. Calhoun. When the Welch fleet was dispersed in 1908 *Archer* went to the Tacoma and Roche Harbour Lime Co. and so into oblivion.

The End of the Matson Sailing Fleet.

It had always been Captain Matson's ambition to found a line of first-class steamers between San Francisco and Honolulu, and he lived to see his ambition fulfilled, for at his death on October 11, 1917, the Matson Line consisted of eight ships, all of them steamers with the exception of the *Annie Johnson*.

Most of his old sailing ships were turned into hulks or barges ; the beautiful *R. P. Rithet*, however, was burnt at sea on July 24, 1917, when bound from Honolulu to San Francisco.

The Alaska Packers Association.

At the present date (1929) there are only three firms left in the world who own more than half a dozen square-rigged sailing ships. These are :

Erikson of Mariehamn, whose fine fleet of old British and German ships are mostly employed in the Australian wheat trade to Europe.

Reederei F. Laeisz of Hamburg, whose magnificent nitrate clippers still race out to the West Coast and back.

The Alaska Packers Association of San Francisco, whose large fleet of square-riggers is now, alas, rapidly being replaced by steamers.

Up till 1909 there was a number of firms running sailing ships from 'Frisco and Puget Sound to the salmon canneries in Alaska, but at that date they were all amalgamated under the flag of the Alaska Packers Association.

This trade—or fishery, perhaps we ought to call it—is entirely different from any other kind of seafaring. Throughout the winter the large fleet of the Alaska Packers is laid up in Oakland Creek; then with the spring the ships are fitted out for their run to the North. They are all painted alike, with black topsides, a bright red boot-top, and with spars and deckhouses of buff colour.

As soon as they are ready for sea they are towed round to their loading docks to receive the cargoes of box-shooks and tinplate, which are needed for the canning of the Alaska salmon.

The larger ships of the fleet sign on crews of thirty A.B.'s and O.S.'s, but besides these they also carry a large number of fishermen, sometimes as many as 150 to 200 men per vessel. These fishermen mostly consist of a rather low type of Mexican; a better class of men would scarcely put up with the hard work for such a small return, the average money earned under favourable circumstances being only about 150 dollars per man. The "trip" money is also mostly swallowed up by outgoings for slop-chest clothes, food, tobacco, etc.

In 1925 there was somewhat of a scandal in San Francisco owing to the alleged ill-treatment of some of these Mexican fishermen, and some very hard things were said in the papers about the employment agencies, who seem to have been mostly to blame.

The captains and officers of the Packers fleet were all very experienced men in the trade, but at the present day, as the older men retire, it is becoming more and more impossible to replace them with younger men who are qualified to handle big square-

ALASKA PACKERS' FLEET.

THE ALASKA PACKERS' FLEET AT OAKLAND, 1923.

HONOLULU HARBOUR, 1889.

Lent by A. Moore, Esq.

rigged sailing ships. There is the same difficulty in getting fore-mast hands who are willing to go aloft and know what to do when they get there. This as much as any other consideration is, I believe, causing the Alaska Packers gradually to sell off their magnificent fleet of sailing ships, which in 1925 consisted of 32 square-rigged ships and barques.

The run to the North is made in from four to six weeks. As the old Packers' shanty has it :

> The Packers' ships are Northward bound ;
> There is one that sails to-day.
> Her skipper's got his orders
> To proceed to Bristol Bay.
>
> The anchor's up, the topsails set—
> The sky looks kind o' murky,
> But fair or foul, she's comin' back
> With choice Alaska turkey.

As soon as the anchors are down in Alaskan waters the fishing begins. Practically the only men who remain aboard the ships throughout the summer are their captains and cooks, but ashore things are busy enough around the canneries which lie along the water's edge.

The length of the fleet's stay in Alaska depends on how the salmon are running, but the extreme limit is four months.

Every kind of labour-saving device is employed on the cannery ships, such as steam winches and windlasses, refrigerating plants, wireless equipment, and so on.

As the cannery wheels begin to slow down, the cargo winches grow busy, and in a very short while the fleet is ready for the run South to San Francisco.

The time taken from Bristol Bay through the Unimak Pass and down the North Pacific to the Golden Gate is usually from four to six weeks, the record being held by the *Sterling,* which made the run from the Bering Sea to San Francisco in exactly three weeks.

As regards the Northward run, a correspondent informs me that the *Star of Lapland* in 1917 ran from San Francisco to Bristol Gulf in 7 days 5 hours. He gives no details, and it would be more

Q

satisfactory to know the anchorage to anchorage time. In 1926 the *Star of Alaska*, ex British ship *Balclutha*, left San Francisco on April 3 and arrived in Bristol Bay on April 17, 14 days out. This was considered a very smart piece of work, but is in no way comparable to the *Star of Lapland's* record.

It is now time to turn to the ships themselves. The *George Skolfield* was the pioneer ship of the fleet, a vessel built at Brunswick, Maine, in 1870 : and registering 1313 tons. At the end of the nineteenth century the Packers fleet consisted entirely of old Down Easters, such as *George Skolfield—Bohemia—Centennial—Indiana—Llewellyn J. Morse—Santa Clara—Sterling—Tacoma*.

In addition to these they owned several smaller vessels, such as *Electra—Nicholas Thayer—Will W. Case—Premier—Prosper*.

Of these ships, *Sterling*, the record holder, disappeared very early, being out of the Register soon after making her fast trip from the Bering Sea.

Wreck of the "Sterling."

On April 27, 1898, the *Sterling* sailed from San Francisco, under the command of C. O. Anderson bound for Koggiung, Alaska, with the usual cargo of cans, retorts, coolers and coal. Besides a crew of 21 seamen she had 150 Chinese cannery hands on board.

At midnight on May 19 the *Sterling* was off the entrance to Nushagak Bay, 18 miles S.W. by S. of Cape Constantine. She then tacked off-shore until daylight, but wore ship towards the land at 3 a.m. on the 20th, the wind being fresh from W. and the ship's course E. by S. so as to clear the shoals to the southward of Cape Constantine. At 6 a.m., when 10 miles S.W. by S. of Cape Constantine, the ship struck heavily on an uncharted shoal with 18 feet of water on it. Captain Anderson immediately sent off the second mate and four men in a boat to Nushagak in order to get the services of a tugboat. The carpenter also was ordered to get up steam in case the pumps were wanted. By 7 a.m. the ship had 12 feet of water in her and was being heavily battered on the shoal, her rudder being carried away and her keel broken. At 8.30 Captain Anderson launched his six boats and landed the 150 Chinese at Cape Constantine. The crew, however, stayed by the vessel, but at 5 p.m. they also were obliged to abandon her, for by this time she was full of water and gave signs of rapidly breaking up. With a S.E. gale blowing on May 21 the destruction of the ship was soon complete, nothing being saved from her in the way of personal effects or cargo.

The *Centennial* was burnt to the water's edge in 1904, but was rebuilt in 1906 and sent to Alaska as a four-mast barquentine. *Santa Clara, Bohemia, Indiana,* and *Llewellyn J. Morse* were sold to the Los Angeles Moving Picture Concerns a few years back and became known as the Movie Fleet. The *Llewellyn J. Morse* has since been run ashore and burnt, whilst the *Santa Clara* is now doing duty as a fishing hulk.

The first British built ships to come into the Alaska fleet were the *Coalinga* ex *La Escocesa, Euterpe, Himalaya,* and *Star of Russia.* The *Star of Russia* has the distinction of being the name ship for the fleet. It was about 1907 that the practice began of renaming all ships as "Stars," and at the same time three more of Corrie's Harland & Wolff built "Stars " came into the fleet, namely, the *Star of Bengal, Star of Italy,* and *Star of France.* These four "Stars" were undoubtedly the pick of the fleet, being not only very fast but beautifully built and in splendid condition.

Captain Wester of the "Star of Italy."

One of the best known commanders in the Alaska Packers Association's fleet was Captain George G. Wester of the beautiful *Star of Italy.* Captain Wester rose to the top of his profession from the fo'c'sle of the famous *Three Brothers.* Many years ago he swam ashore from the big clipper at San Pedro, whence he made his way to San Francisco, where he shipped in a sealing schooner. After several voyages as seaman, hunter, and mate, he was given the command of the *Allie I. Alger.* It was whilst he was in command of this schooner that the late Jack London made two voyages with him to the Bering Sea, resulting in the publication of that great book, *The Sea Wolf.* Wolf Larsen of the *Ghost* was a combined character, part of him being Captain Wester and part of him that fiery American Scot, Alex. Maclean.

Captain Wester himself is a man of immense physical strength, and although, like most sailors, self-taught, is a very well-read and intellectual man.   He gave up sealing in order to go master in the Alaska Packers Association, his chief charge being the *Star of Italy*. Since the War he has commanded the five-masted barquentine *Kate G. Pedersen*, belonging to the Bristol Bay Packing Company, and the *Tonawanda*.   Whilst in charge of the former vessel he made a remarkable passage between Sydney and San Francisco.   The *Kate G. Pedersen*, a soft-wood vessel of 2106 tons register, sailed from Newcastle, N.S.W., on April 16, 1924, with 3500 tons of coal for Iquique.   Three days out the big barquentine ran into a black north-easter.   This strained her so badly that she opened up and began to make over a foot of water an hour, whereupon Captain Wester, after consultation with his mate, the present Captain G. H. Heyen, decided to put back to Sydney.   Here the ship lay for three months, her cargo being sold and discharged.   She was then ordered back to San Francisco in ballast.   At 4 p.m. on July 29 the *Kate G. Pedersen* dropped her tug off the South Head, and on September 16, at 4 p.m., she hove to for a pilot off the San Francisco lightship, her actual sailing time being 49 days 18 hours corrected for longitude.

It must be admitted that Captain Wester had great luck with his winds, for his biggest run was only 280 miles, the total distance being 8608 miles, which made an average of 7.21 knots.   The meridian of 160° W. was crossed on August 9 and the Equator on August 21.   The S.E. Trades were picked up on August 17 in 23° 30' S., and from there to 30° N. not a brace or a sail was touched. Then no sooner had the N.E. Trade been lost on September 2 than a fine south-west wind was picked up.   The ship passed through the Golden Gate at 6 p.m. on September 16, and reached the anchorage at 9 p.m.

Of all the ships in which he has served or been in command, the *Star of Italy* was Captain Wester's favourite, and this is not surprising, for she was one of the smartest vessels ever launched by Harland & Wolff, her record as a jute clipper being probably unsurpassed by any other ship.

None of the wooden built Down Easters was renamed, but the *Coalinga* became the *Star of Chile*; *Euterpe*, *Star of India*; and the *Himalaya*, *Star of Peru*.   By 1910 the following had also been added to the fleet: *Star of Alaska* ex *Balclutha*—*Star of England* ex *Abby Palmer* ex *Blairmore*—*Star of Finland* ex *Kaiulani* —*Star of Greenland* ex *Hawaiian Isles*—*Star of Holland* ex *Homeward Bound* ex *Otto Gildemeister* ex *Zemindar*—*Star of Iceland* ex *Willscott* —*Star of Scotland* ex *Kenilworth.*

Tragic End of " Star of Bengal."

Though there were occasional strandings up in the far North, none of the ships so far had come to grief, with the exception of the *Star of Bengal*, which, in September, 1908, went ashore on Coronation Island, Alaska, when homeward bound with 50,000 cases of salmon. This was the most tragic disaster in the history of the salmon canning industry. No less than 9 Europeans and 101 Chinese were drowned, only 27 men being saved.

The *Star of Bengal* sailed from San Francisco on April 22, 1908, bound for Fort Wrangel, under the command of Nicholas Wagner and with a complement of 146 men, including 110 Chinese cannery hands. Fort Wrangel was reached on May 5, and she left again with a full cargo of salmon on September 19 in tow of two small tugs.

I will now quote from Captain Wagner's report of the loss of his ship, which, besides being a tragic one, is of interest with regard to the curious way in which the *Star of Bengal* was brought to her end owing to those aboard being unable to let the tugs know that they were steering a dangerous course.

Captain Wagner's report runs as follows:

Left cannery at 8.20 a.m. in tow of steamer *Hattie Gage*, Captain F. Farrer, and steamer *Kayak*, Captain P. Hamilton. Weather fine, with light S.E. wind and clear weather. Rounded Point Baker at 3.50 p.m. Course south.

At 1.40 a.m. steamer blew one long and two short whistles, signal to haul in starboard braces. Already braced that way. All went well till 1.54 a.m., when I was called on deck by Victor Johanson, mate, who said we were getting rather close to land. Wind was freshening from S.E., dark and squally. Sighted land through the mist, which appeared rather high. Endeavoured to get ship on starboard tack and tried to hail steamers by use of megaphone and foghorn, to draw their attention to the proximity of the land, yelling "Starboard, starboard," till I got hoarse, but got no response of any kind from either steamer. steamer *Hattie Gage* at this time being on the port beam, steamer *Kayak* about one-half point on starboard bow. Ship's head S.S.W.

Mizen staysail and spanker were set with sheets hauled flat.   Also set mizen topmast staysail to bring ship's head into the wind and head off-shore.   Vessel had but very little headway on, with ship's head coming up to south and west.

Finally, at about 3.30 or thereabouts, vessel's head got pointed to the N.E., when I ordered topsails set, and had just succeeded in getting the main topsail halfway up when ship's head was dragged up into the wind again, and she fell off again on the port tack. I countermanded the order to set topsails and lowered them down again.

I then had cast of lead taken, and found 25 fathoms.   At 3.50 a.m. ordered anchor let go and dropped same in 17 fathoms.   Breakers on the rocks in plain view.   Immediately after dropped second anchor, but ship held to first one, with little or no strain on the other.   Tugs cut hawsers about ten minutes after anchoring.   Burned four blue lights and saw an ugly-looking rocky shore close aboard—about two-thirds of ship's length away.

Secured fore-and-aft sails after hauling same down and immediately set about clearing away the lifeboats on after gallows.   Hung same on davits and lowered them level to the rail.   Secured the main hatches more firmly and got forward boats off gallows. First boat over rail broke painter and drifted out of reach and ashore.   Second boat got swamped, fall carrying away and drifted ashore.

Ordered early breakfast 7.10 a.m., wind freshening and squally.   Ordered all hands into life-preserrvers and had men adjust same on Chinese.   Absolutely no confusion, as I told them that when steamer came I would put all on board and remain by vessel till she struck.   Crew replied they would stand by me till the last.

By 8 a.m. wind had increased to gale, with no signs of either steamer in the offing. Concluded they had abandoned us, and that we must try to get ashore on the rockbound shore.   Knowing it was almost certain death to attempt to send boat, and having no other alternative, I called for volunteers to take line ashore, which was responded to by Harry Lewald, Olaf Hansen, Fred Matson (sailors), and Frank Muir, second cook.   The port lifeboat was then lowered, that being the lee side, and boat slackened away, falls being cut with axes.   Boat was immediately swept clear of stern and towards the rocky beach, striking one of the rocks after being swept twice in the breakers and staving her bottom and stern.

Men jumped out at edge of breakers, boat pulling them back two or three times as the breeches line was made fast to same.   Finally, after great effort, the line was secured and hauled as fast as the entangled kelp and rock would permit, and made fast to a tree amid shouts and cheers of those on the ship, at exactly 9 a.m.   Line was then hove taut from masthead.   Martin Christensen then volunteered to be the man to take the hauling line for the breeches buoy, and had succeeded in getting about halfway when the vessel further dragged and struck at 9.32 a.m., slackening rope and throwing Christensen into the water, jerking now up, now down, till he became exhausted and thrown on rocks and was hauled out by his comrades ashore.

As soon as the vessel struck great waves swept her from stem to stern.   Seeing that the vessel would break up shortly and litter the sea with wreckage I asked the men to jump and swim, but they preferred to remain with me till the last.   Tried to haul broken

"CENTENNIAL."

Lent by A. Moore, Esq.

"STAR OF BENGAL."

Lent by Capt. Lee.

HONOLULU 1903.
Clan Macpherson in foreground, *Foohng Suey* across Wharf.

Lent by A. Moore, Esq.

boat off beach, but line became entangled in kelp and wreckage and boat got smashed to splinters.

Sea was now raising havoc all over ship. Masts commenced to sway and rigging held good, but the pounding on rocky bottom soon demolished the hull, which disappeared in the angry waters in sections with the fall of each mast, the foremast being the first to go, followed by the main and lastly mizen—not more than five minutes elapsing between fall of fore and mizen mast.

With the fall of masts, all hands were swept into the seething mass strewed with wreckage. The more fortunate were cast ashore in a helpless and exhausted condition, numbering 27 souls (17 whites, 10 Asiatics), the first to reach the beach being Andrew Olsen, who was swept off a little in advance of the rest of us. Then came two Chinese and Pat Loftus, cook, and the rest of the survivors, all helpless and crippled, having to be dragged above high water clear of wreckage, which was piling up high, Alf Olsen being the last to reach the shore.

The beach was patrolled all day, looking for other survivors, but only one other was seen, Olaf Petersen, who had just got inside breakers, only to be dragged out by undertow and smothered by a mass of wreckage that tumbled about him.

Most of the survivors being crippled and exhausted from their trying experience, it became necessary to do something to stimulate life in them. Accordingly a fire was built and from among the wreckage was taken a change of clothing and hot coffee made and given to them, which revived them a good deal.

From the time the vessel first struck till she had completely disappeared was exactly 54 minutes, as my watch stopped when I struck the water.

Continuous search was made for the bodies of the rest of the white men, but only nine were recovered and buried, among the missing being Mr. Norman Hawkins, machinist and brother-in-law of Superintendent Babler, and Frank Healy, book-keeper.

Most of the "Stars" had had an interesting history before coming under the Alaska Packers' fleet.

"La Escocesa," "The Scottish Lady."

This beautiful little iron ship was built by Gourlay of Dundee in 1868, and during her early years was owned by Balfour, Williamson & Co. of Liverpool. Captain D. Evans took her from the stocks and made her name as a fast sailer. Perhaps his best record was a run of 10 days 23 hours crossing from Liverpool to New York against the Westerlies.

So great was the reputation of *La Escocesa* for fast sailing that she was actually backed against the famous *Young America* on a passage from Liverpool to San Francisco, in spite of the fact that she only registered 996 tons, as against the *Young America's* 1439 tons. As it happened, the *Young America* made the wonderful run of 96 days from pilot to pilot, and anchored in San Francisco Bay on January 20, 1873, only 99 days out.

La Escocesa had sailed from Liverpool on October 7, five days ahead of *Young America*. Captain Evans made a magnificent run as far as the Equator in the Pacific, which he crossed on December 29, 83 days out, the same time as that taken by the *Young America*. His passage, however, was spoilt during the run in to San Francisco, which took *La Escocesa* 33 days, as against the *Young America's* 17 days. She was thus beaten by 16 days.

Captain Evans put down his beating entirely to the bad luck with the wind on the last leg of the passage, and the following epitome certainly shows that he had some reason for his contention :

	Left Liverpool.	Crossed Equator. (Pacific.)	Arrived 'Frisco.
La Escocesa ..	October 7	Dec. 29, 83 days out.	Jan 31, 116 days out
Young America	,, 12	Jan. 3 83 ,,	,, 20, 99 ,,

La Escocesa evidently found many people, both in San Francisco and England, who were willing to bet that she would beat the *Young America* on the homeward passage round the Horn, for wagers were laid to the amount of close on 50,000 dollars.

The two ships sailed from San Francisco in company on the afternoon of February 27, 1873, both being bound to Liverpool. They were accompanied to the Heads by a tugboat crowded with friends and backers. Neither of them was specially favoured by the winds on the run to Liverpool, but again *Young America* had the best of it. She arrived on June 14 after the excellent passage of 106 days. *La Escocesa* did not reach Queenstown until June 27, having taken 120 days on the passage.

On his next passage Captain Evans loaded in Liverpool for Callao, but before leaving the Mersey *La Escocesa* was run down and sunk. She was raised and refitted, and continued to run out round the Horn either to the West Coast or to San Francisco.

La Escocesa was a family ship during the time that she was commanded by Captain D. Evans, for he always took his wife to sea with him, and his four children—three boys and a girl—grew up aboard *La Escocesa*. At one time Captain Evans had his eldest son as mate, second son as second mate, and third as third mate.

The old shipmaster died at sea, and was succeeded by his eldest son, D. T. Evans. This was at the end of the nineties, and for a while *La Escocesa* had D. T. Evans as captain, one brother as mate, the other brother second mate, and the husband of the sister as third mate. I believe that each son in turn commanded the little ship for a time before going into steam.

In December, 1898, *La Escocesa* was partially dismasted, and after this she was sold to J. L. Howard, reduced to a barque and renamed *Coalinga*. Then in 1902 the Alaska Packers bought her, and we find Captain R. Gundersen placed in command.

Some time before this date Mrs. Evans had died on board, and the family had finally severed their connection with the old ship.

La Escocesa, under the name of *Star of Chile*, remained in active service until September, 1922. She was finally converted into a barge in San Francisco last year (1928).

"Star of India " ex "Euterpe."

This little vessel of 1197 tons was built in the Isle of Man at Ramsey Bay in 1863. She was an early iron passenger ship without any pretensions to speed ; in fact, she was unusually slow for an iron ship of that date.

During the sixties she ran chiefly to Australia, but she was bought by Shaw, Savill & Co. and put on the New Zealand run in 1873. From this date, under Captains Phillips, Hoyle, Banks, and Streeter, the *Euterpe* voyaged steadily in the New Zealand trade until 1899, when she was sold to J. J. Moore & Co. of San Francisco.

Although she must have had many an opportunity of making a fast passage out to New Zealand during her long service in that trade, she never made the run under the 100 days, her best outward passage being 100 days to Lyttelton in the spring of 1876 under Captain Phillips. Her next best was 103 days to Dunedin under Captain Banks in 1896. Her worst passage was 143 days to Lyttelton in 1879. On this trip she was 19 days clearing the Channel and 12 days from the Snares to her port.

At the beginning of the twentieth century the old ship was

purchased by the Alaska Packers, and sailed regularly to the North
under Captain G. A. Swanson for many years. About 1908 she
had the yards stripped off her mizen mast, and Captain Christiansen
took over the command.

A few years ago she was bought by the Zoological Society of
San Diego, California. Their idea was to moor her on a small
lake and convert her into a sort of aquarium and marine natural
history museum. No doubt the portholes, which ran the full
length of her 'tween deck and had for many years been blocked up,
will now be reopened.

"Star of England" ex "Blairmore."

This ship will always be remembered for her tragic capsize
in San Francisco Bay in the spring of 1896. She was built for
Thomson, Dickie & Co.'s "More" Line by McMillan of Dumbarton,
and launched in September, 1893.

Whilst lying at anchor in Mission Bay with only a very small
amount of ballast in her hold to keep her upright, a smart gust of
wind swung her across the tide. Her cable caught across her bow,
and she gradually listed over to port until she capsized. The hands
were all at work in the hold at the time, and only a few of them
managed to reach the deck as she went over. These were picked
up, as also was the captain, who happened to be on the poop. It
was said that he was kept afloat by his dog until he was rescued.

Meanwhile the ship did not sink, owing to the air in her hold,
and the men below could be heard hammering. The fatal mistake
was made of cutting through a plate, artificers being fetched from
the Union Ironworks in order to do this, but directly a hole had
been made the air rushed out and the ship sank like a stone, all
those below being drowned. About three months later she was
raised, and I believe that even at the present day they will show you
a clump of barnacles which were found sticking under the cabin
table.

The ship was bought by R. Sudden and others of San Francisco
and renamed *Abby Palmer*, being granted American registry owing
to the money spent on her refit. She came under the Alaska Packers'
flag in 1905, and is still a member of the fleet.

"Star of Scotland" ex "Kenilworth."

The *Star of Scotland* has always been considered one of the finest ships in the Alaska Packers' fleet. She was built for Williamson & Milligan's "Waverley" Line by John Reid, who was told to use the very best materials in an endeavour to produce the finest steel four-mast ship in the world.

This magnificent vessel was commanded under the British flag by the veteran Captain McNair, but her life under the British flag was a short one. On her maiden voyage she arrived at San Francisco in October, 1887, 181 days from Liverpool. She was one of the six ships which raced from San Francisco to Australia in March, 1888, all of which made wonderful passages, *British Ambassador*, the leader, making the record for an iron ship of 38 days from San Francisco to Newcastle, N.S.W. The *Jubilee* came in second with 40 days, and the *Kenilworth* third with 41 days, the other three ships, *Port Jackson*, *Beecroft*, and *Queen's Island*, taking 44 days.

At Newcastle the *Kenilworth* loaded coal for San Pedro, the run across the Pacific this way taking 88 days. She was then towed up to San Francisco in order to load a grain cargo home. The passage round the Horn to Cork was made in 105 days.

On her second voyage the *Kenilworth* sailed from Liverpool on February 21, 1889, passed the Smalls the next day, and crossed the Line 23 days out, having made two excellent 24-hour runs of 303 and 320 miles. Unfortunately during the rest of the passage very unfavourable winds were encountered, and the Golden Gate was not reached until the 128th day out.

A wheat charter for Liverpool being obtained, the *Kenilworth* was lying alongside at Port Costa under McNear's grain sheds along with the American ship, *Armenia*, and another British ship named the *Honouwar*, when fire broke out in the warehouse. The alarm was first raised aboard the *Armenia* at 4 a.m. during the night of August 26, 1889, and immediately there was a rush on board all three ships to let go their lines and drift clear of the smoke and flames. In this the *Kenilworth* was the luckiest, as she succeeded in getting towed out into the stream before her rigging caught. However, this was simply putting off the evil moment, for presently the steamer,

San Joaquin No. 4, in towing the other two vessels clear, both of which had their rigging in flames, unfortunately allowed the *Honouwar* to foul the *Kenilworth*, and before the two ships could be separated the latter's rigging caught fire and she was soon ablaze like the rest.

When a fireboat from Mare Island arrived on the scene all three vessels were drifting down San Pablo Bay in a mass of flames, and her efforts were of little avail.   The *Armenia* and the *Honouwar* were both burnt to the water's edge, and their crews, unable to bear the intense heat, jumped overboard and struck out for the shore. Some reached this in safety, whilst the rest were picked up by small boats, with the exception of a Chinese cook who was drowned.

The crew of the *Kenilworth* were either smarter or had better luck than the other two, for they managed to scuttle the ship and sink her before she was damaged beyond repair.   Her owners, however, abandoned her to the underwriters, who sold her to Arthur Sewall & Co.   The Bath firm had her repaired by the Union Ironworks, and the cost of repairs qualified her for American registry.

Her first captain under the Stars and Stripes was J. G. Baker, who had previously commanded the Down Easters, *John Rosenfeld* and *Commodore*.   He sailed her in the Cape Horn trade until 1896, his outward passages being mostly from New York to San Francisco, and the homeward from the Hawaiian Islands with sugar.

The first passage of the *Kenilworth* under her new owners was with grain to Liverpool.   On July 27, 1890, she passed Kinsale 99 days out, and anchored in the Mersey two days later.

Captain Baker continued in the command until 1898, when he was succeeded by Captain W. Taylor, who handed over to Captain J. A. Amesbury in 1906.   During these years her best outward passages were the following:

From New York to San Francisco	116, 115, 118, 103 days
From New York to Astoria	119 days

Her best homeward passages were :

Astoria to Cork	111 days
Hongkong to New York	92 days in 1893
Hawaiian Islands to New York ..	93 days in 1895 and 97 days in 1896

In 1893 she went out to China and back in exactly ten months. In 1898, when homeward bound from the Hawaiian Islands, she was compelled to put into Valparaiso with her cargo on fire. After the fire had been extinguished and the ship refitted she sailed from Valparaiso to New York in the excellent time of 65 days.

Captain Amesbury's passage out to San Francisco from Philadelphia was the most unlucky in the whole of the *Kenilworth's* life. Sailing from Philadelphia on August 15, 1906, she arrived at Monte Video in a crippled condition on February 11, 1907, having put back from the latitude of the Horn with her steering gear carried away and damage to her rigging. After two months spent in refitting, she sailed again on April 4, 1907. By this time her hull was so overgrown with barnacles that she would hardly handle, much less sail, and after again being knocked about by the furious Cape Horn weather the ship was obliged to put back once more. This time she arrived in Rio thirteen months out from Philadelphia.

She came into the Alaska Packers fleet in 1909 under the name of the *Star of Scotland*, and has remained one of their favourite ships ever since.

"Star of Holland" ex "Zemindar."

Another very superior British ship to come under the Alaska Packers' flag was Brocklebank's *Zemindar*, a steel full-rigger of 2053 tons built by Harland & Wolff in 1885.

When the sailing ships were ousted from the Calcutta jute trade by steam, the *Zemindar* was sold to D. Cordes & Co. of Bremen, who renamed her the *Otto Gildemeister*. This was in 1900. In February, 1901, the ex-jute clipper was towed into San Francisco dismasted. The repairs cost sufficient money to allow of American registry, and she was bought by Hind, Rolph & Co., renamed the *Homeward Bound*, and registered in San Francisco.

For the next seven years she was sailed by Captain C. J. Thomson, having been re-rigged as a barque. Then in 1909 she came into the Alaska Packers' fleet as the *Star of Holland*. Since then her best sailing performance has been 35 days 4½ hours between Australia and South America. This was in 1916. She dropped her pilot outside Port Phillip Heads at 11.30 a.m. on April 30, and anchored at

Caleta Buena at 4 p.m. on June 3. Her daily average worked out at 201 miles, her best run being only 286 miles.

"Star of Peru " ex "Himalaya."

The *Himalaya* was a very similar ship to the *Euterpe*, though some 300 tons smaller. She was an iron ship built by Pile of Sunderland in 1863, and only registered 1027 tons gross, 976 tons net. Purchased by Shaw, Savill & Co. in 1865, this little ship made as many as twenty-four voyages between London and New Zealand. She was a faster ship than the *Euterpe*, her best passage from the Lizard to the Snares being 78 days, and her best time between ports 90 days from the Thames to Port Chalmers in 1893-4, when commanded by Captain Hill.

The yards were stripped off her mizen mast in 1880. In 1899 Shaw, Savill sold her to J. J. Moore, and two years later she came under the Alaska Packers' flag, her first commander in the cannery trade being T. A. Thomsen.

The first of the Alaska Packers' fleet to be sold were naturally their smallest and oldest ships, and amongst these was, of course, numbered the *Star of Peru*. She has gone to Noumea, New Caledonia, where she is now acting as a coal hulk under the name of *Bougainville*. The *Star of Russia* has also been sold to Noumea.

"Star of Alaska " ex " Balclutha."

By 1928 the Alaska Packers' fleet only numbered fourteen ships, the following five of which were sent North for that season :—
Star of England—*Star of Holland*—*Star of Zealand* ex *Astral*—*Star of Falkland* ex *Durbridge*—*Star of Alaska* ex *Balclutha*.

The *Balclutha*, a steel ship of 1614 tons net, was built by Connell & Co. of Glasgow for R. McMillan & Co. of that port in 1886. She came under the American flag at the beginning of the twentieth century, her first owners being J. J. Moore & Co., then Pope & Talbot of San Francisco. From them she went to the Puget Sound Commercial Co., and finally, in 1904, to the Alaska Packers Association.

Throughout these years, from 1899 to 1904, she was commanded by Captain G. A. Hatfield.

I have already mentioned that she made the best passage of the fleet in 1926.

Wreck of the "Star of Falkland."

The *Star of Falkland* must have been one of the last sailing ships bought by the Alaska Packers Association. She was originally the *Durbridge*, built by W. Hamilton & Co. of Port-Glasgow and owned by Potter Bros. of London. Launched in 1892, she was a steel full-rigger of 2121 tons net. She ran steadily under the Potter house-flag until 1909, when she was sold to Knor & Burchard of Hamburg and renamed the *Steinbek*. Soon after the War we find her listed under the United States Shipping Board as the *Arapahoe* of Seattle. She was then bought by the Alaska Packers, and received the name of *Star of Falkland.*

On May 23, 1928, on her way to Naknek, Alaska, she had managed to get through the Unimak Pass successfully, but that night the wind dropped, and at about 11.30 p.m. this splendid ship drifted on to the N.E. point of Akun Island in the Bering Sea.

In addition to her crew she had close on 400 cannery workers on board, and when these men realised that the ship was fast aground there was something like a panic. However, by means of the radio the lighthouse tender, *Cedar*, and the coastguard cutters, *Unalga* and *Haida*, received notice of the wreck and were soon on the scene, and the crew and fishermen of the *Star of Falkland* were soon removed to the three ships.

Although the weather was calm there was a heavy swell running, but only one life was lost. This man, half crazed with fright, jumped into the sea and never came to the surface.

The *Star of Falkland* had a deck load of fifty live hogs. The work of removing these in the heavy swell was given to the *Unalga*, but it was found impossible to tranship them alive, and they all had to be slaughtered.

When the *Star of Falkland* struck a wake was in progress for one of her crew.

The ship became a total loss, being hard and fast ashore.

Throughout the summer, at any rate until the end of August, she still remained on an even keel, with all masts standing. No doubt she proved a veritable mine of wealth to the natives of the locality.

"Star of Iceland" ex "Willscott."

There was one other British built ship amongst the Alaska "Stars," and that was the *Star of Iceland* ex *Willscott*, a steel barque of 1858 tons net built by W. Hamilton & Co. of Port-Glasgow in 1896 for G. W. Macfarlane of Honolulu, just in time to gain American registry owing to the Hawaiian annexation.

At the beginning of the twentieth century the *Willscott* came under the ownership of G. W. Hume of San Francisco. She was sailed by this firm until 1909, when they sold her to the Alaska Packers' Association.

"Star of Lapland."

The flagship of the Alaska Packers' fleet is the great *Star of Lapland*. She and the *Star of Zealand* ex *Astral* are still to be seen at Oakland, but the *Acme*, renamed the *Star of Poland*, was wrecked on Katsura Island, in the Japan Sea in 1918, when doing U. S. Government work.

No doubt the Alaska Packers will hang on to these big ships until the last, but it is to be feared that the end of square sail on the Pacific coast is fast approaching.

The "E. R. Sterling," Six-mast Barquentine.

It will have been noticed by the reader how often the dictates of economy compelled owners to re-rig the old square-riggers as fore-and-afters. The most outstanding example of this method of sailing ship economy was the case of the six-mast barquentine, *E. R. Sterling*.

The *E. R. Sterling* was built at Belfast in 1883, being one of the superb four-masters from the board of Messrs. Harland & Wolff. She was built of iron, registered 2518 tons, and ran until the end of the nineteenth century under the house-flag of the Belfast Lord Line. She was then sold to the Germans and renamed *Columbia*.

"STAR OF LAPLAND" EX "ATLAS."

"STAR OF LAPLAND" EX "ATLAS."

"LLEWELLYN J. MORSE."

"E. R. STERLING."

In April, 1903, she was dismasted off Cape Flattery, losing everything above the deck on her fore and main. She was picked up and towed into Vancouver. After being docked at Esquimalt she was abandoned to the underwriters on the result of the survey. She next appeared in the Register under her old name and the ownership of the Victoria and Vancouver Stevedoring Company. However, she was very shortly afterwards sold to C. E. Peabody of Vancouver, who renamed her the *Everett G. Griggs.*

She now came under the Canadian flag, and it was under the direction of Captain Delano that she was re-rigged as a six-mast barquentine by Moran Bros. of Seattle. The mizenmast and yards were shifted forward and became the new foremast, and five fore-and-afters of the same height from step to truck were studded along the deck at what one might almost call close interval.

The new rig only spread a total of 6800 feet of canvas, but it saved eleven men before the mast, the fore-and-afters, as well as the upper yards, being hoisted by steam winches. The new crew now only numbered seventeen men instead of twenty-eight. Captain Delano, though admitting that the new rig cost the ship a good deal of her speed, contended that she not only was able to sail closer to the wind, but was easier to handle.

The six-mast barquentine was put into the Pacific lumber trade, and her first cargo consisted of two million feet of Oregon pine, laths and pickets. With this load towering above her topgallant rail she made the run across the Pacific to Melbourne in 88 days. This was in 1906.

Captain Delano, after making a few voyages, handed over to Captain F. Wann. Her passages were mostly in the neighbourhood of 90 days between the Columbia River and Sydney or Melbourne.

In 1910 the well-known American master mariner, Captain E. R. Sterling, late commander of the Down Easters, *Patrician* and *W. F. Babcock*, bought the six-master for £5500, and fitted her with all the up-to-date conveniences and economies he could think of. He wired her from stem to stern for telephone and electric light, and she was also the first sailing ship to be equipped with a wireless installation. Both fore and aft a successful attempt was made to make a home out of the old windjammer. In the cabin a pianola and a gramophone were installed, and concerts for the crew were regularly given by Captain Sterling and his family.

The big barquentine now sailed under the name of *E. R. Sterling*, the captain commanding her himself until 1914, when he handed her over to his son, Captain Ray Sterling, who still further added to the comforts of the ship, both fore and aft. She even was provided with a fast motor-boat and a high powered motor-car, and in her cabin, besides the usual sea-captain's curios, the bulkheads held valuable oil paintings, and the floors Persian carpets and rugs.

During the War the *E. R. Sterling* made a great deal of money in the Pacific lumber trade. She also made several passages between Australia and New Zealand, her best on this run being nine days between Newcastle, N.S.W., and Auckland.

Some time soon after the Armistice Captain Ray Sterling was offered £15,000 for his ship, but he had a real affection for the famous vessel and refused to be tempted.

The Last Passage of the " E. R. Sterling."

On April 16, 1927, the *E. R. Sterling* left Adelaide with a cargo consisting of between 40,000 and 50,000 bags of wheat consigned to the United Kingdom. All went well until the pitch of the Horn was reached, where the *E. R. Sterling* ran into the usual Cape Horn weather.

It was a season, however, when the dangers of the Cape Horn snorter, the snow flurry, the blinding fog, and the mast-testing swell of the Cape Horn calm were still further increased by the dread menace of ice, which, in the shape of large bergs, and fields of the still more dreaded small stuff, blocked the path of the homeward bounder for close on 500 miles.

All these dangers were, however, successfully evaded, and the big barquentine came through the ordeal unscathed. Shortly after passing the Falkland Islands, however, on July 4, Independence Day to be exact, the ship was overtaken by a violent gale of wind, which tore the main and mizen masts out of her. This mishap curtailed her sailing powers very considerably, and when the *E. R. Sterling* was spoken on August 16, 122 days out, she was still some 600 miles south of the Line in 10° S., 31° W.

The lame duck wandered on until she was in the latitude of the Cape Verdes ; then on September 4 she again suffered dismasting in a violent gale. This time the foremast went by the board, and in the usual heroic work of striving to salve the wreck the mate, Mr. Roderick Mackenzie, got badly crushed in the tangle of broken spars and gear. He was carried into the cabin, where Captain Sterling did his best to bring him round, at the same time giving orders for an S.O.S. for a doctor to be sent out. Unfortunately, as the ship lay helpless in the trough of the sea, the aerial had carried away. The young wireless operator, M. B. Anderson, who was a nineteen-year old Australian engaged specially for the trip, risked life and limb in his efforts to refix his aerial, but before this could be done the mate had died from his injuries and was buried at sea the next day.

At last young Anderson succeeded in repairing his aerial, and his S.O.S. calls were speedily answered by the steamer, *Northern Monarch*. By this time, however, Captain Sterling had managed to get something hung up forward, and he decided to run away before the Trade for the West Indies.

After covering 2212 miles under jury rig, the *E. R. Sterling* reached St. Thomas on October 15. Here Captain Sterling found that there were no conveniences or material for re-rigging his vessel. At first he considered transferring his cargo to a tramp steamer, but nothing suitable in this line proved to be within reach, upon which he decided to telegraph for an ocean tug, so that the *E. R. Sterling* could be towed to her destination.

On December 15 the crippled six-master left St. Thomas in tow of the Dutch tug, *Indus*. Horta in Fayal was reached on January 10, 1928, and 18 days later the shipping fraternity of the London River were astonished to see the *E. R. Sterling* come to an anchor in the Thames, 286 days out from Adelaide.

The smart six-mast barquentine, which was the pride of her " old man," was little more than a rust-stained, dishevelled wreck. The fore lower mast was standing, with half the broken lower yard still attached by its crane, but with the yardarm lashed down to the rail. The main and mizen masts were entirely gone, and of the after masts, which had been named spanker, jigger, and driver by Captain Delano, the spanker had only half a topmast; on the jigger was the makeshift aerial; and the driver was without a topmast at all.

At first Captain Sterling spoke hopefully of refitting his vessel, but he soon discovered that this was out of the question, the cost being prohibitive, and so it came about that the heart-broken captain found himself compelled to sell the ship, which had so long been the happy home of himself and his family.

In the end he parted with her for about £4000 to a firm of East Coast shipbreakers, and the old ship was towed away from the Thames for Sunderland on March 26, 1928.

" Monongahela."

This fine four-mast barque, which was or'ginally the *Balasore,* built for the Liverpool firm of Eyre, Evans & Co. by Barclay, Curle & Co. of Glasgow, is one of those ships which came into a new lease of life after the War.

After being used as an oil carrying barge on the Pacific coast, *Monongahela* was refitted and put into the lumber trade between Puget Sound and Australia.

On the last voyage of which I have any note she arrived in Australia from Port Angeles on December 11, 1927, and sailed from Adelaide on February 21, 1928, on the return passage to Seattle, where she arrived 107 days out.

The Beautiful " Tusitala."

There is only one sailing ship in the American Mercantile Marine that still trades regularly between the Atlantic and Pacific ports of the United States. This is the *Tusitala,* once the well-known *Sierra Lucena* of the Liverpool "Sierra" Line. She was launched on the Clyde in September, 1883, from the yard of Robert Steele & Co. of Greenock, the famous builders of tea clippers. Messrs. Steele & Co. failed soon after the launch of the *Sierra Lucena* for the sole reason that they could only put the very best materials and workmanship into their vessels, and this cost more money than sailing ship owners in their last struggles against steam were able to afford. The *Sierra Lucena* was as a matter of fact the last square-rigged ship built by Steele & Co., and she was in no way inferior to any of their other constructions, being most beautifully built in every particular.

She sailed in the "Sierra" Line until 1904, when she was sold to the Norwegians and her name changed to *Sophie*. During the War she was mostly engaged in the Argentine grain trade to Europe under the command of Captain Hans M. Mikkelsen. Then after Peace was declared she made a few trips in the coal trade from Hampton Roads to the Baltic. This evidently did not pay very well, and when the shipping slump came she was laid up. After being inactive for eighteen months she was libelled at Norfolk, Virginia, in 1923, for her master's salary and ship-chandler's bill. The money, however, was paid in time to save the vessel coming under the hammer as she lay in Hampton Roads. Then in April, 1923, she was bought by a syndicate of artists and writers, who called themselves "The Three Hours for Lunch" Club. These sportsmen made quite a ceremony of changing her flag and renaming her. This took place in New York on June 26, 1923. At the selected moment Mr. Will H. Low, the artist, an old friend of Robert Louis Stevenson, made a short speech and renamed her *Tusitala*, at the same time breaking a bottle of champagne over the ship's bell on the fo'c'sle-head. At the same moment Captain Mikkelsen, who was now going to act as mate, blew his whistle and broke out the new house-flag at the main truck and the Stars and Stripes at the monkey-gaff. A letter of greeting was then read by Christopher Morley from Joseph Conrad.

The ship's new owners formed the most ambitious plans with regard to the *Tusitala's* future. These plans, however, all fell to the ground, and the ship found herself in the New York and Rio de Janeiro trade under the command of Captain Coalfleet, taking coal out and manganese ore home. After two voyages the old ship was sold to Mr. James A. Farrell and henceforth flew the well-known house-flag of the Argonaut Line.

Her first voyage under the new ownership was from New York to Honolulu and Seattle by way of the Panama Canal. This was made under Captain Halvor Mikkelsen, with Hans M. Mikkelsen still acting as chief mate. The sailing days from New York to Seattle *via* the Hawaiian Isles were 76, the ship leaving New York on November 4, 1924. At Seattle Captain Mikkelsen handed over his command to Captain Gilbert Gunderson, who brought the ship home to New York, where he and his chief mate both resigned. Since 1925 the *Tusitala* has been commanded by James P. Barker, a British shipmaster, and has made seven voyages between the Atlantic and Pacific ports *via* the Panama Canal. Her cargoes have generally been sulphate of ammonia from New York to Honolulu, then ballast to Seattle, and from Seattle she takes magnesite and lumber to Baltimore. Her round generally takes about six months, and the passages round about the 80 days, her last from Seattle to Baltimore being 77 days.

The *Tusitala* is kept up as probably no other sailing ship in the world is still kept up, unless it happens to be a training ship, and she is equipped with all the modern inventions, such as wireless. Still painted white from truck to waterline, her yachtlike appearance draws the admiration not only of seamen, but of landsmen, wherever she is seen.

The Rolph Navigation and Coal Company.

The last two men to support sail on the Pacific coast were Mr. A. P. Rolph and Captain Robert Dollar. The fleet of the Rolph Navigation and Coal Company, which was got together by Mr. A. P. Rolph, the late Mayor of San Francisco, after the War, must not be confused with that of Messrs. Hind, Rolph & Co., who, previous to the War, owned a number of beautiful little four-mast barquentines and schooners, most of which were built in California.

Of these, the *Koko Head* and her sister ship, the *Puako*, built by Boole of Oakland in 1902, were the largest, with the exception of a couple of old Down Easters, Sewall's *Henry Villard* and the *Invincible*, built by Moses of Bath in 1873, which had been turned into a four-mast schooner. The *Henry Villard* is now a barge in the employ of the Coastwise Steamship & Barge Company of Seattle, but the *Invincible* and the *Koko Head* have both gone. The *Puako* and some half-dozen more of these handsome little four-masters

"GOLDEN GATE."

"KOKO HEAD."
With cargo of Oregon pine.

"JAMES ROLPH."

Lent by Capt. L. R. W. Beavis.

with the South Sea Island names still earn their living in the lumber trade.

The Rolph Navigation and Coal Company also owned a number of wooden barquentines, which were built by the Rolph Shipbuilding Company of Rolph, California, but the most interesting ships in this fleet were the old British built trio, *Annie M. Reid* ex *Howard D. Troop*, *James Rolph* ex *Celtic Monarch*, and *Golden Gate* ex *Lord Shaftesbury*.

Towards the end of 1923 Mr. A. P. Rolph made a valiant attempt to revive the old trans-Pacific sailing ship trade with these three vessels and his four-mast barquentine, the *Rolph*, of 1386 tons, built in 1919.   Of the three ex-Britishers, the *Annie M. Reid* had a great reputation for fast passages.   On her maiden voyage she had crossed the Atlantic from the Tail o' the Bank, River Clyde, to New York against the Westerlies in a little over 13 days under Captain Parker, having only 14 days to save her charter.

From 1905 she was commanded for something like thirteen years by the well-known Blue-nose skipper, Captain J. A. Durkee. In 1906 he sailed her from Sydney, N.S.W., to Falmouth with 3500 tons of wheat on board in 82 days.   In 1909 he drove her from Yokohama to Astoria in 20 days, and during this trip the big four-master made a twenty-four hour run of 851 miles.

Rolph bought her in 1912, paying something under 40,000 dollars for her, and during the War the ship paid for herself many times over.

After making the run from Honolulu to San Francisco in 33 days she was laid up in 1921.

The *James Rolph* ex *Celtic Monarch* was built by Royden of Liverpool in 1884 for the firm of Parry Jones & Co., later Hugh Jones & Co.   This big full-rigger was more noted for the tremendous strength of her construction than for her smart sailing ; nevertheless, she had some good passages to her credit in the Californian trade. In September, 1910, after being completely dismasted, she was allowed to lie rotting on moorings until 1918, when, owing to the War, she came back to life again as a barge.   Then Mr. Rolph bought her and gave her a complete refit.   She ran steadily under the Rolph house-flag until the summer of 1921, when she was laid up in 'Frisco Bay, along with the *Annie M. Reid.*

The *Golden Gate* ex *Lord Shaftesbury* was bought by A. P. Rolph in 1911. She was previously a four-mast ship, but Rolph stripped the jigger mast of its yards. This ship, like the *Annie M. Reid,* has made a number of fine passages across the Pacific in the trade between San Francisco and Sydney.

Unfortunately Mr. Rolph's splendid effort to keep the American flag flying on the old square-rigger soon petered out, and the three ships were once more laid up at their old moorings, but during this last attempt the *Golden Gate* made a very hazardous passage from San Francisco to Runcorn *via* the Panama Canal with barley. She sprang a leak soon after leaving San Francisco, and it was found necessary to work the pumps incessantly in order to keep the water under. Captain Hackell, indeed, confessed that he never expected to bring his ship through.

Panama was reached 48 days out. When the ship was nearing her destination the pumps gave out and a Cunard liner actually stood by the leaking ship whilst they were being repaired. When the *Golden Gate* finally reached the Mersey, 98 days out from San Francisco, she grounded at Ellesmere Port but was refloated again with help from the shore.

The Robert Dollar Company.

The last square-riggers in the Pacific lumber trade were Captain Robert Dollar's British built ships, *Dunsyre* and *Janet Dollar.* The *Dunsyre,* which was built in 1891 by Hamilton & Co. of Port-Glasgow, was one of those big steel full-riggers which were better known as good carriers than fast sailers. She did, however, make a very smart run across the Pacific from San Francisco to Wellington, New Zealand, being only 31 days from land to land and 38 days to port.

The *Janet Dollar* was originally the famous oil sailer, *Eclipse,* which was built on the Clyde in 1902, and when owned by the British-American Oil Co. was considered the fastest ship in their fleet. She went to the Germans just before the War, and under the name of *Egon* was interned in Mexico throughout the term of hostilities, at the end of which she was bought by Captain Robert Dollar.

Her last passage with lumber was made in 1924. After discharging her cargo at Tsingtao she was left at a mooring in that harbour for over three years. At the end of 1927 she was sold to a Chinese firm, and was towed round to Morrison Point, Chin Kiang, where, I believe, she is still used as a hulk by a cement factory.

Captain Robert Dollar bought one other big four-master in his attempt to keep the Pacific lumber trade for sail, and this was the German four-mast barque, *Hans*, which he renamed *Mary Dollar*. This vessel registered 2880 tons and was built by W. Hamilton & Co. of Port-Glasgow in 1904. She was a big carrier, with the modern midship bridge. Like that of the *Janet Dollar* her renewed activity after the War was only of short duration.

All sailing ship lovers should be grateful to such men as Captain Robert Dollar and A. P. Rolph for their self-sacrificing efforts to keep the beautiful square-rigger upon the Seven Seas. Many unavoidable factors combined to defeat their efforts, not the least of which was the difficulty of obtaining officers and foremast hands who were capable of handling and keeping in repair that complex fabric of wood, steel, wire, hemp, and manila, which has been gradually evolved through the ages by numberless generations of burly seamen.

When one remembers, also, that the cost of canvas, rope, wire, blocks and spars has more than doubled since pre-War days, that a suit of sails costs almost as much as a latter-day sailing ship's market value, and that insurance rates are all against the old windjammer, it is easy to realise the difficulties and worries and financial losses suffered by those few old-timers who have clung despairingly to their beloved sailing ships.

Thus it is not to be wondered at that the placid waters inside the Golden Gate reflect the tall spars and web-like rigging of quite a large fleet of idle sailing ships, riding forlorn, neglected, and deserted opposite the wharves of that great city which has owed its prosperity in great part to the ship of masts and sails.

The Down Easters have now followed the famous Yankee clipper, the iron heeler from the Clyde, the green Aberdeen flyer,

the lordly East Indiaman, and the high-pooped Spanish galleon
into the misty seas and sunny, pleasant anchorages of Kingdom
Come, where, as John Masefield sings, we old shellbacks of the mast
and yard may some day hope to find :

> Drowned old wooden hookers, green wi' drippin' wrack,
> Ships as never fetched a port, as never came back—
> Swingin' to the blushin' tide, dippin' to the swell,
> 'N' the crews all singin', sonny, beatin' on the bell.

APPENDIX

Six-masted Barquentine

Five-masted Schooner

Three-masted Barque

Hermaphrodite Brig
(or Brigantine)

Three-masted
Barquentine

Four-masted
Ship

APPENDIX I.

Register of American-Built Ships.

Date	Name	Tons	Length	Breadth	Depth	Builder	Owner
1853	*Young America*	1380	239·6	43·2	26·9	W. H. Webb	George Daniels
	David Crockett	1679	218·8	41	19·7	Greenman & Co.	Handy & Everett
	Great Republic	4555	335	53	38	Donald McKay	Donald McKay
	(When cut down)	3356	335	53	29		
1862	*General McLellan*	1583	191	39·3	28·6	Thomaston	Jas. W. Elwell
1865	*Seminole*	1442	196·5	41·6	25	Maxon & Fish, Mystic, Conn.	A. M. Simpson
1866	*Oneida*	1180	186	36	23	M. Packard	Leon Sloss
1868	*Yosemite*	1104	183	37·2	23·5	Portsmouth	Samuel Blair
	Sovereign of the Seas No. IV.	1502	200·1	50·8	24	Donald McKay	Lawrence, Giles & Co.
1869	*Southern Cross*	1086	176·8	37·5	23·3	Boston	A. H. Brown
	St. Lucie	1263	194·4	37·4	24	Bath	I. F. Chapman
	Augusta	1326				Newbury Port	
	Highlander	1352	190·3	38·8	24	Eoston	F. E. Scammel
	Prussia	1215	184·2	36·5	23·9	Bath	Houghton Bros.
	Glory of the Seas	2103	240·2	44·1	28·3	Donald McKay	J. Henry Sears (1889)
	Great Admiral	1573	214·2	40·3	25·3	R. E. Jackson	W. F. Weld (1889)
	St. Nicholas	1799	206·9	42·8	29	Chapman & Flint	Flint & Co.
	Undaunted	1764	207·3	41·1	27·8	A. & E. Sewall	J. E. Stafford (1894)
	Jairus B. Lincoln	1769	207·7	40·5	28·1	Briggs & Cushing	Hermann of Bremen (1894)
	Cora	1491	200·2	39	23	Belfast, Me.	Wm. H. Burrill
	Enos Soule	1518	193·4	38·1	18·5	Freeport, Me.	Enos Soule
	John Bryce	1958	217	42·2	21·7	Thomaston	E. O'Brien
	Loretto Fish	1840	212	42·2	21·3	Thomaston	S. Watts & Co.
	Imperial	1231	188·7	38	23·5	Quincy, Mass.	Jas. E. Crosby
1870	*John C. Potter*	1244	186	36	23	M. Packard	Chas. Nelson
	St. John	1885	216·3	42·7	20·4	Bath	I. F. Chapman
	Samuel Watts	2384	223·7	40	30·5	Thomaston	S. Watts & Co.
	A. McCallum	1951	215	42	21	Thomaston	E. O'Brien
	Carrie Reed	1352	193·8	39·4	24·9	W. Thompson	
	Agenor	1487	202·3	39·9	24·2	Boston	B. B. Williams
1871	*Matchless*	1198				Curtis, Smith & Co.	James H. Dawes
	Nancy Pendleton	1449	199	39·2	24	Belfast, Me.	Wm. Beazley
	North Star	1357	201·4	38·4	23·9	W. Moses & Son, Bath	
	Columbia	1471	205·9	40	24	Bath	Houghton Bros.
	Harry Morse	1365	198·2	37·5	23·8	Bath	G. E. Plummer
	Independence	952	165·6	34·2	22·9	Boston	Hemingway & Browne

Register of American-Built Ships.—Continued.

Date	Name	Tons	Length	Breadth	Depth	Builder	Owner
1872	Sea Witch	1288	197	37	24	East Boston	E. Lawrence
	Covondelet	1438	202·5	40·5	24	Newcastle, Me.	Cyrus Walker
	Carrollton	1450	198·2	39·6	24·6	Bath	J. Rosenfeld
	McNear	1308	189·9	37·7	24	Belfast	H. A. Thompson
1873	Three Brothers	2972	320	48	29·8	Green Point, Long Island	Geo Howes & Co.
	(Lloyd's 1881)	2936	323	48·4	31·1		J. Williams, Liverpool
	Triumphant	2046	234·5	43	19·1	Quincy	Thayes & Lincoln
	El Capitan	1494	205·3	37·2	25·5	E. & A. Sewall	De Groot & Peck
	Sterling	1732	208·4	42·7	26·1	A. Sewall & Co.	J. Rosenfeld & Sons
	Robert Dixon	1368	194·9	38·7	24·3	A. Hall	J. M. Cushing
	Thomas Dana	1445	203·5	39·5	24·2	J. Currier, Jr.	W. H. Lincoln & Co.
	Wm. R. Grace	1799	218·1	42·8	20·8	Bath	Ben. Flint
	Northern Light	1795	219·7	43·1	19	Quincy, Mass.	Wm. Pickney
	Nearchus	1315	199·1	37·4	24·2	J. Currier	Stephan of Bremen (1894)
	Invincible	1460	202·4	40·3	24	Bath	C. S. Holmes
	Louisiana	1436	202·4	40	24·4	Bath	Houghton Bros.
	North American	1583	219·6	41	24·5	East Boston	H. Hastings
	Antelope	1306	198·3	37·3	24	Belfast	Thos. Peabody
	Grandee	1295	193·6	38·5	23·8	Portsmouth	C. H. Mendum (1889)
1874	St. Paul	1894	228·2	42·1	27·5	Chapman, Bath	I. F. Chapman & Co.
	Spartan	1449	206·6	40·5	24·3	R. E. Jackson	P. B. Cornwall, 'Frisco
	General Fairchild	1428	203·4	38·8	24·3	Briggs & Cushing	W. E. Mighell (1894)
	Frank Pendleton	1414	200	39	25	Belfast	Wm. G. Nichols
	C. F. Sargent	1704	220·3	41·3	26	C. F. Sargent	G. E. Plummer (1894)
	Lucile	1394	200·2	40	23·9	E. C. Soule	J. S. Winslow & Co.
	Mary L. Stone	1459	198·9	39·3	24·3	Goss & Sawyer	De Groot & Peck
	Charger	1444	203·2	39·8	24	Smith & Townsend	H. Hasting & Co.
	J. B. Brown	1551	207·5	40·5	24	Titcomb & Thompson	W. E. Mighell (1894)
	Benjamin Sewall	1434	202	38·9	24·1	Pennell	S. R. Ulmer (1889)
	Saratoga	1449	207·6	39·2	24	Campbell & Brooks	
	Alfred Watts (ex Abner J. Benyon)	2043	227·9	42·1	19·9	Watts	J. S. Burgess
	Leading Wind	1208	186	37	22	Bath	W. A. Rust (1889)
	Gatherer	1509	208·1	40·2	24·2	Bath	Jacob Jenson
	America	2054	232·8	43·1	19·3	Quincy	Chas. Goodall
	Conqueror	1621	215·3	41·8	24	East Boston	P. F. Wells
	Highland Light	1314	194·9	38·1	24·3	Bath	R. C. Byxbee (1889)
	Joseph S. Spinney	1988	230·9	42·6	19·5	Thomaston	Mills Harvey
	Oriental	1688	220·1	42·2	24·9	Bath	Samuel Blair
	Hagerstown	1903	223·7	42·3	17·5	Richmond, Me.	T. Ruger (1889)

Register of American-Built Ships.—Continued.

Date	Name	Tons	Length	Breadth	Depth	Builder	Owner
1875	Occidental	1533	210·6	39·8	24·7	Bath	A. Sewall
	Exporter	1369	199·5	38·2	24	Newburyport	W. Currier
	Landseer	1418	200·5	39·1	24·2		Chas. W. Lord
	Willard Mudgett	875	160·3	34	24·2	Stockton, Me.	Alie Mudgett
	Tam o' Shanter	1603	213·8	41·7	24·3	E. C. Soule	E. C. Soule
	M. P. Grace	1928	229·9	42·1	27·8	Chapman & Flint	Flint & Co.
	Raphael	1543	222	40	24·3	Carleton & Norwood	Carleton, Norwood & Co.
	Isaac Reed	1542	212	40	24·2	A. Reed & Co.	A. R. Reed, N.Y.
	Harvester	1494	210·1	39·7	24	E. & A. Sewall	A. P. Lorentzen (1894)
	Belle O'Brien	1903	237·5	42	26·2	E. O'Brien	E. O'Brien
	Oregon	1431	205·6	30·9	24	W. Rogers, Bath	W. E. Mighell (1894)
	City of Philadelphia	1457	202·3	40·2	24·3	Bath	P. Fitzpatrick
	Centennial	1286	190·4	38	24	East Boston	Sylvanus Smith
	Rufus E. Wood	1477	200·1	40·4	24·5	East Deering, Mass.	W. H. Mighell
	Elwell	1461	212·3	39·1	24·7	Damariscotta, Me.	D. W. Chapman
	Bohemia	1635	221·7	40·2	25·5	Bath	H. L. Houghton
	Big Bonanza	1472	210·2	40·2	24	Newburyport	J. Currier, Jr.
	Continental	1712	220	42·2	25·1	Bath	A. C. Peck
	Daniel I. Tenney	1685	212·4	40·4	22	Newburyport	W. Currier
1876	Henrietta	1266	201·3	39	24	Bucksville	J. C. Nickels
	San Joaquin	1637	219·8	41·6	24·2	E. C. Soule	E. C. Soule
	Samaria	1509	217·6	39·1	24·1	Houghton	Houghton
	Annie H. Smith	1563	200	40	24·5	Calais, Me.	M. P. Smith
	Reaper	1407	211·6	39·2	24	E. & A. Sewall	A. Sewall & Co.
	Sachem	1381	194	39·4	23·8	C. Sampson	M. F. Pickering
	Eureka	2101	230·9	42·1	26·5	T. J. Southard	T. J. Southard
	Harvey Mills	2186				Mills & Creighton	
	Paul Revere	1735	221	41·2	24·6	Smith & Townsend	De Groot & Peck
	R. R. Thomas	1289	202	40·3	24	E. Dunbar	J. C. Nickels
	Belle of Oregon	1169	185·6	38	22·5	Goss & Sawyer	W. H. Besse (1894)
	Josephus	1470	213	29·2	24·4	E. Haggett	Pendleton, Carver & Nichols
	Sania Clara	1535	209·5	40	25·5	Bath	A. G. Ropes
	Portland Lloyds	1242	190·6	38·5	22	East Deering	J. S. Winslow
	Indiana	1488	208·9	40	23·9	A. Sewall & Co.	A. Sewall & Co.
	Palmyra	1360	197	38	24	Goss & Sawyer	Puget Sound Commercial Co
1877	P. N. Blanchard	1582	213·4	40	17·5	Yarmouth, Me.	S. C. Blanchard
	South American	1762	227·5	41·6	25·2	Boston	H. Hastings
	Wandering Jew	737	219·2	40	29	J. Pascal, Camden	Carleton, Norwood & Co.
	Jabez Howes	1648	218·8	40·1	26	J. Currier	J. Rosenfield
	St. Mark	1973	239·9	42·5	27·5	Hitchcock & Blair	G. W. Johnson

Register of American-Built Ships.—Continued.

Date	Name	Tons	Length	Breadth	Depth	Builder	Owner
	St. David	1595	213·4	40·6	17·2	Bath	Ben. Flint
	Levi G. Burgess	1616	217·5	41·2	24·5	Thomaston	Jacob Jensen
	William H. Connor	1496	210·4	40·5	24·2	Searsport	B. F. Pendleton
	Llewellyn J. Morse	1393	198·2	36·6	24	J. Oakes & Son	J. Rosenfeld
	William G. Davis	1669	213·7	41·7	25·4	G. Russell	J. H. Winchester
	Panay	1190	186·7	37	23·5	Boston	Geo. H. Allen
	Challenger	1456	212·4	39·7	23·9	Bath	A. Sewall
	Vigilant	1800	224	40	28	N. L. Thompson	E. Lawrence
	C. C. Chapman	1653	222·3	39·9	25·2	W. Rogers, Bath	J. S. Winslow
	Belle of Bath	1418	203·9	39	24·3	Goss & Sawyer	R. P. Buck & Co.
	Armenia	1698	223·3	40·4	26·1	Bath	Houghton Bros.
	Iceberg	1777	175	37	24	East Boston	J. V. Barnes
	Palestine	1469	209·6	40	24	Bath	Samuel Blair
	Florence	1684	223·1	41	26	Goss & Sawyer	C. Davenport
	Pharos	2001	235	40	27·6	Kennebunk, Me.	T. Ruger
	Daniel Barnes	1485	219·3	39·9	24·1	Bath	Daniel Barnes
	Sintram	1674	215·4	42·9	24·2	E. C. Soule	E. C. Soule
	Red Cross	1300	185·3	38·1	23·1	Richmond	T. J. Southard
	Normandy	1208	188	38	24·2	Damariscotta, Me.	J. M. Turkey
	Amy Turner	900	174	35·4	21·6	East Boston	E. W. Brewer
	Governor Goodwin	1459	212	40	24	Campbell & Brooks	Foster & Pray
	Alex. Gibson	2194	247·3	42·6	29·6	E. O'Brien	E. E. O'Brien
	Granite State	1684	228·9	41·4	24	J. Neal, Kittery	W. Ross
	Sea King	1492	210·6	39·4	24	G. H. Theobald	W. E. Mighell (1894)
	St. Stephen	1392				Bath	Flint & Co.
	Alfred D. Snow	2075	232·7	42·3	21	Watts, Thomaston	S. Watts
	Baring Brothers	2165	243·7	42·3	21·7	Thomaston	E. O'Brien
1878	L. Schepp	1833	224·3	42·1	27·1	Titcomb & Thompson	I. F. Chapman
	Snow & Burgess	1655	228·5	41·5	24·7	S. Watts	A. P. Lorentzen
	Red Cloud	2058	230·5	43·2	21·2	G. Thomas	
	C. D. Bryant	929	172·7	37	21	Pendleton	E. E. Kentfield
	Gerard C. Tobey	1459	208·7	39·1	23·6	Goss, Sawyer & Packard	W. H. Besse
	John A. Briggs	2110	234·2	44·1	28·2	Briggs & Cushing	G. Plummer (1894)
	State of Maine	1536	216	40·1	24·4	Haggett & Co.	J. C. Nickels (1894)
	Eclipse	1594	221·7	40·3	24·3	Bath	G. S. Dearborn
	Standard	1534	212	40·1	24·5	J. M. Hagar	C. V. Minott
	Wachusett	1599	214·7	40·2	26·4	Crawford & Perkins	W. E. Mighell (1894)
1879	Yorktown	1955	227	40·5	20	Richmond	J. A. Delap
	Manuel Llaguno	1733	221·3	41·5	25·5	J. McDonald	I. F. Chapman & Co.
	Commodore	1980	226·9	41·8	27·6	Blanchard Bros.	W. A. Boole (1894)

Register of American-Built Ships.—Continued.

Date	Name	Tons	Length	Breadth	Depth	Builder	Owner
1880	Solitaire	1532	213·7	40·1	24·1	E. Sewall	A. Sewall & Co.
	J. B. Walker	2179	247·1	42·2	29·8	E. O'Brien	E. E. O'Brien
	Guy C. Goss	1572	213·9	39·8	24·4	Bath	Wm. H. Besse
	Paramita	1573	216·6	41·3	23·1	E. C. Soule	E. C. Soule
	Jennie Harkness	1373	206·5	38·3	23·2	Camden, Me.	Carleton & Co.
	Patrician	1254	192·2	36·4	24	Damariscotta, Me.	W. A. Street
	McLaurin	1374	200·8	39	24	Newburyport	F. P. Jones
	George Stetson	1845	232·9	41·3	26·3	A. Hathorne	W. S. Higgins
	Emily Reed	1565	215	40·6	24·1	Reed (Waldebro)	Yates & Porterfield, N.Y.
	Wilna	1483	203	41·9	24	Briggs & Cushing	W. E. Mighell (1894)
	James Drummond	1556	216	40·1	24·2	Phippsburg, Me.	C. V. Minott
	Glendon	1896	235·5	40·6	28·4	Kennebunk, Me.	Geo. W. Rice
1881	Iroquois	2121	239·1	43·6	27·9	A. Sewall	A. Sewall & Co.
	A. J. Fuller	1849	229·3	41·5	26	J. McDonald	Flint & Co.
	Adolph Obrig	1448	208·2	38·6	23	Carleton, Norwood	Carleton, Norwood
	E. B. Sutton	1827	227·8	48·1	25·6	I. F. Chapman	I. F. Chapman
	William J. Rotch	1718	218·2	42·1	24·2	Goss, Sawyer & Packard	W. H. Besse
	Luzon	1391	205·8	40·7	24	Smith & Townsend	De Groot & Peck
	Reuce	1925	229·2	41	27·1	Thompson (Kenne)	G. H. Theobald
	General Knox	2218	251·1	42·4	29·1	E. O'Brien	E. E. O'Brien
	Tacoma	1739	222·2	41	26	Goss & Sawyer	C. Davenport
	Joseph B. Thomas	1938	234·3	42·3	27·2	S. Watts	S. Watts
	Arabia	2080	233·9	43·2	27·7	Newport	Houghton Bros.
	Charmer	1881	221·7	42·4	17·8	W. Rogers, Bath	L. Rosenfeld
1882	Parker M. Whitmore	2205	243·4	43·6	19·5	Bath	P. M. Whitmore
	W. F. Babcock	2130	240·8	43·8	28	A. Sewall & Co.	A. Sewall & Co.
	Charles E. Moody	2203	233·9	43·4	18·2	Bath	J. R. Kelley
	John McDonald	2281	249·4	43·1	28·1	B. Flint	Flint & Co.
	I. F. Chapman	2146	237·5	42·7	27·5	I. F. Chapman	I. F. Chapman & Co.
	St. Frances	1898	231·4	41·8	25·9	J. McDonald	Flint & Co.
	William H. Starbuck	1339	194·1	39	24·3	Goss, Sawyer & Packard	J. E. Stafford (1894)
	Abner Coburn	1973	223	43	26·9	W. Rogers, Bath	Pendleton, Carver & Nichols
	Henry Villard	1553	219	39	24	A. Sewall	A. Sewall & Co.
	Cyrus Wakefield	2119	247	43·7	28·6	S. Watts	S. Watts
	Edward O'Brien II.	2271	259·1	42·5	28·9	E. E. O'Brien	E. E. O'Brien
	George S. Homer	1534	204·9	39·6	20·9	Goss, Sawyer & Pickard	W. H. Besse
	Henry Failing	1976	230·8	43·1	26·3	Goss & Sawyer	W. H. Besse
	John Currier	1945	235·8	42·8	26·8	Newburyport, Mass.	John Currier, Jr.
	Berlin	1634	222·5	40	24·6	Phippsburg, Me.	C. V. Minott
	Elizabeth	1366	231·5	41·8	19·8	Newcastle, Me.	B. F. Pendleton

Register of American-Built Ships.—Continued.

Date	Name	Tons	Length	Breadth	Depth	Builder	Owner
1883	St. James	1566	218·5	41·3	23·7	J. McDonald	Flint & Co.
	S. P. Hitchcock	2292	247·4	44·3	28·6	I. F. Chapman	I. F. Chapman
	Tillie E. Starbuck	2033	257	42·7	23	J. Roach & Son	W. H. Starbuck
	Benjamin F. Packard	2130	244·2	43·3	26·7	Goss, Sawyer & Packard	A. Sewall & Co. (1894)
	Kennebec	2127	237·7	43·3	27·3	W. Rogers	W. A. Boole
	R. D. Rice	2247	252·1	43·7	28·7	S. Watts	S. Watts
	St. Charles	1749	225·2	41·6	16·8	Phippsburg, Me.	C. V. Minott
	T. F. Oakes	1997	255	40·6	23·5	American S.B. Co.	W. H. Starbuck
	Governor Robie	1713	224·1	41	23·8	W. Rogers	Pendleton, Carver & Nichols
	Mary L. Cushing	1658	220·7	40·4	23·7	J. Currier, Jr.	J. R. Kelley
	E. F. Sawyer	1993	230·4	43·4	18·5	Bath	„
	Servia	1867	234·1	41·1	26·7	Houghton Bros.	Houghton Bros.
	Sam Skolfield II.	1593	218·7	39·9	24·2	Skolfield Bros.	Skolfield Bros.
	William H. Macy	2202	254·9	43·2	28·3	Carleton, Norwood	Carleton, Norwood
	William H. Smith	2003	232·4	43·3	17·8	Goss & Sawyer	M. P. Smith
1884	John R. Kelley	2364	256·9	45	27·8	Goss & Sawyer	J. R. Kelley
	Henry B. Hyde	2583	267·9	45	28·8	J. McDonald	Pendleton, Carver & Nichols
	A. G. Ropes	2461	258·2	44·7	28·5	I. F. Chapman & Co.	I. F. Chapman & Co.
	Commodore T. H. Allen	2390	245·3	41·7	28·3	T. J. Southard	T. J. Southard & Son
	Robert L. Belknap	2369	264	43·8	28·6	Rockport, Me.	Carleton, Norwood & Co.
	Clarence S. Bement	1999	259·9	40·6	23·6	American S.B. Co.	J. E. Ridgway
	Adam W. Spies	1232	185	38·4	22·8	Newburyport	J. Cautillion
	George Curtis	1838	234	42·4	25·2	A. R. Reed	A. R. Reed
1885	Frederick Billings	2628	281·7	44·8	28·8	Rockport, Me.	S. D. & C. J. Carleton
	Francis	2077	231	43·4	26·6	N. England S.B. Co.	F. H. Stone
	Holspur	1273	191·9	28·8	22·8	Bath	W. H. Besse
	George R. Skolfield	1731	232·1	39·9	24·6	Brunswick, Me.	G. R. Skolfield
	Willie Rosenfeld	2455	266·5	44·8	27·8	Bath	A. Sewall
	Wallace B. Flint	835	178·4	35·4	17·7	J. McDonald	Flint & Co.
1886 1887 1888	No Square-riggers built—only Fore-and-aft Schooners.						
1889	Rappahannock	3054				A. Sewall	A. Sewall
1890	Matanzas	1028	196·2	37·4	17·4	W. Rogers, Bath	W. D. Munson
	Shenandoah	3154	290·7	39·1	19·9	A. Sewall	A. Sewall
	S. D. Carleton	1788	240	44·4	25·4	Carleton, Norwood	Flint & Co.
	St. Catherine	1264	202·8	39·3	19·1	J. McDonald	„
1891	Susquehanna	2591	273·6	45·1	28	A. Sewall	A. Sewall
	Parthia	2495	260·3	44·4	19·6	Houghton Bros.	Houghton Bros.
	Pactolus	1585	223·7	41·2	24	J. McDonald	Flint & Co.

Register of American-Built Ships.—Continued.

Date	Name	Tons	Length	Breadth	Depth	Builder	Owner
1892	Roanoke	3347	311·2	49·2	29·2	A. Sewall	A. Sewall
	Olympic	1402	224·4	42·1	21·3	N. England S.B. Co.	W. H. Besse
1893	Holliswood	1141	176	38	19·5	J. M. Brooks	E. M. Knight, N.Y.
	Aryan	2017	248·6	42·2	26·3	C. V. Minott	J. W. Elwell & Co.
1894	Dirigo	2845	312	45·1	25·6	A. Sewall	A. Sewall
1898	Erskine M. Phelps	2715	312·1	45·2	25·6	"	"
1899	Arthur Sewall	2919	328·6	45	28·3	"	"
	Edward Sewall	3206	332	45·3	25·5	"	"
	Kaiulani	1571	225·7	42·3	20	"	"
1900	Astral	3262	332·3	45·4	26	"	Standard Oil Co.
1901	William P. Frye	3374	332·4	45·4	26·2	"	A. Sewall & Co.
	Acme	3288	332·2	45·4	26·1	"	Standard Oil Co.
1902	Atlas	3381	332·4	45·4	26·1	"	"

APPENDIX II.

The Searsport Captains.

Compiled by J. H. Sullivan.

COMMANDER	SHIP
Dudley O. Black	*St. James*
Daniel O. Blake	*Harriet McGilvery*
Osias Blake	*Caroline Reed*
John C. Beals	*Richard Nesmith*
Shepard Blanchard	*Louis Walsh*
Elbridge Blanchard	*B. F. Metcalf*
Albert N. Blanchard	*Puritan*
Phineas B. Blanchard	*Bangalore*
Edward D. Blanchard	*Henrietta*
William H. Blanchard	*Governor Robie*
John C. Blanchard	*Wachusett*
James P. Butman	*E. B. Sutton*
Peter C. Cane	*Frank Pendleton*
Benjamin Carver, 1st	*B. Aymar*
Benjamin Carver, 2nd	*L. J. Morse*
James N. Carver, 1st	*Charter Oak*
John A. Carver	*John Bunyan*
Charles G. Carver	*B. F. Carver*
Phineas P. Carver	*Charter Oak*
Nathan P. Carver	*Susan Gilmore*
Frank L. Carver	*S. P. Hitchcock*
Andrew L. Carver	*Mary L. Stone*
William M. Carver	*Susan Gilmore*
Caleb F. Carver	*St. Nicholas*
Jesse T. Carver	*St. Marys*
J. Herbert Colcord	*Elizabeth*
Benjamin F. Colcord	*Centennial*
Theodore P. Colcord	*A. J. Fuller*
Lincoln A. Colcord	*State of Maine*
George W. Colson	*Mary Hammond*
Albert N. Colson	*R. D. Rice*
Edward L. Colson	*Wildwood*
John L. Crawford	*Harvey Mills*
Winthrop S. Crowell	*Flying Eagle*
Lebbens Curtis	*Edward D. Peters*
Eben Curtis	*Tillie E. Starbuck*
Henry G. Curtis	*John C. Potter*
Clifton Curtis	*Belle of Bath*
Samuel Curtis, Jr.	*Henry S. Sanford*
John Dow	*C. B. Carver*
Leory Dow	*John Currier*
Amos A. Dow	*Lucy A. Nickels*
Norman Dunbar	*Louisiana*
George H. Eames	*Mary Goodell*
Oscar G. Eaton	*Oneida*
Thomas B. Ellis	*France*

Josiah L. Emery	..	..	..	..	*Guiding Star*
James T. Erskine	..	..	..	..	*W. H. Conner*
Amasa D. Field	..	..	..	..	*Lucy A. Nickels*
Joseph C. Field	..	..	..	..	*Andrew Jackson*
Alanson Ford		..	..	..	*Kennebec*
James T. Ford	..	..	..	..	*A. S. Davis*
W. Ford	..	..	..	..	*H. McGilvery*
Frank N. Gerry	..	..	..	..	*S. F. Hersey*
Welcome Gilkey	..	..	..	..	*C. B. Hazeltine*
Lincoln Gilkey	..	..	..	..	*Charter Oak*
Isaac F. Gilkey	..	..	..	..	*Dakota*
Philip R. Gilkey		..	..	..	*Josephus*
James C. Gilmore	..	..	..	..	*Henrietta*
J. Locke Gilmore	..	..	..	..	*Western Chief*
Daniel S. Goodell, Sen.		..	..	..	*Mary Goodell*
Daniel S. Goodell, Jr.		..	..	..	*Brown Bros.*
William H. Goodell		..	..	..	*Governor Robie*
Edwin L. Griffin	..	..	..	..	*Charlotte White*
Phineas P. Griffin	..	..	..	..	*Leonora*
Frederick W. Hanson		..	..	..	*Calcutta*
Royal Harriman	..	..	..	..	*Mary Goodell*
George W. Hichborn		..	..	..	*Queenstown*
Sewell Lancaster	..	..	..	..	*W. J. Rotch*
Augustus Lanpher		..	..	..	*B. Aymer*
George McClure	..	..	..	..	*John C. Potter*
Charles C. McClure		..	..	..	*Fort George*
John W. McGilvery		..	..	..	*Pharos*
Freeman McGilvery		..	..	..	*Wellfleet*
James McGilvery	..	..	..	..	*Oneida*
Selwyn N. McGilvery		..	..	..	*David Brown*
Frank W. McGilvery		..	..	..	*Oneida*
Benjamin S. Merithew		..	..	..	*Premier*
John G. Merryman		..	..	..	*Matilda*
James G. Merryman		..	..	..	*R. B. Fuller*
Edward McGrath	..	..	..	..	*Ocean Traveller*
Clarence N. Meyers		..	..	..	*Thomas Dana*
J. C. Nickels	..	..	..	..	*Wild Rover*
David Nickels	..	..	..	..	*Belle of Bath*
J. Fred Nickels	....	..	..	..	*Onward*
Albert V. Nickels	..	..	..	..	*Iroquois*
E. D. P. Nickels	..	..	..	..	*May Flint*
James N. Nickels	..	..	..	..	*Frank Jones*
Sewell L. Nickels	..	..	..	..	*Sachem*
Amos Nickels, Sen.		..	..	..	*Martin Luther*
Charles Nichols	..	..	..	..	*Melrose*
James Nichols	..	..	..	..	*Champlain*
George A. Nichols	..	..	..	..	*Abner Coburn*
Wilfred V. Nickols		..	..	..	*W. H. Conner*
John P. Nichols	..	..	..	..	*Living Age*
Amos Nichols, Jun.		..	..	..	*Governor Robie*
William G. Nichols		..	..	..	*Belle of Bath*
Edward P. Nichols		..	..	..	*Frank Pendleton*

Jasper N. Nichols	*Charter Oak*
Wilson C. Nichols	*Resolute*
Charles M. Nichols	*A. J. Fuller*
Peleg B. Nichols	*R. R. Thomas*
Cyrus G. Nichols, Sen	*Matilda*
Cyrus G. Nichols, Jun.	*R. R. Thomas*
Joshua B. Nichols	*S. P. Hitchcock*
Alexander H. Nichols	*St. Mark*
Daniel C. Nichols	*Wandering Jew*
Allen Noyes	*Mary Goodell*
Benjamin Park	*Henry B. Wright*
Charles C. Park	*Alert*
Melvin L. Park	*Abner Coburn*
Joseph H. Park	*Josephus*
Jeremiah H. Park	*Luazon*
Isaac C. Park	*Leonora*
Oliver C. Park	*Henry B. Wright*
Phineas Pendleton, 2nd	*Vistula*
Phineas Pendleton, 3rd	*Henry B. Hyde*
B. F. Pendleton	*Nancy Pendleton*
John G. Pendleton	*Grace Ross*
John G. Pendleton, Jr.	*Solferino*
James G. Pendleton	*Bell Rock*
Nathan Pendleton	*Dunbarton*
Ephraim Pendleton	*Statesman*
George W. Pendleton	*Henry S. Sanford*
Timothy C. Pendleton	*Louis Walsh*
Frank I. Pendleton	*W. H. Conner*
James N. Pendleton	*Mary L. Cushing*
Charles Pendleton	*Golden Rocket*
Andrew S. Pendleton	*Aryan*
J. Frank Peterson	*Bennington*
Robert Porter	*Matilda*
William A. Rogers	*Hulicon*
Andrew J. Ross	*Premier*
Simon Ross	*Chandos*
Andrew M. Ross	*Henrietta*
Charles K. Sawyer	*B. Aymar*
George C. Small	*State of Maine*
Chandler Smart	*Thirty-one States*
Jeremiah Sweetser, 1st	*Henry Leeds*
Jeremiah Sweetser, 2nd	*Mary Goodell*
Joseph P. Sweetser	*Zephyr*
Forest W. Treat	*St. Paul*
William Treat	*Henry B. Wright*
Joseph W. Wallnutt	*W. R. Grace*
Charles Waterhouse	*Moonlight*
Asa H. Waterhouse	*S. F. Hersey*
Frank Watson	*Jacob C. Ridgeway*
Albert T. Whittier	*Paul Revere*
Oren C. Young	*Reaper*

APPENDIX III.

" Young America "—Complete List of Passages under American Flag.

1ST VOYAGE—CAPTAIN DAVID S. BABCOCK.

Left New York	June 10, 1853	arrived San Francisco Sept.	29	..	111 days
,, San Francisco		,, Honolulu			..	12 ,,
,, Honolulu		,, New York	April	7, 1854	..	96 ,,

2ND VOYAGE.

Left New York	July 2, 1854	arrived San Francisco Oct.	20, 1854	..	110 days
,, San Francisco	Nov. 18, 1854	,, Hongkong	Dec.	30, 1854	..	42 ,,
,, Manila	Sept. 21, 1855	,, New York	Dec.	31, 1855	..	101 ,,

3RD VOYAGE.

Left New York	Mar. 29, 1856	arrived San Francisco July	14	..	107 days
,, San Francisco	Aug. 5, 1856	,, Hongkong	Sept.	18	..	44 ,,
,, Hongkong		,, Melbourne			
,, Melbourne		,, Singapore			
,, Singapore		,, Rangoon			
,, Rangoon	July 31, 1857	,, Falmouth	Oct.	30	..	91 ,,
,, Falmouth		,, Bremen			
,, Bremen		,, Liverpool			
,, Liverpool	April 18, 1858	,, Melbourne	June 20	..	63 ,,
,, Melbourne		,, Singapore			
,, Singapore	Sept. 24	,, New York	Dec.		

4TH VOYAGE—CAPTAIN NATHANIEL BROWN, JR.

Left New York   Jan. 30, 1859   arrived San Francisco July   24   ..   175 days
(Put into Rio dismasted March 18, left after repairs, May 15.)
Left San Francisco   arrived New York   ..   100 days

5TH VOYAGE—CAPTAIN CARLISLE.

Left Liverpool	1860	arrived Melbourne			..	79 days
,, Melbourne	..	,, Callao			..	49 ,,
,, Callao	Nov. 8, 1860	,, Liverpool	Feb.	2, 1861	..	86 ,,
,, Liverpool	Mar. 27, 1861	,, New York	April	26, 1861	..	30 ,,

6TH VOYAGE—CAPTAIN CARLISLE.

Left New York	July 27, 1861	arrived Liverpool			
,, Glasgow	Nov. 1, 1861	,, Oamaru	Feb.	2, 1862	..	93 days
,, Oamaru		,, Callao			
,, Callao	Aug. 4, 1862	,, Antwerp			
(Put into Plymouth October 30 dismasted.)					
,, Antwerp		arrived New York	Mar.	21, 1863	..	32 days

7TH VOYAGE—CAPTAIN JONES.

Left New York	May 28, 1863	arrived San Francisco Sept.	22, 1863	..	117 days
,, San Francisco	Nov. 3, 1863	,, Liverpool	Mar.	8, 1864	..	125 ,,
,, Liverpool	April 15, 1864	,, New York	May	14, 1864	..	29 ,,

8TH VOYAGO—CAPTAIN GEORGE CUMMING.

Left New York		arrived San Francisco	Dec.	9, 1864 ..	120 days
„ San Francisco	Jan. 14, 1865	„ Hongkong	Feb.	28, 1865 ..	45 „
„ Hongkong		„ Manila			
„ Manila	April 16	„ New York	July	24, 1865 ..	99 „

9TH VOYAGE—Captain GEORGE CUMMING.

Left New York	Nov. 12, 1865	arrived San Francisco	Mar.	10, 1866 ..	118 days
„ San Francisco	June 9, 1866	„ Liverpool	Oct.	5, 1866 ..	108 „
„ Liverpool		„ New York			

10TH VOYAGE—CAPTAIN GEORGE CUMMING.

Left New York	Mar. 2, 1867	arrived San Francisco	July	11, 1867 ..	130 days
„ San Francisco	Aug. 12, 1867	„ New York	Nov.	19, 1867 ..	99 „

11TH VOYAGE—CAPTAIN GEORGE CUMMING.

Left New York	Jan. 9, 1868	arrived San Francisco	April	27, 1868 ..	109 days
„ San Francisco	May 21, 1868	„ New York	Sept.	8, 1868 ..	110 „

12TH VOYAGE—CAPTAIN GEORGE CUMMING.

Left New York	Oct. 23, 1868	arrived San Francisco	Feb.	17, 1869 ..	117 days
(Dismasted in a pampero, refitted at sea.)					
Left San Francisco	April 10, 1869	arrived New York	July	21, 1869 ..	102 days

13TH VOYAGE—CAPTAIN GEORGE CUMMING.

Left New York	Sept. 21, 1869	arrived San Francisco	Jan.	21, 1870 ..	122 days
„ San Francisco	Mar. 15, 1870	„ New York	June	6, 1870 ..	83 „

14TH VOYAGE—CAPTAIN GEORGE CUMMING.

Left New York	Aug. 22, 1870	arrived San Francisco	Jan.	8, 1871 ..	139 days
„ San Francisco	April 7, 1871	„ New York	July	2, 1871 ..	86 „

15TH VOYAGE—CAPTAIN GEORGE CUMMING.

Left New York	Sept. 1, 1871	arrived San Francisco	Jan.	10, 1872 ..	131 days
„ San Francisco		„ Liverpool		..	105 „

16TH VOYAGE—CAPTAIN CEORGE CUMMING.

Left Liverpool	Oct. 12, 1872	arrived San Francisco	Jan.	20, 1873 ..	100 days
(96 days from the Tuskar.)					
Left San Francisco	Feb. 27, 1873	arrived Liverpool	June	14, 1873 ..	107 days
„ Liverpool	July 16, 1873	„ New York	Aug.	8, 1873 ..	23 „

17TH VOYAGE—CAPTAIN JOHN L. MANSON.

Left New York	Oct. 29, 1873	arrived San Francisco	Feb.	13, 1874 ..	107 days
„ San Francisco	Mar. 12, 1874	„ Liverpool	June	23, 1874 ..	103 „

18TH VOYAGE—CAPTAIN JOHN L. MANSON.

Left Liverpool	Aug. 30, 1874	arrived San Francisco	Dec.	25, 1874 ..	117 days
„ San Francisco	Feb. 9, 1875	„ New York	May	12, 1875 ..	92 „

19TH VOYAGE—CAPTAIN JOHN L. MANSON.

Left New York	July 9, 1875	arrived San Francisco	Oct.	29, 1875 ..	112 days
„ San Francisco	Dec. 21, 1875	„ New York	Mar.	28, 1876 ..	97 „

20TH VOYAGE—CAPTAIN E. C. BAKER.

Left New York	May 16, 1876	arrived San Francisco Sept.	18, 1876 ..	125 days
„ San Francisco	Oct. 20, 1876	„ New York Jan.	27, 1877 ..	99 „

21ST VOYAGE—CAPTAIN E. C. BAKER.

Left New York	Mar. 22, 1877	arrived San Francisco Aug.	5, 1877 ..	136 days
„ San Francisco	Sept. 12, 1877	„ New York Dec.	13, 1877 ..	92 „

22ND VOYAGE—CAPTAIN E. C. BAKER.

Left New York	Feb. 6, 1878	arrived San Francisco June	3, 1878 ..	117 days
„ San Francisco	July 20, 1878	„ New York Oct.	29, 1878 ..	101 „

23RD VOYAGE—CAPTAIN E. C. BAKER.

Left New York	Jan. 20, 1879	arrived San Francisco May	16, 1879 ..	116 days
„ San Francisco	June 8, 1879	„ New York Sept.	3, 1879 ..	114 „

24TH VOYAGE—CAPTAIN E. C. BAKER.

Left New York	Dec. 26, 1879	arrived San Francisco April	7, 1880 ..	102 days

CAPTAIN H. T. BAKER.

Left San Francisco	May 20, 1880	arrived Liverpool Sept.	3, 1880 ..	106 „

25TH VOYAGE—CAPTAIN H. T. BAKER.

Left Liverpool	Oct. 11, 1880	arrived San Francisco Jan.	30, 1881 ..	111 days
„ San Francisco	Mar. 9, 1881	„ Antwerp July	5, 1881 ..	118 „

26TH VOYAGE—CAPTAIN H. T. BAKER.

Left Antwerp	Sept. 6, 1881	arrived San Francisco Jan.	27, 1882 ..	143 days
„ San Francisco	Mar. 22, 1882	„ New York July	2, 1882 ..	102 „

27TH VOYAGE—CAPTAIN H. T. BAKER.

Left New York	Sepr. 7, 1882	arrived Portland (O.) Feb.	5, 1883 ..	151 days
„ Portland (O.)		„ San Francisco	1883 ..	7 „

CAPTAIN CHARLES MATTHEWS.

Left San Francisco June 2, 1883 arrived New York Oct. 6, 1883 .. 126 days
(Put into Rio leaking, 20 days under repair.)
Sold to Austman's for 13,500 dollars.

APPENDIX IV.

Cape Horn Passages of "David Crockett."

1ST CAPE HORN VOYAGE—CAPTAIN SPENCER.

Left New York		arrived San Francisco July	19, 1857	..	122 days
,, San Francisco	Oct. 6	,, New York Jan.	10, 1858	..	96 ,,

2ND VOYAGE—CAPTAIN SPENCER.

Left New York		arrived San Francisco July	19, 1858	..	117 days
,, San Francisco	Oct. 7	,, New York Jan.	15, 1859	..	89 ,,

3RD VOYAGE—CAPTAIN ROWLAND.

Left New York	Mar. 16, 1859	arrived San Francisco July	27, 1859	..	131 days
,, San Francisco	Oct. 15, 1859	,, New York Jan.	16, 1860	..	93 ,,

4TH VOYAGE—CAPTAIN JOHN A. BURGESS.

Left New York		arrived San Francisco July	3, 1860	..	123 days
,, San Francisco	July 24, 1860	,, Callao		..	47 ,,
,, Callao	Nov. 28, 1860	,, Hampton Roads		..	72 ,,

5TH VOYAGE—CAPTAIN JOHN A. BURGESS.

Left New York		arrived San Francisco	..	113 days
,, San Francisco		,, New York	..	88 ,,

6TH VOYAGE—CAPTAIN JOHN A. BURGESS.

Left New York	May 8, 1862	arrived San Francisco Sept.	2, 1862	..	117 days
,, San Francisco	Nov. 1, 1862	,, Liverpool Feb.	17, 1863	..	108 ,,

7TH VOYAGE—CAPTAIN JOHN A. BURGESS.

Left New York		arrived San Francisco Oct.	21, 1863	..	110 days
,, San Francisco	Dec. 5, 1863	,, Liverpool Mar.	14, 1864	..	100 ,,

8TH VOYAGE—CAPTAIN JOHN A. BURGESS.

Left New York		arrived San Francisco Jan. 27,	1865	..	107 days
,, San Francisco		,, Valparaiso April 4,	1865	..	40 ,,
,, Paquica		,, Liverpool			

9TH VOYAGE—CAPTAIN JOHN A. BURGESS.

Left New York		arrived San Francisco Aug.	26, 1866	..	114 days
,, San Francisco	Sept. 21	,, Philadelphia Dec.	25, 1866	..	94 ,,

10TH VOYAGE—CAPTAIN JOHN A. BURGESS.

Left New York		arrived San Francisco July	22, 1867	..	110 days
,, San Francisco	Aug. 28	,, New York Dec.	20, 1867	..	114 ,,

11TH VOYAGE—CAPTAIN JOHN A. BURGESS.

Left New York		arrived San Francisco July	16, 1868	..	137 days
,, San Francisco	Aug. 24	,, New York Nov.	27, 1868	..	95 ,,

12TH VOYAGE—CAPTAIN JOHN A. BURGESS.

Left New York		arrived San Francisco	..	106 days
,, San Francisco		,, Liverpool	..	114 ,,

13TH VOYAGE—CAPTAIN JOHN A. BURGESS.

Left New York   April 27, 1870   arrived San Francisco Aug.   23, 1870   ..   118 days
,, San Francisco   Mar. 11, 1871   ,,   Liverpool   ..   111 ,,

14TH VOYAGE—CAPTAIN JOHN A. BURGESS.

Left New York   Nov. 6, 1871   arrived San Francisco Feb.   17, 1872   ..   103 days
,, San Francisco   May 12, 1872   ,,   New York   ..   102 ,,

15TH VOYAGE—CAPTAIN JOHN A. BURGESS.

Left New York   arrived San Francisco   ..   108 days
,, San Francisco   Mar. 22, 1873   ,,   Liverpool   ..   98 ,,

16TH VOYAGE—CAPTAIN JOHN A. BURGESS.

Left New York   Nov. 9, 1873   arrived San Francisco Mar.   2, 1874   ..113 days
,, San Francisco April 20, 1874   ,,   Liverpool   Aug.   10, 1874 ..   107 ,,
(Captain Burgess washed overboard off the Plate: the mate, John Anderson, took the ship on.)

17TH VOYAGE—CAPTAIN JOHN ANDERSON.

Left New York   Nov. 22, 1874   arrived San Francisco   ..   104 days
,, San Francisco April 11, 1875   ,,   Liverpool   Aug.   5, 1875 ..   116 ,,

18TH VOYAGE—CAPTAIN JOHN ANDERSON.

Left New York   arrived San Francisco Mar.   27, 1876   ..   109 days
,, San Francisco   May 30, 1876   ,,   Queenstown Sept. 27   ..   120 ,,

19TH VOYAGE.

Left New York   arrived San Francisco June   14, 1877   ..   113 days
,, San Francisco   Nov. 12   ,,   New York   Feb.   24, 1878 ..   104 ,,

20TH VOYAGE.

Left New York   April 2, 1878   arrived San Francisco July   27, 1878   ..   116 days
,, San Francisco   Oct. 22, 1878   ,,   New York   Jan.   30, 1879 ..   100 ,,

21ST VOYAGE.

Left New York   Mar. 26, 1879   arrived San Francisco   ..   136 days
,, San Francisco   Oct. 21   ,,   New York   Jan.   30, 1880 ..   100 ,,

22ND VOYAGE.

Left New York   Mar. 22, 1880   arrived San Francisco July   28, 1880   ..   128 days
,, San Francisco   Oct 18, 1880   ,,   New York   Feb.   11, 1881 ..   116 ,,

23RD VOYAGE.

Left New York   Mar. 22, 1881   arrived San Francisco July   23, 1881   ..   124 days
,, San Francisco   Aug. 31, 1881   ,,   New York   Dec.   8, 1881 ..   99 ,,

24TH VOYAGE.

Left New York   arrived San Francisco July   27, 1882   ..   157 days
,, San Francisco   Sept. 3,   ,,   New York   Dec.   14, 1882 ..   102 ,,

25TH VOYAGE.

Left New York   Feb. 10, 1883   arrived San Francisco June   28, 1883   ..   138 days
,, San Francisco   Aug. 22, 1883   ,,   New York   Nov.   22, 1883 ..   92 ,,

APPENDIX V.

Abstract Log of Ship "Glory of the Seas"—J. N. KNOWLES, Master.
San Francisco to Sydney, March-April, 1875.

Date	Lat. ° '	Long. ° '	Distance	Remarks
March 14		126 22 W	miles 50	Tug *Rescue* took us in tow at 6 a.m.: 8.30, cast off; 9.30, dropped pilot just outside bar.
„ 15	33 27 N.		278	At noon, South Farallone bore N. 24 miles. Strong N.W. wind. Ship making 12 knots. Ship very cranky and cannot carry as much sail as otherwise. Strong and fresh winds from N.W. and N.N.W.; cloudy.
„ 16	30 30	128 50	216	Moderate breezes from North to N.N.E.; cloudy.
„ 17	28 04	131 18	196	Same.
„ 18	25 34	133 33	193	Same.
„ 19	22 28	135 20	215	Moderate Trades from N.E. cloudy; squally.
„ 20	18 52	137 10	235	Fresh Trades from N.E.; squally. Carried away fore topmast stunsail boom.
„ 21	15 18	138 13	223	Same Trades and weather made 1006 miles past week.
„ 22	11 30	139 15	236	Same. Sea smooth.
„ 23	7 45	140 15	233	Same. Sea smooth.
„ 24	5 30	140 51	138	Light, baffling, moderate winds from N.E. to E.S.E., S.E. and East.
„ 25	3 1	142 31	180	First part light from East; middle and latter fresh Trades from East to E. by S. Occasional rain squalls throughout.
„ 26	0 29 N.	145 06	216	Moderate S.E. Trades. Occasional rain squalls. Pleasant hot weather.
„ 27	1 39 S.	147 36	198	Light Trades from E.S.E. Strong current setting W.S.W. 1¼ knots per hour.
„ 28	4 20	150 25	235	Fresh Trades. Heavy rain. Squally.
„ 29	7 11	153 10	238	Moderate S.E. Trade throughout, clear, pleasant. Current 14 miles S.W.
„ 30	9 20	155 34	192	Same Trades and weather. Current 15 miles west.
„ 31	11 03	157 27	152	Light Trades, pleasant. Occasional rain squalls. Made by log 163 miles.
April 1	12 40	159 10	141	Light Trades; baffling N.E. to E. Pleasant, sea smooth, hot.
„ 2	14 40	161 20	175	Light winds. Rain squalls, middle and latter. Moderate Trades from S.E.
„ 3	15 58	163 26	145	Light Trades from S.E. to N.E. Occasional rain squalls, hot.
„ 4	17 30	166 17	188	First and middle parts same, ends strong Trades.
„ 5	19 38	170 18	261	Strong Trades at 8 a.m., Savage Islands bore North 10 miles distant.
„ 6	21 53	174 44	284	Strong Trades. Squally. At noon, Eooa Island bore North 23 miles distant.
„ 7	2 58	179 38 W	278	Strong Trades. Rain squalls.
„ 8	23 58 D.R.	175 36 E.	270	Same throughout. Crossed 180° meridian so drop a day. Made 270 miles by log.
„ 10	25 05	170 55	264	Fresh Trades from East. Sailed by log 275 miles.
„ 11	26 06	166 23	252	Moderate from E.N.E. to East. Clear, pleasant.
„ 12	26 58	163	192	Same with occasional rain squalls. Sailed by log 201 miles; made 1801 miles past week.
„ 13	27 48	160 22	148	Light breezes from N.E. to E.N.E. Current setting S. 10 miles. Sailed by log 154 miles.

Abstract Log of Ship "Glory of the Seas."—Continued.

Date	Lat.	Long.	Distance	Remarks
	° ′	° ′	miles	
„ 14	28 22	158 42	94	Light baffling airs from E.N.E. to N.E. Ends cloudy and overcast.
„ 15	28 46	156 58	94	Light, baffling, calm. Rain squalls, Ends moderate from S.E.
„ 16	29 47	154 55	124	First strong from S.E. to S.S.E. Middle and latter light to calm.
„ 17	30 25	154 22	47	First and middle light and baffling. Latter strong gales from S.E. Current strong to N.N.E.
„ 18	31 42	154 12	78	Strong moderate from S.E. to E.S.E.
„ 19			185	First part moderate from E.S.E. to S.E. Cloudy and frequent rain squalls. At 12 midnight, Port Stephens light bore N.N.W. 20 miles. At 5 a.m., Newcastle light bore N.W. 20 miles. At 8 a.m. made North Head and at 9 o'clock took Sydney pilot. At 11.30, anchored in Sydney Harbour. Passage anchor to anchor 35 days 11 hrs. 15 min.; pilot to pilot 35 days 5 hrs 15 mins. Total distance 6844 miles; sailed 7026; average 8¼ knots.

APPENDIX VI.

Register of Foreign-Built American Ships.

Date built	Name	Old Name	Tons	L'gth (ft.)	Br'dth	Depth (ft.)	Builders	Owners
1888	Foohng Suey		1048	214	34.5	19.2	Napier, Shanks & Bell	C. Brewer & Co.
1891	Helen Brewer		1582	247.7	38.9	22.5	R. Duncan & Co.	„ „
1876	Iolani	Thurland Castle	1306	226.1	34.8	21.5	Harland & Wolff	„ „
1882	Nuuanu	Highland Glen	1028	211.3	34	19.6	Ramage & Ferguson	„ „
1885	Santago		979	207.6	33.1	20	Harland & Wolff	Matson Nav. Co.
1873	Roderick Dhu		1534	257.1	40.2	22.8	Mounsey & Foster	„ „
1866	Antiope		1486	242.3	38.4	23.7	J. Reid & Co.	„ „
1872	Annie Johnson	Ada Iredale	997	112.1	31.1	21.6	Williamson & Co.	„ „
1882	Marion Chilcott	Kilbrannan	1738	256.4	38.2	22.8	Russell & Co.	„ „
1878	Falls of Clyde		1809	266.1	40	23.5	Russell & Co.	„ „
1878	Monterey	Cypromene	1889	260	39.5	24	Oswald, Mordaunt & Co.	„ „
1892	R. P. Rithet		1097	206.5	38	19	C. Connell & Co.	„ „
1888	Andrew Welch		903	185.6	36.1	18.5	Russell & Co.	S. „ Francisco Shipping Co.
1892	John Ena		2842	312.9	48.1	25	R. Duncan & Co.	A. Nelson
1892	Hawaiian Isles		2097	270	43.1	23.6	C. Connell & Co.	I. E. Thayer
1891	Manga Reva	Pyrenees	2243	284.5	42.5	24.7	G. „Peverall"	J. S. Walker
1863	Mauna Ala	Pak Wan	779	186.2	32.6	19	C. Lungley	S. C. Allen, Honolulu
1866	Diamond Head	Gainsborough	1012	206	31.4	20.4		
1874	Coronado	J. C. Pfluger ex Waikato	1007	210.5	34.1	19.2	J. Blumer & Co.	J. D. Spreckels & Co.
1876	Archer	Coalinga ex La Escocesa	900	189.1	32	18.7	R. Thompson, Jr.	Welch & Co.
1898	Star of Chile	Euterpe	1001	202	34.2	21.3	Gourley Bros.	Alaska Packers Assoc.
1863	Star of India	Himalaya	1318	205.5	35.2	23.4	Gibson & Co.	„ „
1863	Star of Peru	Balclutha	1027	201.6	33	20.5	Pile, Hay & Co.	„ „
1886	Star of Alaska	Abby Palmer ex Blairmore	1716	256.3	38.5	22.7	Connell & Co.	„ „
1893	Star of England		1943	264	39	23.5	A. MacMillan & Son	„ „
1885	Star of Holland	Homeward Bound ex Zemindar	2131	292.6	39.7	23.5	Harland & Wolff	„ „
1887	Star of Scotland	Kenilworth	2293	300.2	43.1	24.2	J. Reid & Co.	„ „
1877	Star of France		1644	258	38	22.8	Harland & Wolff	„ „
1896	Star of Iceland	Willscott	1981	267.3	40.1	23.7	W. Hamilton & Co.	„ „
1874	Star of Bengal		1877	262.8	40.2	23.5	Harland & Wolff	„ „
1892	Star of Falkland	Durbridge	2121	276.8	42	24.2	W. Hamilton & Co.	„ „
1877	Star of Italy		1497	257.1	38	22.8	Harland & Wolff	„ „
1883	E. R. Sterling	Lord Wolseley	2577	308.2	42.9	25.1	Harland d &Wolff	Captain E. R. Sterling

Register of Foreign-Built American Ships.—Continued.

Date built	Name	Old Name	Tons	L'gth	Br'dth	Depth	Builders	Owners
				ft.	ft.	ft.		
1892	Monongahela ..	Balasore	2724	311	43·6	24·5	Barclay, Curle & Co.	U.S. Shipping Board
1883	Tusitala ..	Sophie ex Sierra Lucena ex Inveruglas	1621	260·4	39	23·5	R. Steele & Co.	Three-hours for Lunch Club.
1892	Annie M. Reid ..	Howard D. Troop	2165	291·3	42·2	24	R. Duncan & Co.	Rolph Nav. & Coal Co.
1884	James Rolph ..	Celtic Monarch	2119	277·3	42·5	24·2	T. Royden & Sons	,, ,,
1888	Golden Gate ..	Lord Shaftesbury	2341	293·3	42·8	24	Whitehaven S.B. Co.	,, ,,
1891	Dunsyre ..		2149	277·8	41·8	24·4	W. Hamilton & Co.	Robert Dollar Co.
1902	Janet Dollar ..	Eclipse	3090	326·8	46·4	26·2	A. Rodger & Co.	,, ,,
1904	Mary Dollar ..	Hans	3102	335·5	46·9	26·5	W. Hamilton & Co.	,, ,,

APPENDIX VII.

"*Paul Jones,*" an Early Down Easter.

I have included the fine photograph of the *Paul Jones* amongst the illustrations of this book so that the Down Easter of the forties may be compared with her successor of the seventies and eighties. The *Paul Jones* was a very fine example of the type of ship built for the trade to China and the East just before the advent of the out-and-out clipper. Indeed, the vessel which many shipping historians contend was the first of the American clippers was modelled and planned in her cabin during her maiden voyage. I refer to the famous *Houqua.*

The *Paul Jones* was built in 1842 by Waterman & Elwell of Medford, U.S.A., for John M. Forbes and the Canton firm of Russell & Co. She was a full-built ship of 620 tons (750 old measurement) and was a fair cargo carrier, being considered by Captain R. B. Forbes about as fine a specimen of a merchant ship as could be built in America at that period. And, like many another full-built old timer of pre-clipper days, she was by no means slow, as the sailing records below prove clearly enough.

Her first commander was Captain Nat Palmer, one of those enterprising seamen who were in great part responsible for the flourishing condition of the American Mercantile Marine in the forties and fifties.

Captain Robert B. Forbes, another shipmaster and owner to be numbered amongst the architects of America's greatness on the sea, was a partner in Russell & Co., and was mainly responsible for the rigging specifications of the new East Indiamen. It was owing to him that the *Paul Jones* was fitted with Robinson's screw steering apparatus. Steering by machinery—as this screw gear was called—came into use in America in the year 1840, and the *Paul Jones* was one of the first vessels fitted with Robinson's patent, which was the best. Nat Palmer, like many an old seaman, was very suspicious of such an innovation, and insisted on a common wheel being put aboard in the event of the patent gear failing. However, he was soon enthusiastic in its praise.

The *Paul Jones* sailed from Boston on January 15, 1843, for China. The Equator was crossed 26½ days out in longitude 25° 41′ and the ship was off the Cape of Good Hope 54 days out, reached the Straits of Sunda on April 10, 88 days out, and arrived at Hongkong 111 days out, having logged 13,289 miles.

On her homeward passage William H. Low, brother of Abiel Abbott Low, of the New York firm of A. A. Low & Brother and a member of the firm of Russell & Co., took a passage for himself and his wife, and it was during this homeward run that Nat Palmer and William H. Low discussed the building of a clipper ship for the China trade. Nat Palmer had been much impressed by the American clipper brig, *Antelope,* which was making a fortune in the opium trade, running between Bombay and China. His first plan was to build a brig of the same type, but his ideas, coinciding with those of W. H. Low, were gradually enlarged until the whittled out model of the clipper ship, *Houqua,* 706 tons, was the result; and at the end of the voyage Palmer handed over the command of the *Paul Jones* to Captain James T. Watkins in order to superintend the building of the *Houqua,* which he subsequently commanded.

To return to the *Paul Jones*: she made a very fine run home, being only 79 days from Anjer (left August 1, 1843) to New York, her best day's run in the S.E. Trades being 266 miles.

On her second passage home from China the *Paul Jones,* commanded by Captain Watkins, left the Canton river on September 28, 1844, and experiencing very light and baffling winds in the China Sea did not clear the Straits of Sunda until October 27. She was off the Cape 66 days out, her best run in the S.E. Trades being 240 miles. The Line in the Atlantic was reached on the 88th day out, and New York on January 18, 1845, 113 days from China.

Here is another excellent passage made by Captain Watkins. The *Paul Jones* sailed from New York on October 13, 1847. The Line was crossed 31 days out, and the Meridian of the Cape 57 days out. St. Paul's Island was passed on December 22, 70 days out, and Sandalwood Island reached on January 7, 86 days out. On February 4, 1848, the *Paul Jones* anchored at Hongkong after a passage of 113 days, the total distance sailed being 16,554 miles. Her best day's run on this passage was 252 miles, and the average of her best ten days was 214½ miles.

The ship was given a quick turn round, and sailing from the Canton river on March 2 cleared the Straits of Sunda on April 5, was off the Cape 32 days from Java Head, her best run in the Trades being 253 miles, and reached New York on June 20, 110 days from Canton and only 76 days from Anjer.

On her next voyage the *Paul Jones* was very nearly lost. Captain Watkins had left her in order to take over the opium clipper, *Antelope.* In a letter dated May 21, 1848, written whilst on his passage from Macao to Bombay, Captain Watkins wrote:—

On May 6th, Latitude 1° 33′, Longitude 107° 17′, we fell in with hundreds of tea chests. I sent a boat and an officer to ascertain what ill-fated ship they were from, and very soon my worst fears were realised, for the packages were marked *Paul Jones*. Our only child was a passenger in her, and we naturally feared the worst, so that you can imagine our feelings. I subsequently learnt that he was all right, and that he had been on shore at Anjer with Captain Gordon ; I learnt there that my dear old ship had not sustained any damage, and that she had been on shore near Gaspar Island.

The *Paul Jones*, commanded by Captain Joseph R. Gordon, had grounded on the west side of the Straits of Gaspar, not far from Wilson Bank, to the south-south-east of Berikat Point. After jettisoning a considerable portion of her tea cargo and listing the ship over, the *Paul Jones* was brought off without sustaining any damage and proceeded on her way to New York.

Captain Gordon was afterwards unfortunate enough to lose the clipper ship, *Memnon* on Gaspar Island.

With the boom in clipper ships which started with the advent of the *Houqua* and the *Rainbow*, such vessels as the stout little *Paul Jones* sank into obscurity. She continued, however, to earn her living on the high seas for another forty years. The end came in the year 1887, when it is to be feared that the little white painted beauty had achieved some notoriety as a hell-ship. After being loaded at Melbourne, she was delayed from sailing because of the difficulty of shipping a crew, even the most reckless sailormen being unwilling to trust themselves aboard her. At last, however, the usual mixed lot of dead-beats were shanghaied aboard her, and the *Paul Jones* sailed for home; but she was barely outside Port Philip Heads before she caught fire, or possibly, was set on fire by one of her crew, and that was the end of this old-time Down Easter. She was eventually abandoned off the Otway, her crew being taken off by the Heap clipper, *Antiope.*

"MATANZAS" ON WAYS AT BATH, MAINE.

"PAUL JONES."

Lent by Capt. Schultze.

INDEX